Conversations on the Edge of the Apocalypse

Interviews by David Jay Brown *with*:

Kary Mullis

Noam Chomsky

Candace B. Pert

Edgar D. Mitchell

Rupert Sheldrake

Dean Radin

John E. Mack

Ray Kurzweil

Hans Moravec

Clifford Pickover

Bruce Sterling

Douglas Rushkoff

Robert Anton Wilson

George Carlin

Paul Krassner

Peter Russell

Deepak Chopra

Ram Dass

Valerie Corral

Jeff McBride

Alex Grey

Conversations on the Edge of the Apocalypse

Contemplating the Future with Noam Chomsky, George Carlin, Deepak Chopra, Rupert Sheldrake, and Others

David Jay Brown

CONVERSATIONS ON THE EDGE OF THE APOCALYPSE
© David Jay Brown, 2005.

First published in 2005 by
PALGRAVE MACMILLAN™
175 Fifth Avenue, New York, N.Y. 10010 and
Houndmills, Basingstoke, Hampshire, England RG21 6XS
Companies and representatives throughout the world.

PALGRAVE MACMILLAN is the global academic imprint of the Palgrave Macmillan division of St. Martin's Press, LLC and of Palgrave Macmillan Ltd. Macmillan® is a registered trademark in the United States, United Kingdom and other countries. Palgrave is a registered trademark in the European Union and other countries.

ISBN 1–4039–6532–3

Library of Congress Cataloging-in-Publication Data is available from the Library of Congress.

A catalogue record for this book is available from the British Library.

Design by Newgen Imaging Systems (P) Ltd., Chennai, India.

First edition: May 2005

10 9 8 7 6 5 4 3 2 1

Printed in the United States of America.

For
Oz Janiger

Contents

Acknowledgments

PUTTING THIS BOOK TOGETHER WAS AN INCREDIBLE ODYSSEY AND A tremendous amount of fun. It's every writer's dream to be able to explore the frontiers of thought with the greatest minds on the planet. As with most books, many people played valuable roles in its creation. It would have been impossible for me to do this book without the support and inspiration that I have received in abundance from my incredible and amazing friends and family.

First and foremost, I would like to thank Joseph Wouk and Clifford Pickover. Joe built the *Mavericks of the Mind* Web site (www.mavericksofthemind.com) out of interviews from my previous books, and, after discovering the site, Cliff put me in touch with his editor at Palgrave Macmillan, thus making this book possible.

I would also like to thank my editor at Palgrave, Amanda Johnson, for her encouragement and excitement about the project. Extra special thanks go to Suzie Wouk, Robin Rae and Brummbaer, Arleen Margulis, Jesse Houts, Amy Barnes Excolere, Sherry Hall, Valerie Corral, Robert Anton Wilson, and Carolyn Mary Kleefeld, for their supernaturally generous levels of support and for their continued belief in my work over the years.

I'd also like to thank the following individuals for their valuable help: Nancy Mullis, Marlene Rhoeder, Carole Myers, Jeremy Tarcher, Annie Sprinkle, David Wayne Dunn, Robin Atwood, Colette Phair, Nina Strohminger, Emily Brown, Paul Krassner, Sherri Paris, Mike Corral, Michael Horowitz, Denis Berry, the members of WAMM and the RAW Group Mind, Senta Rose Hernandez, Katherine Covell, Bethan Carter, Rebecca McClen Novick, Rupert Sheldrake, Dean Radin, Mimi Hill, Dana Peleg, Michael Brown, Serena Hall, Sammie and Tudie, Heather Hazen, Anna Damoth, Karen Lieberman, Bernadette Wilson, Randy Baker, Nick Herbert, Heaven Gainsbrugh, Jean Hanamoto, Jessica Ansberry, Jody Lombardo, Robin Chase, Matthew Steiner, Nancy Crowley, Sylvia Thyssen, Dina Meyer, Cheryle Goldstein, Linda Meyer, Gene Goldstein, Ann and Gerry Brown, Carolyn Rangel, Jeremiah Sullivan, Mike Shane, Will Bueche, Jessica Pariente, John Morgenthaler, Arlene Istar Lev, Shahab Geranmayeh, and Angie Rodrigez.

This book also owes a great deal to several people who have passed on from this world yet remain quite alive in my heart and mind: Terence McKenna, Timothy Leary, John C. Lilly, Oscar Janiger, Arlen Wilson, Rosemary Woodruff-Leary, Elizabeth Gips, and Nina Graboi.

I would also like to express my sincere gratitude to all the extraordinary people I interviewed for their valuable time, generous help, and thoughtful speculations. John Mack, one of the people that I interviewed for this collection, was tragically killed by a drunk driver in London on September 27, 2004. John was a brilliant, compassionate, and open-minded man. His passing was a huge loss, and he will be missed.

Conversations on the Edge of the Apocalypse

Introduction

David Jay Brown

THE FUTURE HAS NEVER LOOKED BRIGHTER OR MORE BLEAK. NEVER BEFORE IN human history has there been so much cause for both hope and alarm. We are living in a world of increasing uncertainty, and each day brings new reasons for both celebration and concern. Are we headed toward a glistening new world of technological marvels and wonders or our own extinction?

We are facing a looming environmental crisis and an incalculable loss of biodiversity, as well as threats from AIDS and new antibiotic-resistant pathogens. Recent terror attacks left many Americans alarmed by the specter of more terrorism and war and concerned about the fate of their vanishing constitutional rights. At the same time, new technological advances and scientific breakthroughs offer hope bordering on the miraculous—the Internet, genetic engineering, stem cell research, advances in neuroscience, quantum computing, artificial intelligence, robotics, and nanotechnology promise to end poverty and eliminate disease, provide society with cheap, pollution-free energy, and predict a future so fantastic it staggers the imagination.

In these pages you'll find in-depth conversations with cutting-edge visionaries that explore the future evolution of the human race and the mystery of consciousness, from scientific, philosophical, and spiritual perspectives. Some of the world's most brilliant (and entertaining) minds—world-class experts in genetics, neuroscience, language, artificial intelligence, robotics, space flight, science fiction, comedy, magic, visionary art, and Eastern philosophy—discuss life's most ancient and compelling philosophical puzzles, such as the origin of human consciousness and the notion of teleology in evolution. Reflecting on these timeless mysteries creates fertile ground from which to contemplate important questions regarding humanity's future. The human species is headed down a path that could very well lead to its own destruction. This book was inspired by the hope that in viewing our precarious situation from a larger, more evolutionary perspective, we may be able to glean some valuable insights and, possibly, some enlightening proposals for our potential future.

As with my two previous interview books, *Mavericks of the Mind* and *Voices from the Edge*, the people I chose to interview are some of the most creative and controversial thinkers on the intellectual frontiers of science and art—the mavericks, those who have stepped outside the boundaries of consensus thought. These are experts from various fields who have seen beyond the traditional and conventional view, who dare to question authority and think for themselves. It is often the capacity for independent thought in these remarkable individuals that lies at the heart of their exceptional abilities and accomplishments. In questioning old belief systems and traveling beyond the edges of the established horizons to find their answers, they have gained revolutionary insights into the nature of consciousness, and they offer some unique solutions to the problems that are facing modern day society.

I chose people who were not only courageous and controversial, but largely people whose work has influenced one another. The interviews are designed not only to be interdisciplinary, but also to connect with each other, by exploring what the interviewees think about some of the same questions as well as about one another's ideas. For example, controversial areas of science—such as the study of psychic phenomena or the alien abduction phenomena—are debated in the following pages by having the interviewees respond to one another's work and comments. Giving the interviewees an opportunity to discuss one another's opinions helps to create a lively, more interactive debate as well as a larger, more holistic point of view. By running common threads through the conversations and interlinking the interviews, the very format of this book also helps to demonstrate one of its primary themes: that the world is a deeply interconnected place.

What emerges from these interviews—as a whole—is far more than one might expect from viewing them separately. No single person has the answers to the Big Questions. But when we put our best minds together a collective vision begins to form, a meta-intelligence is created that transcends that of any individual. We start to see a balance between perspectives—such as rational analysis and intuition, serious thought and playful humor, practical application and imaginative speculation. Like the social insects that cooperate in highly coordinated ways to form complex hives and colonies, we too seem capable of a type of group intelligence that transcends our limitations as individuals and behaves in a manner akin to that of a single organism. Each one of us holds a piece to the puzzle, and the pieces begin to come together when our best minds explore the frontiers of thought together.

Some of the questions that I will be discussing with the extraordinary individuals I interviewed for this book have grand implications. Will the human species survive, or is it doomed to destroy itself? How will our current political trends affect the future? How is technology affecting the biosphere, our chances of survival, and the evolution of human consciousness? What happens to consciousness after death? What is God? Is there any teleology in evolution or intelligent design in nature? Are psychic phenomena real? Do intelligent extraterrestrials exist? Can science and spirituality be compatible? If we do survive, what does the future evolution of the human race hold in store? Speculating on these important questions can help us to understand ourselves better and to chart the course of our future—if, indeed, we have one. Let's take a look at some of these questions more closely.

WILL THE HUMAN SPECIES SURVIVE?

We are living in a time that is marked by one of the most widespread mass extinctions in the history of our planet. Conservation biologists tell us that climate change, habitat destruction, ozone depletion, toxic chemicals, and invasive or infectious species are driving biodiversity on this planet back 65 million years, to the lowest level of vitality since the end of the Age of the Dinosaurs. During that period at least half of all species went extinct, more or less overnight. "The same thing is happening right now," physicist Peter Russell told me. "Species are becoming extinct at a fantastic rate. It's suggested that three species an hour are becoming extinct in the world." If current trends continue, one-half of all species on Earth will be extinct in one hundred years.

Although it's natural for species to go extinct, and, in fact, the majority of species that have lived on this planet have gone extinct (only about one in a thousand species that ever lived on Earth is still living today), during only five other periods in our planet's 4.5-billion-year history have there been mass extinctions on the scale that we are currently witnessing. Mass extinctions, defined as episodes when an exceptional global decline in biodiversity takes place, affect a broad range of life-forms over a relatively short period of time. Various explanations have been given for these five previous mass extinctions in our planet's history—such as the effects of glaciation, ultraviolet radiation from the sun after gamma rays from a supernova explosion destroying Earth's ozone layer, or the widespread climatic impact of an asteroid striking Earth.

When I interviewed Nobel laureate Kary Mullis for this book, he told me he thought that the ever-present possibility of an asteroid colliding with Earth poses the biggest threat to the human species. Our solar system is filled with massive asteroids, and their shifting paths collide with planets on occasion. One such collision may have ended the reign of the dinosaurs 65 million years ago. According to Mullis, it could happen again at any time.

However, the driving force behind the current episode of mass extinctions is not due to any wayward asteroid but rather to the impact of a single species— *Homo sapiens*. Human actions have resulted in the widespread loss, fragmentation, and poisoning of natural habitats and the gross disruption of the numerous intricate natural processes that affect the delicate balance of our planet's ecosystems. Humanity could very well be driving itself into extinction.

A 2004 U.S. Pentagon study entitled "An Abrupt Climate Change Scenario and Its Implications for United States National Security" warns of the possibility of global warming pushing the planet into a new ice age. According to the Pentagon report, the question is not *if* abrupt climate change will happen, but *when*. The study goes on to describe a world where riots and wars over food and drinkable water become commonplace, as 400 million people are forced to migrate from uninhabitable areas.

THE MIGHTY NEW SUPERTECHNOLOGIES

If these current environmental trends weren't alarming enough, then there are the new technologies that are emerging on the horizon. Many of the new technologies that we are developing are like double-edged swords. Bill Joy, chief scientist for Sun Microsystems, proposed in his widely reprinted *Wired* magazine article "The Future Does Not Need Us" that biotechnology, nanotechnology, and robotics may result in the creation of unnatural entities that can self-replicate beyond human control. Although nanotechnology and robotics may allow us to create marvels of medical science that will extend human life indefinitely and tap into a vast abundance of new resources (topics that technology experts Ray Kurzweil and Hans Moravec address in this book), there are much darker possibilities as well.

When contemplating the power of these mighty new supertechnologies, I can't help but think of the warnings from science-fiction movies. HAL, the psychotic computer in *2001: A Space Odyssey*, the deadly superrobots in *The Matrix* and *Terminator* films—and who can forget the haunting slogan from *Westworld*, Michael Crichton's 1973 movie about robots gone berserk—"Nothing can possibly go wrong . . . go wrong . . . go wrong." The late neuro-scientist and consciousness explorer John C. Lilly had once warned that superintelligent machines from the future—"Solid State Entities"—represented the largest threat to organic life on the planet. Science-fiction/science writers Bruce Sterling and Clifford Pickover address some of these possibilities in the pages that follow.

Even more unthinkable than machines evolving beyond human control or a nanotechnological accident is the possibility of misguided individuals delib-erately using these powerful technologies to further their nefarious agendas. A nation-state government blinded by rage, or an angry terrorist group, could do far more destruction with nanotechnology than with a nuclear bomb or a deadly weaponized virus. Like the protoplasmic creature that arrived on a meteorite from outer space in the movie *The Blob*, self-replicating nanomachines could reduce all organic life on this planet to a giant mass of gray goo, as nanotechnology expert Eric Drexler warns in his book *Engines of Creation*.

Ecological disasters, technological malfunctions, and terrorist nightmares aside, there are some people who believe that an end to humanity's reign on Earth is inevitable. They say that humanity lies on the brink of Armageddon, the end of the world is near, and we are currently witnessing the "Last Days" prophesied in the Judeo-Christian Bible. However, in Yuri Rubinsky and Ian Wiseman's book *A History of the End of the World*, they demonstrate how throughout all of human history some people have proclaimed that "the End" was near.

Nonetheless, only in the past few decades have we developed the technology actually to drive ourselves into extinction, and the situation in the world today has truly never seemed more dire. There are thousands of thermonuclear bombs on this planet and vast stores of genetically modified pathogens that have the capacity to end life as we know it. Every day the U.S. military is working to produce faster, lighter, more deadly weapons. Meanwhile, the political situation on the planet appears to be growing more chaotic and unpredictable.

Some of the people I interviewed spoke with great urgency and concern about the dangers. "We've come very close to terminal nuclear war a number of times. It's kind of a miracle that the species has escaped, in fact. And those threats are increasing," warned U.S. foreign policy critic Noam Chomsky when I spoke with him. "For example, the development and the expansion of military systems into space—with highly destructive space-based offensive weapons that are probably on hair-trigger alert—is almost a guarantee of devastation, if only by accident."

This colossal potential for devastation is difficult and disturbing to contemplate, but what if our worst fears are realized and the human species *does* drive itself into extinction: Then what?

WHAT HAPPENS TO CONSCIOUSNESS AFTER DEATH?

What happens to consciousness after death? From where does consciousness arise? Is consciousness an emergent property of complex information-processing systems, like brains (and possibly computers), or can it exist independent of a physical structure? This is one of the most ancient of all philosophical debates.

Death—what the late ethnobotanist Terence McKenna called "the black hole of biology"—is perhaps the greatest mystery known to human beings. While there is compelling evidence that consciousness survives death and there is compelling evidence that it does not, the truth is that no one knows for sure what happens when we die. Although the postbiological fate of human consciousness is a truly magnificent mystery, beliefs about what happens to consciousness after death generally fall into four traditional categories: reincarnation, eternal heaven or hell, union with "God," or complete nonexistence. This limited range of possibilities is likely due to our strong fear of death, which creates a powerful emotional charge and makes playful speculation on this topic difficult for most people. But if our fears can be suspended or transcended, and we can set our hopes aside, how might we explore this mystery and come up with alternative possibilities? Is it possible, as some people claim, that altered or mystical states of consciousness can give us insight into what happens after death?

Some people I spoke with, such as spiritual teachers Deepak Chopra and Ram Dass, believe that some aspect of our consciousness survives death. "Nothing happens to consciousness after the death of the body," Chopra told me. "Consciousness just loses a vehicle to express itself." Ram Dass told me he thought that after death, consciousness "jumps into a body of some kind, on some plane of existence, and it goes on doing that until it is with God. From a Hindu point of view, consciousness keeps going through reincarnations, which are learning experiences for the soul . . . I think that if you have finished your work and you're just awareness that happens to be in a body, when the body ends it's like selling your Ford—it's no big deal."

Psychologist and psi researcher Dean Radin told me that part of us dies and part of us lives on after the death of the body. "I expect that what we think of as ourselves—which is primarily personality, personal history, and personality traits—all goes away, because it's probably captured, in some way in the body itself," Radin said. "But as to some kind of a primal awareness, I think it probably continues. . . ."

Other people that I interviewed, such as Noam Chomsky and Kary Mullis, doubt that there is any type of afterlife. "I think that consciousness decays to nothing after death," Mullis said. ". . . as your body dies, I think your consciousness probably dies with it." "I assume it's finished," Chomsky told me. "Death is the end of the organism, and the end of everything associated with it."

Hans Moravec proposed a multiple-universe theory to explain what he thought happens to consciousness after death. "In the space of all possible worlds," he told me, "there are certainly going to be continuations of consciousness in some of them, no matter what happens to us . . . no matter how we die, in some possible world there's a way in which we, through some mechanism or other, continue on."

Biologist Rupert Sheldrake told me that he thought death might be like going into a dream from which we cannot awaken and that our belief about what happens after we die may affect what actually happens. He said, "What happens [after death] may indeed depend on our expectations. It may be that materialists and atheists who think death will just be a blank would actually experience a blank. It may be that their expectations will affect what actually happens. It may be that people who think they'll go to a heavenly realm of palm oases and almond-eyed dancing girls really will. It may be that the afterlife is heavily conditioned by our expectations and beliefs, just as our dreams are."

Comedian George Carlin told me that he just accepted the mystery of death. He said, "It's obviously one of the most fascinating things that we don't know. . . . And I'm satisfied not knowing, because it allows me to be filled with speculation, and imagination, about all the possibilities."

Although most of the people I interviewed responded to my query about the possibility of an afterlife in accordance with the four traditional views, others entertained less conventional notions, and a few said that they just accepted the mystery. Exploring ideas about what happens after we die with these remarkable individuals only deepens the mystery because it expands the range of possibilities. Although no one can be certain about evidence of an afterlife from near-death experiences, supposed spirit communications, psychedelic experiences, or spiritual revelations, contemplating the possibilities of a post-death existence cannot only be psychologically liberating and thought-provoking, it can deeply inspire the imagination.

EVE OF THE APOCALYPSE OR DAWN OF A RENAISSANCE?

Although each of us will ultimately die, most of the people I interviewed for this book told me that they didn't believe that the human species was headed toward extinction. As Bruce Sterling said, "It would be difficult to exterminate a broadly spread species. It's like asking Do you think that every rat will be gone in the next hundred years? I mean, we're at least as inventive as they are." Celebrated stage magician Jeff McBride echoed this by saying, "I think we're just a bit smarter than cockroaches, and look how long they've lasted."

Although everyone that I spoke with recognized the dangers, most expressed cautious optimism. For example, computer scientist and entrepreneur Ray Kurzweil told me, "We have enough nuclear weapons to destroy all mammalian life on the planet. . . . When nuclear weapons were exploded in the 1940s, who would have predicted that, nearly sixty years later, not a single other atomic weapon would have been used in anger? . . . There's a lot of things that we don't like about human behavior, and yet we have actually been successful in not only not destroying the world, but in not even having a single weapon go off. Now, we can't say, okay, we solved that problem, because we still have the enormous danger. But that does give us some cause for optimism."

Some of the people I spoke with actually expressed great optimism about the future—such as *Cosmic Trigger* author Robert Anton Wilson, who told me that he was even more optimistic now than he was thirty years ago, "because I don't think politics has as much importance as most people imagine. The real changes occur first in pure science, then in technology, then in social forms; the politicians then run around in front of the parade and pretend they're leading it—like Al Gore claiming he invented Internet. If you only look at Dubya and Osama, the world looks like a Dark Age madhouse, but look at biotech, computer science, and space colonies, and a much more hopeful scenario dawns."

Just as there have always been people who thought that the end of the world was near, so too, it seems, there have always been people who have proclaimed the opposite—that humanity is on the brink of a New Age or a quantum leap in evolution. The Human Potential Movement claims that we are evolving into a higher species and headed into a golden age of enlightenment. This is not new—the mystical artist and poet William Blake and the founder of the Theosophical Society, Madame Blavatsky, began talking about the dawning of a New Age in the 1800s. The Italian philosopher Giodorno Bruno made similar claims in the 1500s.

Ironically, it is the very same technologies—nanotechnology, artificial intelligence, and advanced robotics—that give us the power to reduce all organic life on the planet to a puddle of gray goo that also hold the keys to a utopian world free of aging, disease, poverty, and possibly even death. With incredible speed, replicating-molecular nanomachines, capable of precisely sequencing atoms, could be programmed to repair any type of cellular damage in the body. They could completely reverse the aging process, as if they were changing graphics on a computer screen.

We know that this powerful subLilliputian technology is possible because the inspiration for it comes from nature. All living things are already built by biological molecular assemblers. This is simply the most precise way to build (or rebuild) material forms, as well as the cheapest and the fastest. Nanotechnology expert Eric Drexler says that this submicroscopic technology is inevitable given our current line of technological development in microelectronics, computers, and genetic engineering.

Through advances in computer science, software design, and the reverse engineering of the human brain, Ray Kurzweil predicts that computer intelligence will exceed human intelligence in just a few decades—and that it won't be long after that before humans start merging with machines, blurring the line between technology and biology.

Hans Moravec envisions "bush robots" that will be able to repair virtually any type of damage to the human body. "A bush robot," according to Moravec, "is a branched hierarchy of articulated limbs, starting from a macroscopically large trunk through successively smaller and more numerous branches, ultimately leading to microscopic twigs and nanoscale fingers." This would make virtually any type of medical procedure possible, as "even the most complicated procedures could be completed by a trillion-fingered robot, able, if necessary, to simultaneously work on almost every cell of a human body."

Through the combination of nanotechnology, advanced robotics, and escalating artificial intelligence, virtually anything that we can imagine really does become possible. So it's true, for the first time in human history, that we really do stand on the brink of a miraculous New Age. Likewise, for the first time in human history, we are perilously close to engineering our own extinction.

But again, we must remind ourselves that it has *always* seemed this way to some people. Perhaps this is because the human adventure is simply an expression of deeper forces that are present at every level of organization in our universe—driving the cosmos simultaneously toward both higher order and more pronounced chaos. Through the eons, the whole evolution of life and technology that percolates up from the the primordial oceans and into the heavens is locked in a constant battle against the forces of decay and the second law of thermodynamics. One force always seems ready to devour the other, yet somehow they have remained in balance for around 15 billion years. Perhaps this is because these forces are ultimately part of larger whole, as the Chinese philosophy of Taoism would say.

However, there does seem to be an escalation in the intensity of these two driving forces in the realm of human history, and the rate of change appears to be ever accelerating. The "dark" seems to keep on getting darker, while the "light" appears to be getting brighter. Because of this apparent escalation, many people believe that we are headed toward a final showdown, and that one of these forces—chaos or order—will finally prevail. When I interviewed Terence McKenna for my book *Mavericks of the Mind*, he predicted that a momentous evolutionary shift is going to occur in the year 2012 that will change human life forever. His Timewave Theory of novelty acceleration gave a semiscientific basis for the otherwise Christian notion that we are headed into the "Final Days," what McKenna called a "descent into novelty."

DISSOLVING BOUNDARIES AND SHIFTING PARADIGMS

McKenna believed that our planetary biosphere is not only conscious but highly intelligent, and that the evolution of life and the universe is guided by a grand teleological process. Whether there is any conscious design in nature is one of the themes in this book. Although many scientists remain dubious about McKenna's theories, some share his idea that the planetary biosphere may be operating in a manner akin to a single organism. Viewing the biosphere as a single, self-regulating system is paradigm shifting, and this perspective casts the whole process of evolution in a new light. It sees weblike connections and symbiosis where the classic Darwinian perspective sees only genes selfishly competing for their survival.

Interconnection is an important theme in this book, and virtually all fields of science—from quantum physics to environmental biology—are revealing how interconnected the world truly is. Neuroscientist Candace Pert spoke to me about how her research into brain receptors and neuropeptides is demonstrating a strong interconnection between mind and body. When I interviewed psi researchers Rupert Sheldrake, Dean Radin, and Edgar Mitchell for this book, they spoke of compelling scientific evidence for telepathy and other psychic phenomena, which imply that our minds are also more interconnected to one another than previously thought. These scientific perspectives have dramatic implications when they become the basis for how we see the world, where we define our boundaries, and how we view the process of extinction.

Most people, including most scientists, are unaware of the vast abundance of compelling scientific evidence for psychic phenomena, which has resulted from over a century of parapsychological research. Hundreds of carefully controlled studies—in which psi researchers continuously redesigned experiments to address comments from their critics—have produced results that demonstrate small but statistically significant effects for psi phenomena, such as telepathy, precognition, and psychokinesis.

According to Dean Radin, a meta-analysis of this research demonstrates that the positive results from these studies are significant with odds in the order of many billions to one. Princeton University, the Stanford Research Institute, Duke University, the Institute of Noetic Science, the U.S. and Russian governments, and many other respectable institutions have spent years researching these mysterious phenomena, and conventional science is at a loss to explain the results.

Just as fascinating as the research into psychic phenomena is the controversy that surrounds it. Although surveys conducted by Rupert Sheldrake and me reveal that around 78 percent of the population has had unexplainable "psychic" experiences, and scientific evidence supports the validity of these experiences, many scientists I've spoken with have difficulty accepting the results of psi research. In my own experience researching the possibility of telepathy in animals and other unexplained phenomena with Dr. Sheldrake, I discovered that many people are eager to share personal anecdotes about psychic events in their life—such as remarkable coincidences, uncanny premonitions, precognitive dreams, and seemingly telepathic communications. In these cases, the scientific studies simply confirm life experiences. Yet many scientists I've spoken with haven't reviewed the evidence and remain doubtful that there is any reality to psychic phenomenon.

When Dr. Sheldrake and I investigated whether pets could anticipate their owner's arrival in ways not easily explained by conventional science, we approached the phenomena of telepathy as if it were part of the natural world, an adaptive ability that evolved through the process of natural selection, like any other biological trait. But this perspective is unusual in the scientific community. Although the scientific evidence strongly supports the existence of telepathy, and even though quantum physics provides a foundational basis for understanding it, most conventional scientists are unaware of this evidence and think that direct brain-to-brain communication is impossible. This ignorance demonstrates the enormous power that a scientific paradigm can hold over a generation of scientists, and it makes me wonder: Just how else might our concepts and assumptions be limiting our view of the universe?

ARE WE ALONE IN THE UNIVERSE?

Robert Anton Wilson once told me that he sees dozens of UFOs every week. He said that he also sees a lot of UNFOs—unidentified nonflying objects—as well, and that much of what he sees can't be positively identified. But what about the possibility of extraterrestrials? Organic compounds are known to be present in space, and they are found in meteorites. The majority of biologists I've spoken with agree that life probably has evolved elsewhere in the cosmos. Francis Crick—who codiscovered the structure of the DNA molecule—once told me he thought it possible that life may have arrived on Earth as the result of directed panspermia, a deliberate attempt to seed life on other planets, by an older, more advanced species from a distant star system.

The discovery of "extremophiles"—organisms that live in extremely harsh environments that would kill most other organisms—have increased speculations about the possibility of extraterrestrial life. "Recent discoveries of life living miles under the Earth in utter darkness, or in ice, or even in boiling water, tell us: Whatever is possible in nature tends to become realized. My personal view is that almost everything happens in our universe that is not forbidden by the laws of physics and chemistry. Life on Earth can thrive in unimaginably harsh conditions, even in acid or within solid rock. On the ocean floor, bacteria thrive in scalding, mineral-laden hot springs. If microbes thrive in such miserable conditions on Earth, where else beyond Earth might similar life-forms exist?" Clifford Pickover said.

Extraterrestrial microbes may be as close as the planets in our own solar system. Some of the strongest evidence of extraterrestrial life came in 1996, when a meteorite was discovered that contained the first organic molecules thought to be of Martian origin; several mineral features characteristic of biological activity; and possible microscopic fossils of a primitive, bacteria-like organism that may have lived on Mars more than 3.6 billion years ago. If it's true that life has evolved elsewhere in the universe, how much of this life is intelligent?

There are over 10 billion stars in our galaxy, and if only one-tenth of 1 percent of those have planets with the right conditions for life, then there are 10 million suitable planets in our galaxy alone. According to the calculations of astrophysicist Frank Drake, there may be as many as ten thousand advanced extraterrestrial civilizations in our Milky Way galaxy, and there are at least a billion other galaxies out there. The discovery of a single extraterrestrial civilization holds the power to cause us to entirely reevaluate ourselves and our position in the universe. But if this is true, then where are they?

"Given that the universe is so vast, with so many stars that must have planets like ours, why is it that there aren't people down here trying to trade us beads and trinkets for Manhattan? Why aren't flying saucers all over the place setting up little shops to deal with us? We must have something that they'd think was cool, and yet it just doesn't seem to be the case. If it is, they're not making themselves known," Kary Mullis told me.

However, when I interviewed Pulitzer Prize-winning, Harvard psychiatrist John Mack for this book, he told me that he took seriously the reports that aliens were abducting human beings for the purpose of study and experimentation. He described how a substantial number of credible and mentally sound people he has worked with claim to have been abducted by otherworldly visitors—taken aboard strange spacecrafts in a beam of light and subjected to intrusive medical exams by small, spindly-limbed, gray-skinned beings, with large pear-shaped heads and big black almond-shaped eyes.

The evidence that Mack presents for this unexplained phenomenon is truly compelling, as there is a great deal of similarity in the details of the accounts that the "abductees" give. It is very difficult for a thoughtful person to examine the evidence and not look up into the sky and wonder about the truth of these claims.

Perhaps even more interesting is the claim that an alien superintelligence is accessible to human beings in special states of consciousness. Even though Terence McKenna mockingly referred to the supposed beings behind the alien abduction phenomena as "the pro bono proctologists from Zeta Reticuli," he believed that an advanced extraterrestrial intelligence had arrived on our planet long ago, encoded inside the spores of hallucinogenic (psilocybin) mushrooms. By consuming the mind-expanding mushrooms in a shamanic context, he believed, one could telepathically communicate with these ancient alien beings. I've spoken with dozens of people who have ingested this hyperdimensional fungus and share McKenna's belief that such a discourse is indeed possible. In the pages that follow, I discuss this possibility with Clifford Pickover, John Mack, and Robert Anton Wilson. Contact with an intelligent extraterrestrial mind could have extremely profound effects on our understanding of consciousness.

Popular science fiction films such as *Independence Day*, *Contact*, and *Close Encounters of the Third Kind* reveal how we are at once both frightened and fascinated with the possibility of extraterrestrial contact. If we make physical contact with an intelligent species of extraterrestrials, what would they think of us, and what would we have in common with them? Assuming that we could find a way to communicate with them, what would we talk about? How would contact with an advanced extraterrestrial civilization influence our ideas about science, politics, art, and religion? Questions like this help us to understand ourselves better and develop a less species-centric point of view.

To understand the mind and culture of an advanced extraterrestrial species, we need first to consider that an alien brain and nervous system, which evolved under conditions very different from Earth, may experience states of consciousness that are completely unlike our own. It is also possible that interstellar travel itself, with its spectacular views of the heavens and the weightless environment of space, may allow for the evolution of new states of consciousness in otherworldly species as well as in ourselves. I've spoken with several astronauts who have told me about the changes in consciousness that they experienced while in space.

When I interviewed Edgar Mitchell, the sixth Apollo astronaut to walk on the moon, he described in poetic detail how his journey through space led to a life-changing mystical experience. While on his return trip to Earth, he said, "Every couple of minutes you'd get to see the Sun, the Earth, the Moon, the heavens, and that was a pretty wild experience. . . . I suddenly realized that the molecules of my body, the molecules of the spacecraft, and those of my partners had been prototyped in some ancient generation of stars . . . and okay, that was nice intellectual knowledge, but all of a sudden it hit me at the gut, and—wow—*those are my molecules*. It became personal. I could see the stars, see the separateness of things, but felt an inner connectedness of everything. It was personal. It was wild. It was ecstatic."

THE EVOLUTION OF FUTURE SPECIES

The term "neotony" refers to the mechanism in evolution whereby a new organism evolves by retaining juvenile or larval characteristics from the organism that it evolved from into its adulthood. The result is a sexually mature organism with juvenile appearance that goes on to become a new species. Neotony can be seen in many animals and is a common occurrence in the domestication of animals. According to evolutionary biologists, vertebrates evolved in this way from invertebrates, and amphibians in this manner from fish.

Humans tend to resemble young, relatively hairless apes. Isn't it interesting that many of the descriptions of extraterrestrials—in both the alien abduction phenomenon and in science fiction movies—actually resemble young human children or even human embryos? Extraterrestrials are often envisioned in science fiction, and reported in alien encounters, as having unusually large eyes, rudimentary noses, hairless heads, and bodies of small size. These descriptions sound almost as if they could be an intuition about ourselves in the future. Perhaps we can learn about the future evolution of our species by paying more attention to children.

When I asked media theorist Douglas Rushkoff what he thought adults can learn from youth culture, he replied, "Why, they can learn about the future. Everybody tries to forecast the future using all sorts of strange methodologies about what's going to happen. So much effort has been expended exploring the question, Where's the human race going? When all that you have to do is look at a kid. A kid is basically the next model of human being. So, if you want to know where evolution is taking us—whether it's physical evolution or cultural evolution—you look at kids, because they are quite literally the future."

The late psychologist and futurist Timothy Leary often spoke of humanity being at a larval stage in its development, humans being analogous to caterpillars that have not yet evolved into butterflies. Leary pointed out that most animal species on this planet live in either the ocean or the air. If there is any type of teleology—design or intelligence—inherent in the evolutionary process, it would seem that gravity-bound creatures might be a transitional stage in evolution. Leary suggested that the human species might evolve into thousands of new "post-terrestrial," or "post-larval," species, as different as the various mammals of today are from one another.

Certainly, when we consider our evolutionary history, a quick survey of our situation on this planet does seem to indicate that our species is at some sort of evolutionary crossroads. Could humans be the common ancestor to a vast array of future species, more varied in their form and abilities than the superpowered mutants in the *X-Men* movies? Could we be on the verge of branching off into a diverse extraterrestrial zoology that lives beyond the horizon of our imagination? Our wayward species may indeed be headed toward extinction, but maybe our descendants will evolve into something that does survive.

Perhaps the dinosaurs provide a compelling metaphor for the human species. No one is completely sure what killed off these massive, small-brained reptiles that ruled Earth for 125 million years; some evidence indicates that dinosaur populations began dwindling before the mass extinction of 65 million years ago. But when you think about the Big Picture, what really happened? The dinosaurs—these extremely large, cumbersome creatures, whose genetics favored size over intelligence—were, over time and evolution, replaced by mammals and smaller, smarter, more mobile creatures that spend their days singing and soaring in the sky. In other words, the smarter dinosaurs didn't die; they grew wings and evolved into what are today their only living descendants— birds. There may be a message here for human beings. Could we currently be facing an evolutionary crossroads similar to the one the dinosaurs faced 65 million years ago?

Douglas Rushkoff told me that the larger a multinational corporation grows, the smaller its brain becomes by comparison and the less control it has over what its doing. Like the dinosaurs, part of us—the military industrial complex, for example—may have grown disproportionately huge at the expense of other parts. The challenge we currently are facing is due to an imbalance that comes from within ourselves. With the exception of natural disasters such as earthquakes, hurricanes, and possibly asteroids, every problem that the human race currently is facing is entirely self-created. All that we really need to do in order to survive is learn how to get along with each other. If we can just learn to live together without killing each other, and can be careful not to trash the environment, the human species will pass through a golden threshold into an age of miracles—but, apparently, this just isn't as simple as it sounds.

In fact, avoiding our own destructive tendencies seems to be our biggest challenge, and this is why when science-fiction writers envision intelligent extraterrestrial civilizations, they tend to equate advanced technology with advanced social and spiritual development. There just doesn't seem to be any other way to survive. The escalating dangers of combining high technology with violence and greed on our own planet make it clear that the potential for a global-scale disaster dramatically increases as a technologically sophisticated species matures. Unless a species' social and political capacities evolve with its technological advances, and unless members of the species learn how to get along with each other and their biosphere, the species appears likely to destroy itself.

In his book *Critical Path*, the late inventor and architect Buckminster Fuller calculated that if the human race redirected all the money that is currently being spent on military budgets around the world, there would be enough resources on this planet for each person to live the lifestyle of a multimillion-aire. Just think of how utterly ridiculous our species would appear to an advanced extraterrestrial if we take this fact into account. If our planet's resources were redirected—away from what Robert Anton Wilson calls the "Death Sciences" (where the goal is to develop "faster and faster ways to kill more and more people") and into the "Life Sciences" (where the goal is to improve the quality of human life)—we could be living in a world that is truly limited only by the boundaries of our imaginations.

PUTTING THINGS IN PERSPECTIVE

Life has been evolving on Earth for a few billion years, and the earliest fossil records show that human beings first appeared on the scene around 100 or 200 thousand years ago. For the first 60,000 to 160,000 years of our existence, not a whole lot happened. Then, around 40,000 years ago, human culture suddenly appeared: Art, tool use, and religion began. Humanity was on its way to becoming a technological species. No one knows what triggered this explosion of human intelligence, but it happened all at once, over the entire planet. All of a sudden, humans were painting pictures on cave walls, making crude tools, adorning their bodies with jewelry, and burying their dead with religious objects. Forty thousand years later, we have cell phones, space shuttles, MTV, and the World Wide Web.

Most of what we know of human history only occurred in the last 4,000 years. "We're as ephemeral as mayflies," Terence McKenna said. Our time here has been so short. Our senses detect only the smallest slice of the electromagnetic spectrum—which is how we perceive the universe around us—and our brains allow only the tiniest fraction of those signals into our conscious awareness. The models of the world that we create in our minds are extremely limited and highly biased due to our genetics and social conditioning. We're pretty much in the dark here. In fact, astrophysicists tell us that the 200 billion galaxies that are detectable by our best telescopes add up to only about 4 percent of the whole cosmos. Around 96 percent of the universe is composed of "dark matter" or "dark energy" that we can't see. Nobody knows what this is, but we know it's there because it massively outweighs all the atoms, in all the stars, in all the galaxies, across the whole detectable range of space.

From the perspective of cosmic time, we've had barely a moment to try to figure out what's going on here. The last few hundred years of scientific progress have opened up worlds to us, with discoveries our ancestors could hardly have imagined. Science may yet crack the neural code, extend human life indefinitely, and create computers with extraordinary intelligence. Science may help us to discover intelligent life elsewhere in the universe, and it may allow us to enhance the powers of our mind. Ultimately it may allow us to completely master matter and energy, time and space.

Yet no matter how much our knowledge expands or how godlike our abilities become, there always will be a burning mystery in the center of it all. Even if the ultimate mystery—the origin of our existence—is eternally unsolvable, that doesn't mean that we should stop trying to figure it all out. Socrates believed that "the aim of life is to know thyself." Searching for the origin of the universe and the genesis of consciousness helps us to understand ourselves better—and therein may lie the key to our survival as a species. The process of self-discovery—as individuals and as a species—helps to create a sense of purpose and passion in our lives, and history has shown us, again and again, that life guided by purpose, and driven by passion, will forever triumph over chaos.

The following interviews shed some light on the timeless mysteries of the mind. They explore the unexplained and illuminate the unknown, but perhaps their greatest treasure lies in the maps that they provide us with for navigating out of our current crisis and into a boundless future.

*　*　*

Note: Due to spatial constraints, I had to shorten the length of some of the interviews. Whenever a section of text was removed, the deleted passage is marked by an ellipsis (. . .).

Chemistry and the Mind Field

An Interview with Kary Mullis

Kary Mullis won the 1993 Nobel Prize in Chemistry for his invention of the polymerase chain reaction (PCR), which revolutionized the study of genetics. The journal Science *listed Dr. Mullis's invention of PCR as one of the most important scientific breakthroughs in human history. It has influenced popular culture, science fiction, and even paleobiology. Dr. Mullis earned his Ph.D. in biochemistry from the University of California at Berkeley. He is the author of numerous scientific papers as well as the book* Dancing Naked in the Mind Field, *in which he makes a compelling case for the existence of greater mystery in the world around us. He was inducted into the National Inventors Hall of Fame in 1998 and is a Distinguished Professor at Children's Hospital Oakland Research Institute in Oakland, California.*

* * *

DAVID: Where do you think humanity should be focusing its scientific efforts right now?

KARY: I think that if we, as a society, want to survive for a long time, then we've got to put up an umbrella over our heads to protect us from the things that are obviously going to fall on our planet.

I often wonder, given that the universe is so vast, with so many stars that must have planets like ours, why there aren't aliens down here trying to trade us beads and trinkets for Manhattan? (*laughter*) We must have something that they'd think was cool, and yet it just doesn't seem to be the case. If it is, they're not making themselves known.

Maybe it's because cultures tend to get wiped out by asteroids. We have gotten to the point where we can look into the near vicinity of space and see the things that are a serious danger to us. The asteroid belt is full of things that don't have stable orbits. Maybe by the time a culture can recognize that, it's too late, because they have gone off on some ridiculous tangents. I think we've done that, in terms of our science.

We're not pragmatists anymore. For at least a couple of hundred years Americans have always been thought of as pragmatic philosophers—if it doesn't matter, we're not going to worry about it too much. We've spent billions and billions trying to understand something called "the Grand Unified Theory of Everything"—and all you have to do is take LSD one time to realize that that is not going to happen. (*laughter*) You're just not going to find "the Grand Unified Field of Everything."

You can pretend to find it by spending vast sums of money and building huge machines. We're building this great big thing called BABAR, which looks like an elephant. It's an attachment that detects B-mesons, and will sit on top of the Stanford Linear Accelerator. They're making something that's going to produce a lot of what's called B-mesons, and, from its particular properties, physicists hope to understand enough to provide the final structure of the universe—"the Grand Unified Theory of Everything."

But human beings, who are paying for this whole endeavor, will never understand this. I've been studying it since I was a little boy, and it's not really clear to me that this particular theory of everything is anything more than just a myth. You can find evidence for anything if you look hard enough.

DAVID: What do you think is the biggest threat to the human species?

KARY: We need to know where the asteroids are and which ones could be on a course for Earth sometime in the next five hundred years, or even right now. If something two miles wide crashed on this planet going 17 thousand miles per hour—which it probably would be by the time it got here—it would destroy everything. It's done it before. We know for sure it happened 65 million years ago. That seems like a long time, but it's not an infinitely long time. It's just a long time.

You have to have a sense of a long-distant future for man to be concerned about something like that. There are many asteroids, and every now and then, because of interactions among themselves, one of them will flip itself out of the band between Mars and Jupiter. It will generally head sunward—that means that it comes toward us. It only takes one, and in two minutes the whole planet will be uninhabitable. Maybe a few of us will survive. Perhaps a couple of people up in Denver will be able to hang on.

The last time it happened something five miles wide landed north off of present-day Yucatán. It left a hundred-mile-wide hole and kicked up a tidal wave that, when it passed where Kansas City is today, was five hundred feet high. Denver would have escaped the tidal wave, but the world was totally changed in a matter of minutes.

We can prevent this from happening if we put enough attention toward it and take our physicists off of things like quarks, which most of us are not too concerned about. We were worried that the Russians would get there first, and make a superbomb that we wouldn't be able to make. Now that's over, so let's put an umbrella of protection over our culture—so that we have a million years or so to ponder what our options are. Who are we? That sort of thing.

DAVID: Do you think it's possible to blow up an asteroid that's headed toward us before it strikes the Earth?

KARY: I think so. The next time one of them is about to land here, whether we've prepared for it or not, we'll probably try to do that. There have been a couple of movies where people make an emergency attempt to, and there have been technical papers written about it; but we shouldn't wait until one is almost here. We need to be watching them. There are now about seventy-five catalogued Earth-orbit-crossing asteroids. Astronomers are watching their orbits, but every now and then a new one appears, or someone suddenly discovers a new comet. Comets and asteroids both have that very unpredictable aspect. Some amateur astronomer in Arizona will suddenly see something, and say, Jesus, that's heading right toward us. It's going to be here in a month.

I think the problem is that when our physicists think of something fundamental, they assume that it is either the tiniest little thing or the hugest. It's either the whole universe, or it's a vibrating string ten to forty-five meters wide or something like a quark that has absolutely no volume. It's more romantic, I guess, to talk about and study those sorts of things. I love it, but it's not as practical as studying and understanding the solar system. There are dangers to us right here.

If you look at the surface of the Moon, where weather has not been destroying the evidence of impacts, what do you see? The whole place is full of holes. Mars is the same way. There are all kinds of craters around, because things have been smashing into them. We watched eight or nine almost Earth-size objects crash into Jupiter in 1994. They left huge holes, bigger than the Earth. Any one of those impacts would have destroyed us.

We need to have space stations. We need to get away from here and have people up there ready to defend us. This is not a fanciful idea. There's more evidence for this than for anything else that's dangerous to us. That's the way our civilization is going to end, when something big smashes into this planet. We're going to get to watch it on CNN, and we're going to be helpless.

DAVID: Do you think that the human species is going to survive the next hundred years, and if so, how do you envision humanity's future evolution?

KARY: I think the probability is good that we're going to exist for a whole longer than that, but exactly what the conditions will be, I have absolutely no idea. I see a lot of science fiction movies that I think are probable, and they're all different. I'm kind of an optimist. I don't think it's going to get terribly worse.

DAVID: It's just that the human species has reached a point in its evolution where it has the potential to drive itself into extinction.

KARY: I am optimistic that we won't do it. That optimism does not arise from evidence, it's just my feeling that we won't. We've had the ability to wipe ourselves out for quite a while now.

DAVID: Do you see any teleology in nature, or think that there is any direction in evolution? Or do you think it's purely a random process?

KARY: My feeling about evolution is that it seems to have a teleology, but it doesn't really. It's just the operation of selection on random changes, as far as I can tell. I accept that theory as being the way evolution works.

I think there is so much more in existence besides matter, energy, and time. Nineteenth-century physics had those in an orderly arrangement, but it is too weird to be just that. There are other things going on, so evolution might not actually be without some kind of presupposed or predestined direction. But I think it's possible that it all happens through random changes.

There's a book by Richard Dawkins called *Climbing Mount Improbable* that I like. I think that the evolutionary mechanism makes it possible for very bizarre things to evolve in very slow steps. In his book Dawkins talks about the fact that you don't go straight up the face of Mount Improbable (Mount Improbable being the end, or the present state of being, of some particular species). You always go in little steps, back and forth, crisscrossing, finding the trails.

If you look at any one of the little steps leading to something as improbable as the human eye, it doesn't seem like such a magical thing. In fact, if random steps aren't the mechanism whereby very complex things like those form, then the next possible choice is somebody did it. Then you have to figure out, well, where did that somebody come from? The beauty of evolution is it says it can happen anywhere and it will get really freaky. (*laughter*)

You don't have to know who or why. The laws of evolution say that if you have random chances of species undergoing changes, then the ones which are best fit to reproduce in the environment they find themselves in will survive and continually create weirder and weirder things. You'll end up with giraffes, elephants, crocodiles, and people.

DAVID: I'm sure you're aware that there's evidence that *E. coli* bacteria don't always mutate randomly—that there's actually a response to the environment with regard to how their genetic mutations occur, so as to be more adaptive. How do you account for that?

KARY: There's something like that in *E. coli* and several other organisms. With the passage of a particular kind of retrovirus through several different species, there are certain DNA changes that happen that are actually not random. But if you look for the mechanism of those, you'd find that those mechanisms themselves are in place probably due to random things. In other words, the fact that you can change your DNA in a way that's not random does not mean that most of evolution doesn't occur due to random changes.

I think it's not an unlikely hypothesis that we're here simply because we survived, and there were changes all along that were random. It doesn't take any more than that, because time is so long. Four billion years means a lot of generations, and little tiny changes at every stage of the way, selected by whatever was there, the environment at the time, could very likely produce things like this. Nobody's ever shown that experimentally. There is really no experimental evidence for Darwinian evolution ever creating a new species.

DAVID: I guess it might take awhile to run the experiment. (*laughter*)

KARY: Yes, it takes time. But there are processes that help us to understand this. For instance, there are a lot of PCR-based permutation experiments, where you try to make a whole bunch of different kinds of the same molecule— millions and millions of variations of it. You select for the one that has a property that you like, and then you take that one and do the same thing to it. You can increase the ability of, say, some RNA species that you're making, or some protein that you're finally making from it, to bind to some specific protein receptors, thousands-fold that way—just doing it randomly.

You just reproduce the thing over and over in a way that will make little mistakes. Then you pick the best one, and do the same thing to it. Then pick the best one from that bunch and do it again. Eventually you end up with something that's almost qualitatively different, something that has a property that you've been selecting for which is so much greater than the thing you started with. You can almost say this is a different species of molecule.

That's sort of a test tube proof of the principle. The principle is almost like a tautology, in a sense, that, once you see it, you don't feel like you need proof for it. You say, well, of course that would happen. How else could it happen?

DAVID: What about the possibility of a strange attractor, like we find in the dynamic systems of chaos mathematics? When I interviewed Terence McKenna, he suggested that something at the end of time may be pulling us through evolution.

KARY: There may be something pulling us, and if so, that's going to be scary. (*laughter*) We're going to have to say, well, where the hell did that come from? (*laughter*) I like the idea that we have an independent existence that depends on nothing at all, except for the properties of matter and time. I like that because that's something we know about.

If there's some strange attractor driving us toward some particular evolution, then some people might feel more comfortable with that, but I wouldn't. I like that cold, clean feeling on the far side of the Moon, where there's nothing but us—just us and the chickens. (*laughter*)

DAVID: Terence McKenna also told me that he thought that time was a type of wave, having a beginning point and an end point. What is your perspective on time?

KARY: It's clearly nature's way of keeping everything from happening at once. (*laughter*) It may be that it flows along in a straight line, or it may be that it has a lot of curlicue things in it. It might be that it's got a shape that we have no idea what that would even look like.

I enjoy fractal geometry as a sort of hobby. Fractal geometry does not have any straight lines in it. It doesn't have any edges, any background or foreground, and yet it's really pleasant to look at.

DAVID: Just like nature.

KARY: Yes. I think nature is more like fractal geometry than it is like Euclidian geometry. Euclidian geometry says there is such a thing as a line—except a line is an infinitesimally thin thing. It's not a pencil line—that's a sort of an approximation to a line. But a real line doesn't have any thickness. A real point doesn't have any volume. A real square doesn't exist anywhere I've ever seen on the planet. No triangles either. Everything is an approximation to that, and the finer you look at it, the less of an approximation it is.

Let's say you ask: What is the perimeter of England? You could take a map of England, draw a circle around it, and say that is the perimeter. But if you get down really close, it becomes more difficult. How do you measure the perimeter of England? Let's say you take a rod and you see how many times it takes to walk around England with this rod end over end, and the rod is ten meters long. Then you say, Well, it took me a million times, so it must be 10 million meters around England.

But now if you get a smaller rod, perhaps five meters long, and do the same thing, it will turn out that you'll measure a larger perimeter of England, because that will work itself in and out better. The smaller the rod, the longer the perimeter of England gets. You finally have to conclude that it doesn't have a perimeter. (*laughter*)

DAVID: Or that it has an infinite perimeter.

KARY: A perimeter is a practical word that we use to approximately measure something that we think about, like skin surface. But it's the same as with the perimeter of England. It goes in and out, and in and out. There's not really an edge of you. You really stick out into everything, and it sticks into you.

DAVID: So, in other words, the boundaries that we perceive in the world are merely arbitrary creations of our own minds?

KARY: Yes. I think that the Buddhists have a name for that. It's the interpenetrability of things—like when you close your fingers together like this. (*Kary intertwines his fingers together.*) That's how you are with the universe. That's another thing, just like evolution, that you don't really need to prove to yourself. You just look at the principle and you say, Yeah, that's got to be true.

DAVID: From a psychological point of view, sometimes it seems as though time is composed of all these little discrete moments, like the stills of a movie, and we string them together somehow through our memories.

KARY: Yes, there do seem to be moments. I've experienced that, and I go through the moment concept also. It's as if there are moments and then there is space between them somehow. It's a subjective feeling that I get that probably relates to something, but I don't know how to set up a scientific experiment to measure a moment.

In the physicist's view, until the twentieth century, time was a continuous function. There weren't any punctate parts of it. It didn't stop and start—it was always there and it was running smoothly. Maybe the cogs and the gears of the clocks that we made were discrete—they made little movements, and you had seconds—but it was considered that those were due to our limitations, because we didn't have anything that would just totally and continuously measure time. We still don't.

But now, in our physics, it's not really clear that that is what is happening. The moment concept might be much more like what modern physics would say. Things do not run completely smoothly and even sometimes get ahead of themselves, in the sense that the cause of something happens after the effect of it.

DAVID: That seems to run completely counter to the entire way that we perceive the flow of time. How do you think that happens?

KARY: I don't know. In quantum mechanics there's a fuzziness about precisely locating anything in time or space, so it is possible that the cause of some phenomenon occurs after the phenomenon has already happened. I mean "after" in tiny little increments like tiny fractions of picoseconds, or something like that.

The probability that the cause of something occurs after the effect decreases with the size and complexity of the thing that's happening, and with how much later you're talking about. But it's always there. It's always finite. It is not absolutely impossible for the cause to happen a long time after the effect. It's just a matter of some little mathematical function that drops off exponentially. So there's really no "now" ever, anywhere.

DAVID: Of course the Buddhists would say that there's nothing else except "now."

KARY: It's almost the same thing when you get down to it. (*laughter*) When you say there is absolutely not a "now," then everything is "now" in a way.

There are parts of your brain that do not respond to time. In other parts, for example, emotional areas, everything is happening now. There's no saying, well, that's over, so I don't feel sorry about it anymore. You keep it. One of my favorite quotes in my book was that there was a particular part of your brain that deals with the melancholy of things past, and, as you age, it grows and prospers, until finally, against your better judgment, you listen to country music. (*laughter*)

DAVID: When I interviewed parapsychologist Dean Radin, he described experiments that he did showing people images on a video screen that were either pleasant or shocking, while a galvanic skin response system continuously monitored the people's reactions. A computer randomly chose the image five seconds before displaying it. The fascinating thing was that there was a significant change in the electrical conductivity of people's skin five seconds *prior* to their seeing a shocking image.

KARY: I sat wired up in front of Radin's machine myself one morning. I was intrigued. My skin conductivity could respond, not every time, but a statistically significant percentage of the time, to what sort of stimulus his absolutely random machine was going to present to me. I don't know what it means, but five seconds is almost an infinity compared to fractions of a picosecond, so I don't think that what Radin is investigating is the same thing as what Heisenberg is suggesting with the Uncertainty Principle and the fuzziness of time over ultra-short intervals. Both are weird from the standpoint of our normal sense of reality, but in a very different way. Picoseconds are not in our personal reality. Radin is addressing something to do with human minds on our time scale; whether our minds are really localized in space and time, like we normally think of them. He is not presenting a theory about things almost incomprehensibly small. He is demonstrating an empirical fact, a strange and unexpected property of things, on a scale of seconds, with which we are personally familiar, and he is doing it in a technically convincing way. I don't know what it means, that's why it's intriguing.

On a related but very different note, in one of the chapters of my book, I was talking about whether a computer could be ahead of you by looking at your brain activity. Before you would know you were going to do something, it would know. I feel like that's probably possible, but it doesn't suggest any radical new concept.

What Radin is getting at is something more curious. If you think about yourself as something going through time, how thick are you? You've got to have a certain finite "thickness" in time, or you wouldn't exist. So you might be a fraction of a second, or a second wide, or five, sliding through time.

DAVID: And your "thickness" may change, depending on your neurochemistry at the time. (*laughter*)

KARY: Yes.

DAVID: Perhaps our conscious experience of "now" has a thinner "thickness" than other unconscious aspects of our brains? I've wondered if this possibility might be an explanation for what people have described as precognition. What do you think?

KARY: It might be that certain parts of you are weeks, months, or years wide. Or maybe some part of you is "now" all the time—from your birth (or maybe even before birth) to your death. Some part of you is in the future at any moment, and some part of you is in the past, because you couldn't possibly be just in this infinitesimally thin thing we call "now"—because there wouldn't be room for you in there. (*laughter*)

That's using a lot of concepts that come out of physics and maybe don't belong in that context, but I've always thought that a little bit of me has got to be in the future.

DAVID: Or part of your brain can be processing information about an aspect of "now" that you're not quite conscious of.

KARY: Not yet conscious of, or maybe you won't ever be. Maybe it sticks out in lots of directions. (*laughter*) I mean, there's no need for this place to be just three-dimensional space and time. We have a subjective sense of physics that is consistent with three-dimensional Euclidian geometry. Euclid probably did too. But a lot of modern physics says that this place has more dimensions than that. String theory says that it is all made of strings, vibrating in eleven dimensions. We are made out of things that are eleven dimensional.

DAVID: At least.

KARY: This physics claims that eight of those dimensions have shrunk to such proportions that we can't perceive them in our normal life. They're just not wide enough to see. But we can infer them from the properties of tiny particles that we can see with enormous machines that we can build at great expense. And we can only understand the properties of all the particles we know about, from those machines, if the strings that compose them exist in eleven dimensions. That is to say, if these things which we are postulating to explain the things that we can see with machines are really things—meaning they have a finite spot where they are sometimes, and they have a certain energy associated with them—then they have properties that can only exist in an eleven-dimensional space. This concept would be helpful if you could imagine an eleven-dimensional space, which I can't. I'm still having trouble with five.

In my book I try to express this. I don't like to preach to people and tell them what I think they should be, but a lot of people need to be waked up to the fact that they follow like sheep. They think that the world has gotten too complex and that they can't decide for themselves about complicated issues.

Let's look at global warming. If those guys with the satellite sensors and the banks of computers running global circulation simulation programs call a press conference to say "If you don't stop burning fossil fuels, the Earth is going to get hotter and hotter until you're dead," most people will believe them. They don't think about the fact that with every scientific utterance that you hear or read, somebody's making a living.

Scientists get paid for making statements like that, and the more impact that their statements seem to make on our life, the more we're willing to support that sort of research. I make a case in my book for the fact that we're supporting a lot of research for very foolish things. We're still living on the frontier. We should be worrying about practical things.

DAVID: Like the asteroids that may come crashing down on us.

KARY: Yes, like the asteroids. We're spending three million dollars a year on that. We've spent three *billion* dollars on trying to figure out some way to experimentally confirm the existence of something called the Higgs particle. Nobody on this whole block cares about it, and nobody's going to care about it, unless they happen to be in the group that discovers it.

We're putting money into things that often don't matter. If we believe there is a hole in the ozone, and the "experts" say we must replace the former refrigerants with new ones, patentable to a company like Monsanto, there is more profit to be made. The freon patents have run out. We will spend trillions on replacing it with something equally likely to be bad for us in some way, and creating a black market for freon.

It's a ridiculous waste of the world's resources to be doing things like that, because there's no evidence for a hole in the ozone. Some labs were probably about to go out of business and needed a reason to exist and be funded.

If you really care about the planet, you don't have to always be torn by the latest fad, or the latest substitute for Catholicism—which I think environmentalism is in a way.

DAVID: In other words, question authority and think for yourself.

KARY: And ignore alien orders. (*laughter*) Yes, absolutely question authority, because there isn't any real authority. It's a democratic place in a way. The whole concept of evolution says that we all have the same sort of beginnings. We don't come from something above, telling us what's right and what's wrong. We have to figure it out for ourselves.

We're here, and we each have a spirit inside of us somehow that can make those decisions—if you keep informed. Don't read trash all the time. Every now and then read something that attempts to be factual, and try to make sense out it. But don't accept it as being factual. Just accept the fact that if you look at enough information, for a long enough time, you will start being one of the people in the world that can make decisions about what's really good for the planet.

DAVID: What do you think happens to consciousness after death?

KARY: I think that consciousness decays to nothing after death. My approach is to ask myself: What do I have evidence for? It seems like every living process does end at some point. It's a fuzzy thing, but as your body dies, I think your consciousness probably dies with it. Now, that's what I think—but what I would like to believe might be different from that. I'm not absolutely certain that that's a question that I have enough evidence to answer. In science you're supposed to have evidence.

It's all right to have a hypothesis, but you still have to have some evidence. You need to have something, like an indication, to make the hypothesis more than just a wish. Of course, being a scientist doesn't mean you don't have wishes. But, from a scientific point of view, I would say consciousness is definitely asso-ciated with the body as we know it. There's no reason to make up stories about things that we don't know anything about.

However, when I'm thinking about what's possible, then anything is possible. I think it would be pretty neat if we didn't dissolve after our death. It's not a question that there is an answer for. There's no reason to think that conscious-ness continues after death, besides just the fact that we would like it, and that we don't want to dissolve—but that's not really a reasonable kind of a scientific premise.

You couldn't get a National Science Foundation grant to study it properly, because we don't have any kind of indication that consciousness survives death. There are a lot of people that think that consciousness continues after we die, but I don't think that is reason for the scientist part of me to give it any truck at all. But there is a part of me, just like the rest of those people, that feels immortal and would like it to be that way. That question does not really have a rational answer.

DAVID: It's a question that fascinates me because I think it really stimulates the imagination.

KARY: Yes, it does. If you were to take a vote around the planet, it would definitely come out that we are eternal and responsible somehow for ourselves and our actions forever. But that's not a rational point of view. There's nothing that we accept like that in science except for mathematical truths. The universe itself, we would say it changes, and it has a lifetime. And at some point, it will either return to a singularity, or it will just expand itself out of existence, or whatever. I mean, there's nothing around us that has that property of being immortal.

DAVID: When I spoke with Rupert Sheldrake, he told me that he questions the idea that there are these eternal, unchanging mathematical laws that govern the universe.

KARY: He questioned that too?

DAVID: Yeah, he thinks of them more like habits than laws, and that they could be evolving, just like everything else in the universe is evolving.

KARY: Our idea about mathematics is that, once a theorem is proven, that it will always be true, because of the whole interwoven structure of mathematical logic. But a lot of things that we think are true in terms of physics, which is different from mathematics, have changed—like Newtonian gravitation, for instance. In the seventeenth century it seemed to be true, then, after three hundred years, with more thinking and better observations, it turned out not to be exactly true. Relativity came along and said no, you're dealing with elements like mass and length as though they were absolute and none of them are. Space is not absolute. Only the velocity of light is absolute. So everything had to be changed. But in mathematics, as long as we keep the definitions clear, it seems that a mathematical truth is eternal. The fly in the ointment, of course, is that mathematics does not say anything directly about reality. We make the associations intuitively, and we also up the axioms for want of any other way to get them. But we wouldn't want it to be simple here, would we?

DAVID: What Rupert questions is the idea that universal constants, like the speed of light, or gravitational constants, remain eternally unchanging.

KARY: There's no reason to think that those things can't change.

DAVID: Yet that's the assumption that most scientists have.

KARY: The speed of light is something that actually is a measurement that we make, and special relativity says it will always be the same for everyone. But special relativity is just a theory in the same way that Newtonian mechanics was a theory. We could find out that in certain circumstances, special relativity wasn't quite true. What we found out from Newtonian mechanics was that, in certain circumstances, Newton was wrong. The mass of something does seem to increase if it is going, relative to us, at a speed near the speed of light. In fact, it doesn't even have to be going near the speed of light. If it's just moving at all, the mass increases. It's just that the increase is kind of small until it gets up to a very high velocity. Newton thought that mass would always stay the same.

DAVID: Has your use of psychedelics influenced your scientific work, and how has it affected your perspective on life in general?

KARY: I would say that it was a mind-opening experience. It showed me that it might be a lot weirder here than I thought it was. So pay attention. Know what your assumptions are, and which of those are just arbitrary. Notice that things might be a little bit different than you think they are. I wouldn't say that it led to any particular developments in my thought, except that it just expanded it a little bit. I think almost anyone who's had those experiences would say that this place might be a little weirder than it appears. I'm not so certain anymore that the world is exactly the way I think it is. Most people get fairly stuck in ways of thinking that really are the current fashion, the current theory—like Newtonian mechanics seemed to be the way that things were for two hundred years.

DAVID: What is your perspective on the concept of God?

KARY: It's a notion that really doesn't solve any philosophical questions; it just puts it off a little bit. On the other hand, it's a concept that occupies the minds of a heck of a lot of humans, so it's an important concept to keep in mind. But if you look at it in a philosophical way, it simply puts off any kinds of thoughts that you might have of your origins or of your purpose. To just say I'm here because of Allah, and I'm here to do his will, doesn't really tell you what to do, or why you're here. It just gives it a name, and there's nothing really specific about anything of it.

DAVID: Do you think it's possible that there could be any type of intelligence or consciousness inherent in nature?

KARY: Well, what we know of the universe is so big, and so complex—on a large scale or on a small scale—that nothing really should be all that shocking to us. If it turns out to have properties that echo various religious beliefs, I don't think it would be terribly shocking.

But there's no evidence for such a thing. If you read and follow the thinking of those theories that are prominent today in terms of physics—like how physicists envision the whole of existence—and when they start talking about things like quantum mechanics, you realize that this place is so complicated, and so nonintuitive in a way, that anything is really possible, and nothing should surprise you.

But, on the other hand, there's no evidence that we are being led by some divine purpose. There's no evidence for that, and there's no evidence against that. It's not a question that science really needs to address, because there's no evidence to support it. But we often ignore some of the weirdest things on the planet.

DAVID: Like what?

KARY: Crop circles, for example. People might say that they don't exist, or they're all a hoax, but that's pretty silly. I don't think anyone could make some of the ones that I've seen. Either the pictures are faked, or the things are made by some kind of forces that we don't quite understand. They're not made by people going out in the middle of the night with sticks and ropes. There are a lot of things like that that we don't understand.

If you ask people the question, Have you ever had any experience that you just could not explain at all, but you couldn't deny it? most people will say, yes, that happened to me at least once. I consider that the experiences that I've had in my life are real in a sense. I don't make them up. Some things have happened to me that I can't explain, and I can't deny that they happened.

DAVID: What are some of the things that have happened to you that you can't explain?

KARY: All kinds of things have happened to me that I can't explain. They happen all the time. Don't you ever have what you might call an intuition, but really it seems that you have seen into the future?

DAVID: Sure.

KARY: I have that happen a lot. My wife has that happen. Just simple little things that are kind of contrary to any sort of scientific explanations that I can see. Actually, there's nothing in present-day physics that says that you can't have precognitive experiences. Like I was saying earlier, part of you exists in the future. Present-day physics says that the percentage of you that exists in the future drops off exponentially, and there's not much of it really, but how much does it take to see something in the future? I have all kinds of experiences that don't fit with the very simple and Newtonian picture of causality. Things seem to be connected by more dimensions than I can perceive with my vision, and modern physics says that's true.

DAVID: Why do you think it is that so many conventional scientists are opposed to the idea that telepathy or precognition might have a basis in reality?

KARY: Maybe they think there's scientific reason to doubt that those things could possibly exist. I don't think there is scientific evidence for these phenomena. Science has been silent on those things because scientists don't know how to deal with them. They don't really present a side we can grasp.

DAVID: Actually there has been quite a bit of serious research done trying to measure things like telepathy and other forms of psychic phenomena.

KARY: Yes, but it's not been terribly successful. Some people claim to have telepathic powers, but they can't always do it on demand.

DAVID: When I interviewed Dean Radin for this book, he told me that he did a meta-analysis of all the psi research that's been done over past hundred years. He said that, statistically, the odds of these hundreds of experiments—which tested for things like telepathy and psychokinesis—working out as positively as they did, were in the order of billions to one. The effects were small, but very statistically significant.

KARY: That may be so, but if I try to play the California lottery, for the life of me, I can't get it right. (*laughter*) I know that once in a while somebody does, but never me. My wife, Nancy, had this dream that she won the lottery. It was a powerful dream, and it woke her up. In the dream she won 16 million dollars. It was Saturday, and the lottery was at 13 million. She bought a ticket but didn't get close. The following Wednesday, the lottery was 16 million. She bought a ticket, got four numbers right, and made eighty-five dollars. She would have made a huge amount of money if she had gotten the Mega number correct. Amazingly, her incorrect numbers were only digits away from the correct numbers.

DAVID: Do you have any kind of model that you use to explain experiences like that?

KARY: I just say that was something I don't understand. It was mystifying that she would get four out of six, because that's hard to do. After that happened, we tried doing it more often. I thought maybe she would be good at it. That's what a scientist would think. If you could get four of them one time, maybe the next time you can get all six of them. But it didn't work that way. On that particular day, the chances were high that she was going get it for some reason. Otherwise, it was just a complete coincidence that she had that dream.

DAVID: It would be interesting to know how many other people got four out of six numbers right that day—and how many of those people had similar dreams.

KARY: Yeah, there are a whole lot of little questions like that. Do the people that win it just pick it by chance? Obviously, if enough people try, then somebody's going to win eventually, because that's the way it's set up.

DAVID: I don't think that anybody ever wins it repeatedly. Or at least, I've never heard of anybody doing that.

KARY: I don't think people do. If somebody could, they probably would, wouldn't they?

DAVID: You'd think. (laughter)

KARY: If people can really see into the future consistently, then they ain't telling me that. Nobody's ever told me they could see into the future anytime they wanted.

DAVID: But then weird things do happen though.

KARY: Yes, they do. Weird things like Nancy dreaming the lottery. She doesn't normally buy tickets. It has that element of somehow seeing into the future, but you can't really understand how it works. Anyone who doesn't think the world is much more mysterious than the simple picture that a physics laboratory would give you has not really been watching closely. If you think that everything that goes on here follows a set of Newtonian rules of mechanics, or even Einsteinian kind of stuff, then you're not paying attention.

DAVID: There are a lot of people like that.

KARY: Yes, they're not noticing it in their own life. They think it's just a coincidence. It's hard to say what the probability is that you will have a dream in which you've won the 16-million-dollar-lottery and, in a few days, it *is* 16 million, and you damn well almost win it. What is the probability of that? There's no way to compute what the probability of having a premonition dream is, and having it be close.

DAVID: You could start keeping a log of your dreams.

KARY: If you do keep a log, and you're paying attention, then there will be more chances to notice things. There are more weird things going on in your life then you expect by pure chance. I've never had any luck moving things with my mind, like making a penny fall the right way. I know there are people who can guess them sometimes, but they can't do it all the time. So, I would say that this place is not as well behaved as our theories about it would have it be.

And exactly what we are—which goes back to your question about whether or not consciousness vanishes when we die—is something that we don't know. Most of the people in the world think that there is a nonphysical part of people. By nonphysical, I mean that you can't weigh it. But if it weren't physical in some way, if it never had any effects on what you think of as real, it wouldn't matter whether it was there or not, would it?

There are a lot of people who feel this weird thing about their soul. However they define the soul, they think it's there. They say that the soul has certain properties, and you can make it be either happy for you or sad, after you die, by doing certain things. I consider these people to not be deep thinkers.

DAVID: Do you think their beliefs are some kind of psychological defense mechanism, or that their religious ideas come out of their fear of death?

KARY: I don't know where it comes from. Different cultures have all kinds of myths that are strongly adhered to by people. Christianity is one, and Islam is another. There are things in Buddhism that I would look at in the same way. They're just little myths that we don't really know much about, yet some people feel very strongly about them. So if you are studying humans, you certainly would not ignore religion, because it's probably one of the strongest forces that have affected us in the last three or four thousand years, and probably from long before that.

If you are studying what you think to be "the entirety of existence"—like somebody who studies physics would think—and you can't put an experimental framework on it, then it's not really useful to entertain that sort of myth. In other words, if there's nothing you can do about it—you can't measure it, use it to predict something with, or do something with it that you can't do without it—then you have to ignore it. One of the principles in scientific investigations is that you keep it as simple as possible. You don't introduce an extraneous idea that doesn't have some sort of meaning in terms of an experimental proof that you can do.

So introducing this idea of a greater-than-human force—a god, with human characteristics (which is usually the way religions picture this thing) who has it all figured out—has no basis, as far as I'm concerned, in my experience, or in the experience of reliable observers that I have access to. I don't see any reason to use that as a hypothesis and try to figure out an experiment to prove it or not.

DAVID: A lot of people claim from their experience with psychedelics that they've had religious or mystical experiences, which caused them to suspect that there might be some kind of intelligence operating in nature.

KARY: Yeah, and after a six-pack of beer a lot of people think they're invincible, which they're not. I'm not discounting the fact that psychedelics might open you up to see things that are true, which you wouldn't have seen without them. But a couple of six-packs might also show you something. It doesn't prove anything. You don't assume that what you see while your mind is under the influence of some drug is truer than what your mind sees when it's not.

Language, Politics, and Propaganda

An Interview with Noam Chomsky

Noam Chomsky revolutionized the study of linguistics and is one of the leading critics of U.S. foreign policy. Three different citation indices show that Dr. Chomsky is one of the most cited individuals in human history, and the New York Times *called him "arguably the most important intellectual alive." Between 1980 and 1992 Dr. Chomsky had 3,874 citations in the Arts and Humanities Citation Index, making him the most cited living person in that period and the eighth most cited source overall (just behind Sigmund Freud, Plato, The Bible, Aristotle, and Shakespeare). Dr. Chomsky received his Ph.D. in linguistics from the University of Pennsylvania. He teaches at the Massachusetts Institute of Technology, where he was appointed Institute Professor, and he held the Ferrari P. Ward Chair of Modern Language and Linguistics. In addition to authoring more than eighty books on language and politics, Dr. Chomsky also*

lectures widely and is one of America's most popular speakers, drawing standing-room-only audiences all over the country.

*   *   *

DAVID: All previous forms of media—television, radio, and newspapers—have been monopolized by corporations. It seems that they can't monopolize the Internet. Do you think that this will make a difference sociologically?

NOAM: First of all, historically, that's not really true. I don't know about other countries, but the history of media in the modern period—the last two centuries—has been studied pretty closely in England and the United States, and the period when the press was most free was probably the nineteenth century. There was a very substantial press in the nineteenth century, and it was very diverse. There was a working-class press, an ethnic press, and so on—with a lot of participation and involvement. It reached a great many people, and it presented a variety opinions and point of views.

Over time this changed. Actually there was an effort, first in England, to try to censor the independent press by various government means, such as taxation and others. Now, that didn't work, there were too many ways around it. It was finally recognized that through the forces of capital concentration and advertiser reliance, the independent press would simply be eroded since it would not be able to gain business support, either capital investment or advertising. And over time the press has narrowed, very sharply, in fact. It's been going on for the last few years, and the mass-based independent press has largely disappeared.

In the United States, for example, as recently as the 1950s, there were about eight hundred labor-based newspapers which reached, maybe, 30 million people a week. Of course, that's completely disappeared. If you go back to the early part of the century, about a century ago, popular-based, what we would call left-oriented journals, were on the scale of commercial press, and the same has been true in England. So it's not entirely true that it's always been monopolized, that's a process that takes place through capital accumulation and reliance on advertising.

The Internet is a very important case. Like most of the modern economy, it was developed in the state system, and for about thirty years it was either within the Pentagon or later the National Science Foundation. It was only privatized in the mid-'90s, and since then it has changed. So far it's been impossible to really control, so if people want to use it for their own purposes they can. But there are major efforts being made by the corporate owners and advertisers to shape the Internet, so that it will be mostly used for advertising, commerce, diversion, and so on. Then those who wish to use it for information, political organizing, and other such activities will have a harder time. Now, that hasn't happened yet, and it's really a terrain of struggle. But what's going on with the Internet is, in some respects, similar to the early days of print press, later radio, to some extent television.

DAVID: What sort of difference do you think the Internet has made politically? Do you see it as a tool for improving human rights and democracy?

NOAM: The appearance of the Internet has had a big effect. So a good deal of the organizing and activism of the past say ten years has been Internet-based. Now, that's true inside particular countries. So, for example, the overthrow of the dictatorship in Indonesia was very much facilitated by Internet contact among people, many of them students, who were able to organize and overthrow the dictatorship. Now we've just seen it in South Korea very dramatically.

Like just about every major element of capitalist society, the media are highly concentrated and very business-run. But South Korea is the most wired-up country in the world, I think, and through the use of the Internet, it was possible to develop what amounted to alternative media, independent media, which were on a very substantial scale. And they a were major factor in the political victory of the current president, who was reformist—a party which had plenty of popular support, and was able to organize it through Internet-based media.

The same is true much more generally. So, for example, international organizing that blocked the multilateral agreement on investments was done almost entirely by Internet. The media simply wouldn't cover the issue. Groups—like, say, the World Social Forum, which is now a huge organization, like a hundred thousand people show up at the meetings, and many more are involved from all over the world—are almost entirely Internet organized. The mass media won't permit any information to appear about it. There are many other examples.

. . .

DAVID: Do you think that our species is making progress with regards to human rights and democracy?

NOAM: Well, there's progress and there's regression, so it's a difficult trajectory to plot. By and large, with regard to human rights, I think there is notable progress. With regard to democracy, it's a much more complicated story. Formal democracy is increasing. So democracy in the sense of, say, the ability to vote for people in office is increasing. On the other hand, the barriers to effective use of democratic rights are also increasing. That's why skepticism and disillusionment with democracy are very notably increasing throughout a good part of the world, including the United States.

So, in the United States, for example, which is one of the most free and democratic societies there is, by now about three-quarters of the population regard presidential elections as basically a farce—just some game played by rich contributors and the public relations industry, which crafts candidates to say things that they don't mean and don't understand. And those proportions have been increasing. The same has been happening through Latin America and much in of the world. So formal democracy is definitely increasing, but with regard to substantive democracy, I don't think one can easily draw that conclusion.

DAVID: What do you think can be done to help bring about greater democracy in America and the world?

NOAM: The greatest American social philosopher of the twentieth century, John Dewey, once said—correctly I think—that politics is the shadow cast over society by big business. What he meant by that is, as long as you have a massive concentration of private power and wealth, there will essentially be dictatorial systems within the economy. A business firm is basically a dictatorship, with orders coming from top to bottom. As long as those phenomena continue, democracy's going to be very limited. The way to extend democracy is to overcome this massive concentration of power and wealth and to introduce democratic procedures throughout all institutions—what Dewey called going from industrial feudalism to industrial democracy. And not just in industry, but in every other institution. That's a traditional view—Dewey's not a far-out Leftist—and I think it's correct.

DAVID: Has your work in linguistics led you to believe that there is anything like a universal morality, similar to a universal grammar, that is inherent in people?

NOAM: Well, my work in linguistics hasn't led to that, but I think it's correct. In fact, the insight goes back well beyond the emergence of modern linguistics. The eighteenth-century British philosopher David Hume pointed out correctly that—as he put it—the number of duties is infinite. This means that we have an understanding of what we ought to do in a unbounded range of circumstances, many of them novel. And this can only happen, he said, if there were some fixed principles of human nature from which we derive an understanding of what our moral responsibilities are. And that's obviously got to be given to us, as he put it in the eighteenth century, by "the original hand of nature." You could say it's evolved as part of our nature.

It's hard to see what other possibility there could be, and that's very similar to the question of how linguistic knowledge develops. It must be part of our nature, and it is available for a unbounded range of circumstances.

So you and I, for example, may be producing expressions right now which neither of us have ever heard in our lifetimes, or may never have been produced before, but we understand them, because we have a fixed nature that provides the computational and interpretive mechanisms to use and understand them over an unbounded range. So in that sense there's a similarity, you could say, but it seems to be that Hume's observation is correct, whether or not you know anything about language.

DAVID: How do you think the innate structure of our minds imposes limits on our understanding?

NOAM: Well, if we are organic creatures and not angels, then our innate characteristics provide scope for our development, as well as limits on it. The fact that I have human genes and not mouse genes determined that I could become a human being, but I was unable to become a mouse. The same has to be true of our cognitive capacities. So whatever the genetic basis for our cognitive capacities is, it plainly provides a rich scope of options. But it must also provide limits on those options. They're logically connected—if there's a cognitive scope, then there's cognitive limits, just as with physical capacities.

DAVID: How do you think language affects consciousness and what we experience as reality?

NOAM: Your guess is as good as anyone else's. I mean, what we know is mostly by introspection. If you pay attention for, say, the next few hours, you'll discover that you're constantly talking to yourself. It's almost impossible to go through a moment of time without internal dialogue taking place, and that's just an enormous part of our consciousness. And it's in language, most of it, at least the part that's accessible to our consciousness is in language. How it affects our thought, and our general awareness, it's pretty hard to say. The thing is, we have no real access to thought or consciousness, except through language. So it's hard to ask the question.

DAVID: Bodily expressions and pheromones aside, do you think that language usage pretty much explains human communication? Or do you ever entertain the notion that telepathic, or other means of communication currently unrecognized by conventional science, can play a role?

NOAM: First of all, language by no means exhausts human communication. We communicate in all sorts of ways—by gesture, by the clothes we wear, by our hairstyles. All sorts of interactions are communicative. Language is just one of many modes of communication. But as for things like, say, telepathic modes, I don't have any reason to believe in their existence. I can't prove with certainty that they don't exist, but we need some evidence for it. It seems very unlikely because it would be quite inconsistent with, at least, what's understood about the nature of physical reality. It doesn't necessarily prove that it's wrong, but just that it's unlikely. It raises very high the bars to belief in it.

DAVID: What is your perspective on the concept of God, and do you see any teleology in evolution?

NOAM: I don't think there's any reason to suspect that there's any validity to any such notions.

DAVID: What do you personally think happens to consciousness after death?

NOAM: I assume it's finished.

DAVID: It's finished. That's the end?

NOAM: That's the end. Death is the end of the organism, and the end of everything associated with it.

DAVID: What do you think is the biggest threat to the human species, and what do you think we can do to help avoid it?

NOAM: The biggest imminent threat, I suppose, is nuclear war, which is not far away. We've come very close to terminal nuclear war a number of times. It's kind of a miracle that the species has escaped, in fact. And those threats are increasing. For example, the development and the expansion of military systems into space—with highly destructive space-based offensive weapons that are probably on hair-trigger alert—is almost a guarantee of devastation, if only by accident.

Now, those are very imminent threats and they're being increased, and the same is true with other weapons of mass destruction. For the moment, nuclear weapons are by far the most destructive, but bioweapons are increasing in lethal character and being spread. The failure to develop a bioweapons treaty is a serious danger to the species. Actually the United States has been in the lead in blocking any implementation of bioweapons treaties. In fact, it just undermined the latest bioweapons treaty, and is in fact also in the forefront of developing new nuclear weapons and the militarization of space.

Now, those are *extreme* dangers. In fact, if you were watching from Mars, a rational person would be amazed that the species has survived this long, and wouldn't put very high odds on it for the future. Now, beyond that, there are many other dangers. I mean, nobody really understands very much about the environmental threats, but there's a very broad consensus among scientists that they're serious. It could be that a nonlinear process is taking place—meaning that small differences, small changes, could have massive effects. This could have unpredictable consequences, and many of the possibilities are lethal. And there are a list of others. The species is in a very hazardous state. A rational person wouldn't put very high odds on survival.

DAVID: Do you think that the human species is going to survive, or do you think we're headed toward extinction?

NOAM: It depends whether we can take control of our own destinies. We have the means to do it. I mean, there's no law of nature that says you have to put destructive weapons in space or that you have to destroy the environment by wild overconsumption of hydrocarbons. Those are choices.

. . .

DAVID: What gives you hope?

NOAM: The short answer is that it doesn't really matter. How hopeful one or another of us may be is an insignificant matter of personal assessment of incalculable possibilities. We should do exactly the same things no matter what our subjective probabilities are. But when we see people all over the world struggling courageously under conditions of really terrible adversity, it seems to me not our business to pay much attention to our personal guesses, but rather to make use of the legacy of freedom and privilege that most of us enjoy.

Molecules of Mind and Body

An Interview with Candace B. Pert

Candace B. Pert is a neuroscientist who conducted groundbreaking research that changed the way scientists view the relationship between mind and body. While still a graduate student at Johns Hopkins University, she discovered the opiate receptor, the molecular docking site where opium-derived drugs like morphine and heroin bind to nerve cells in the human brain. Many people believe that Dr. Pert should have won the Nobel Prize for her discovery of the opiate receptor—which is considered one of the most important discoveries in the history of neuroscience—but that internal politics interfered with her being properly recognized for her work. Dr. Pert received her Ph.D. in pharmacology from the Johns Hopkins University School of Medicine, and she conducted research at the National Institute of Mental Health. Dr. Pert is Research Professor in the Department of Physiology and Biophysics at Georgetown University Medical Center in Washington, D.C., where she conducts AIDS research. She is the

author of numerous scientific papers and the book Molecules of Emotion: Why You Feel the Way You Feel, *which offers a personal and insightful reinterpretation of neuroscience and mind–body medicine. To find out more about Dr. Pert's work, visit her Web site: www.candacepert.com.*

* * *

DAVID: What were you like as a child?

CANDACE: My first thought is I was bad (*laughter*), but I'm working on my self-esteem so I don't want to say that. I was the kind of child who thought she was the only person in the world. I called out in class and never gave anyone else a chance. The adults in my life treated me like I was the Sun, the Moon, and stars. My mother says I was incredibly curious—that was her spin. She said I was always saying "what?" "why?" and asking millions of questions from a very early age.

DAVID: What inspired your interest in neuroscience?

CANDACE: I got interested in neuroscience because I got interested in my first husband. I think a lot of my interests come from the people I meet. I absorb. I kind of do a "mind meld" with people. That's my style—to get very close to people. So my first husband was (and is) a physiological psychologist. He wasn't just interested in the laws of behavior and psychology, but also in the actual physiological mechanisms in the brain—how things are happening beyond the black box. So I became a biology major. This is in the late '60s, early '70s. I think that we used to just basically fantasize together about the whole world of what is now neuroscience.

DAVID: Why is seeking truth important to you?

CANDACE: Seeking truth is extremely important to me just because it feels good. Everything else is below me, in the political world. Early on I saw that there's no standards without truth. I think I got mad at some teacher who gave me a C on an English paper about this. I'm particularly interested in things that have eternal truth. I don't know. It's part of my heritage and background, and maybe my crazy Connecticut Yankee blood—you know, congregationalists are into truth, honesty, and integrity. Truth is everything. What else is there? Everything else is fluff. (*laughter*)

DAVID: How has your sense of intuition helped to guide your research?

CANDACE: More and more. It's astounding. I mean, I always went with what I had an emotional connection to in choosing my projects—what seemed interesting and exciting—but now I'm finding that my intuition plays an even bigger role. Its almost eerie. I'm using "syncho-destiny" in my life. You know about "synchro-destiny," right?

DAVID: I know about synchronicity.

CANDACE: Synchronicity, of course, is the term that Carl Jung coined to describe meaningful coincidences, but Deepak Chopra developed this idea further. I hate to push Deepak, but he is great. He's got a new book called *Syncho-Destiny*, where you not only observe about synchronicity, but you harness synchronicity in your life to actually make decisions. One of the things that I noticed when I began meditating around fifteen years ago (and it was a double-blind experiment, because nobody told me this would happen) was that I was having more and more synchronicity experiences. And Deepak, or some other people, said, oh, yeah, that's typical of what happens when you meditate. Of course I asked why, and nobody knew why exactly. But yes, that's happening to me more and more—to the point that it actually guides what I do.

DAVID: That's interesting, Candace. In my own life, and with quite a few other people that I've spoken with, the number of uncanny synchronicities also seems to dramatically escalate in the weeks that follow a psychedelic experience. What's an example of how synchronicity has helped to guide your research?

CANDACE: Here's an example. My husband, Michael, and I were at the Society for Neuroscience meeting last November, and it was just weird. Every time I turned around, up would pop the members of this very interesting lab, the Wenk Lab, who have the leading-edge animal model for Alzheimer's disease— as an neuroinflammatory disease, as opposed to other approaches to the disease, where, I think, there's an overemphasis on plaques and tangles, which may be some kind of epiphenomenon and not the actual source of the disease. But there was literally twenty thousand people at this meeting, and every time I would turn around there would be someone from this lab. (*laughter*)

It's really weird. Finally, at the end of the conference, we had breakfast at that famous place in New Orleans, Café du Monde, with Susanna Rosi, and we plotted out a series of experiments. And they're just turning into the most exciting things—where the drug that we had originally invented for AIDS turns out be incredibly efficacious in this animal model for Alzheimer's. So that's an example. I mean, it was like, yeah, let's work with her. We keep bumping into her, so there's got to be a reason.

DAVID: What sort of model do you use to explain the synchronicities that you've experienced?

CANDACE: In two words, my model for explaining synchronicities in my life is "God's work." It's proof of God, whatever God is. It's just kind of like all of the laws of the universe—the ones we understand and the ones that we don't understand. It's action at a distance. It's timelessness. It's the final psychological manifestation of the laws of quantum physics. That's what's synchronicities are about.

DAVID: In your your book you mention experiences with both "synchronicity" and "serendipity." How do you define the difference between these experiences?

CANDACE: It's funny, and it's interesting, now I hardly ever use the word "serendipity." I think serendipity has an element of chance, and that it's not purposeful. Since I now think there are no accidents, I think that's probably why I don't use the word "serendipity" any more.

DAVID: Can you talk a little about women in science? Why is the system so stacked against them, and what do you think needs to be done to correct the situation?

CANDACE: That's a big question. I just went to a very nice event. There was a wonderful opening at the National Library of Medicine of a fabulous exhibit on the history of women in medicine. It was put together by a group called the Advancement of Metropolitan Area Women in Medicine and Science, or something horrible like that. (We're trying to find a new name.) But they had lots of good data and statistics.

Basically, you can see how wonderfully women have gone from being 1 or 2 percent of the medical school classes and graduate school programs in the '40s, '50s, and even '60s, compared to today when most of them are now at 50 percent. It's even skyrocketed up in the armed forces medical school. The armed forces is a big deal. They have commandant, and they're getting up to 40. So there's progress, but then when you get to a certain point, it's the glass ceiling all over again. When you get to the percentage of women who are department chairs or deans, then it just starts to plummet. For example, Georgetown University, where I am, has only one female department head in the whole medical school.

This is a terrible thing to say, but more and more, I'm appreciating that there are certain innate tendencies and patterns that people have, and women, on the whole, truly are less aggressive than men. They're less able to toot their own horn, and are more able to promote others and work as a team. These are not things that make them wonderful people, but don't necessarily let them rise to be the head of the department or full professor. That's what some of the women think—that the women are just not down there complaining enough, and they're not aggressive enough. So if that's what it's about, then women are different, and then you might say, oh, it's never going to happen.

But since they're also incredibly talented maybe there's going to be some shift in how we perceive the way science should really be done. For example, like right now in the AIDS field, there's this thing about the experts, and who gets the most money. It's almost an entirely male-dominated field, and maybe people will learn that the women really make an unusually high number of breakthroughs for their numbers. They're sort of like the Swedes of science. There's very few Swedish scientists, but they've discovered all kinds of incredible things. I think women are that way, although a lot of times they don't actually get full credit for what they do, since they do have this innate tendency to be less pushy. Not me, of course. (*laughter*)

DAVID: Can you talk a little about the positive potential that you see for combined male/female energy in research labs?

CANDACE: Oh, of course that's the ultimate—the two working together, the male–female energy. One obvious example is husband-and-wife teams. I work, and have worked, really closely with my wonderful husband, Michael Ruff, for many years. This allows you to have a real "mind meld," particularly if it's another person who has a different background. Michael is a immunologist/virologist and I'm a neuroscientist. Strangely enough—I don't know if we created this with our minds or if it was an independent event—but it turns out that now more and more people are appreciating the neuroinflammatory aspects of many diseases. We see this from Parkinson's to Alzheimer's, and even schizophrenia and autism. We've spent a lot of time talking about pioneering in this the idea that the brain and the immune system really are communicating. It started out being "closely connected," but now there's also kinds of cell sharing.

Male and female energy—just get more women in the lab, and then you'll have more male and female energy! There's nothing wrong with funding initiatives so that more women can get their own money. There's so many terrific women that wind up as being like kind of gal Fridays, or fabulous first lieutenants for men. You see that all the time. It's kind of an amazing how the scientific system lends itself to that. You have a hierarchy. The person who gets the most money gets the postdocs, and can pay someone to stay on. And even through their title is Assistant Professor or even Associate Professor, they're kind of often indebted to the big alpha male. So I think there should be some funding initiatives to get more women as heads of their own labs and financially independent of men. That's another thing I'm learning in my old age (*laughter*)—money is power.

DAVID: Why do you think it's so difficult to get new ideas accepted in science?

CANDACE: That's a very interesting question. I was just thinking about that the other day. The Pollyanna answer is, hey, it's wonderful for science because otherwise there would just be all this crap creeping in its way. It's critical, things have to be tested out, and blah blah blah. But, I think, it's just like human nature to do this. I mean, I used to be responsible for it too. People only believe their own things. So if they haven't seen something, they tend to not believe it, I guess. Then there's like some jealousy of new ideas. But it is part of the scientific culture that we don't dare accept a new idea. It's wrong. That would be a major setback. You gradually let ideas in one by one, after they've been really proven. But, of course, there's Thomas Kuhn's ideas about paradigm shifts and all that. We know that it doesn't really work that way, and it tends to be like more revolutionary. So I don't know. But like the thing that I'm really interested in right now is neurogenesis. You know about this?

DAVID: The birth of new brain cells.

CANDACE: Yeah, and the idea is twofold, one more amazing than the other. The idea is that we are making new neurons everyday in our brains, and the other is that stem cells come normally out of bone marrow, move through the blood, and actually wind up in the brain as neurons.

DAVID: Which goes against everything that I learned in school! My psycho-biology professors taught me that we were all stuck with this limited number of neurons, and they're slowly dying as you age, with no ability to regenerate. So you just have less and less as you go, and your cognitive functioning is gradually slipping away.

CANDACE: Exactly. I mean, the fights that the scientists have had to go through to get this accepted. Finally, what's happened is, it's an interesting Mexican standoff. There's lots of struggle, and people now accept that this is true. But the people making these observations had to jump through a hundred hoops of carefully controlled experiments to refute every possibility of it being an arti-fact. Now it's accepted as a fact, but for a long time it wasn't. Two long-term colleagues, who are really smart, and they're great scientists, sat there and they were poo-pooing the actual biological importance of it. They were saying, all right, so there are neurons, yes, it's been proven—there's evidence from humans that many of these new cells are maturing every day—but we have no evidence that it's important, and the whole thing just may have nothing to do with anything. And that's the position they're holding right now.

DAVID: I find that astonishing. They don't think that the discovery of new brain growth is important?

CANDACE: Well, they're just taking a very conservative scientific view, that you're not allowed to imagine. I'm getting ready to give a lecture in New York on Sunday, and it's the cornerstone of my lecture. I'm going to talk about the impli-cations for our own mind, body, health, and how we can utilize this discovery. I mean, it's no longer just a truism to think positively, choose positive thoughts, and to make an effort to not put negativity into words. Every time you repeat something, you're stabilizing this neuronal network that's forming. There's always a nascent network that's forming, and there's a constant living and dying of neurons. And what lives and what dies depends on how often it's used. So the more negative things you think or say about yourself, you're just reinforcing those circuits. So to me this is huge. I still can't get over it. (*laughter*)

DAVID: You mention having "psychic hunches" in your book. What is your perspective regarding research on psychic phenomena like telepathy or precognition?

CANDACE: From what I know about parapsychology, I certainly think there's interesting, valid research going on. Lots of mainstream scientists would dis-miss it, but—from a research perspective—I don't. It's another area to study. There's so many interesting things that aren't in psychic science that I'm like excited about that I wouldn't be so interested in that. But, in terms of psychic phenomena, I'd be interested in the mechanism. I mean, it's spooky. Nothing springs to mind at the moment, but I've experienced these things myself, and I've had so many amazing things happen that I have no doubt. But I am way less interested in proving that there is such a thing statistically than I am in trying to understand the mechanism by which it happens. Because I assume that stuff happens. I've experienced it.

DAVID: In your book you mentioned once saying a prayer over an experiment, which was something that early alchemists actually did, believing that it could have an effect on the outcome. British biologist Rupert Sheldrake has suggested that scientific researchers might want to consider always doing double-blind experiments—not just in psychology and medical research, but also in hard science fields like physics and chemistry—to control for the possibility that a researcher's intention may be subtly influencing the outcome of the experiment. Do you think that our beliefs and intentions could possibly affect the outcome of experiments in ways that are not currently recognized or understood by conventional science?

CANDACE: Rupert is one of the main reasons I got this crazy dog that's changed my life. Yeah, I think there's work on that. You might want to speak to Bill Tiller. I think that's interesting. That's possible. But once again, what do I want to say? I mean, there is just a whole eerie quality. It makes me nervous, because I've had a career as a straight scientist, but it's pretty astounding. It gets to be very philosophical, and I hated philosophy. It was the only course I ever flunked in my life. So I get nervous about all this. But like the opiate receptor—which has now been renamed the opioid receptor—did I discover it? Or did I invent it? It's like, if you believe in something enough, maybe somehow you can organize reality around it. Do you know what I mean?

DAVID: I wonder about that a lot actually. It certainly appears that way sometimes.

CANDACE: Yeah. Do I believe the concept? There's something going on that's pretty weird. I mean, my mind is still boggled on the peptide T front. We just came from the NIH [National Institute of Health], where we saw talks relevant to HIV. At the time peptide T was invented, no one ever heard of the word chemokine. The word had not been coined yet. This is a class of peptides that are found in both the brain and the immune system. Their role in how cells move and divide and survive had not yet been done, and it wouldn't be done for ten more years. And just today we heard it again. Now it turned out five years ago that HIV uses the receptors for this class of peptides, and every company is now saying that the best thing to target is the chemokine receptor, and specifically the type of chemokine receptor, which is called CCR-5. Now, it turns out, not only does peptide T target this, but it targets this exact receptor. Not just chemokine receptors in general, the one that everyone's trying to make a drug for. Now, come on, is that weird or what? To me, that is the ultimate, and in some ways peptide T's discovery is the ultimate psychic phenomena, because it's just truly unbelievable.

Now it's starting to have these applications in other fields as well. So its not just in AIDS. I mean, it's huge. And how did this all happen? It's so strange the way it came to be invented. So when you pose that question—yeah, there was something where I was really really wanting to make a discovery, to help people with AIDS, at the time the discovery was made. So I don't know what that state of mind of is, where you're really in some godlike mental state, where your consciousness is going everywhere and coming from everywhere. I've written about it. I had hiked up this crater in Maui and come down it, and it was pretty astounding. I was in some very out-there state of mind when I had the idea for how to proceed, and it's almost twenty years before what people are trying to do now. It stills blows me away.

DAVID: What do you think happens to consciousness after death?

CANDACE: That's a great question. Years ago I had to answer that question to get a big honorarium, so I participated, and what I said then is still relevant. It's this idea that information is never destroyed. More and more information is constantly being created, and it's not lost, and energy and matter are interconvertible. So somehow there must be some survival, because one human being represents a huge amount of information. So I can imagine that there is survival, but I'm not sure exactly what form that it takes. I think Buddhist practice is interesting. There's this whole idea that you're actually preparing yourself for death, and if you do it just right you can make the transition better.

DAVID: What is your concept of God, and do you see any teleology in evolution?

CANDACE: We don't have to say that evolution is guided by an intelligence, but it's very clear to me that the process itself—stars cooling, entropy, evolution—is always leading toward more and more complexity and more and more perfection. So the actual physical laws of the universe are God. You don't have to invoke anything beyond that. I mean, God is not incompatible with the laws of science. God is a manifestation of that. There's no incompatibility. We're not talking about the Bible; we're talking about the true laws of science. So I guess that's why I'm so into truth-seeking—because truth-seeking is God-seeking at the same time.

DAVID: Do you think that the human species will survive the next hundred years, or do you think we're danger of extinction?

CANDACE: Oh, I don't know about the next hundred years, but I'm very nervous about that. The estimates vary, but my understanding is we're going to run out of fossil fuels between two hundred and five hundred years. God knows what's going to happen during that point. We used to all be afraid of the nuclear threats, and all that, although I'm more afraid of this. But first of all, let me say I'm an optimist. We're going to escape it. It's going to work. But people have to start paying attention. I think that before we have an extinction of our species we might have the extinction of advanced intelligence. We've got this terrible problem with our food, that I'm more and more interested in. I've actually bought a farm with a group of friends, and have this totally insane plan to turn it into some kind of learning, educational, and research center to continue to educate myself and others more about food.

So I'm concerned about this. Genetic engineering is only the tip of the iceberg. Forget genetic engineering. It's the fact that the food we eat today is not chemically what it was even ten or twenty years ago. If you list every chemical found in an apple today, and make a graph, it takes only about three typed pages to write them all down. But if you compare this to an old apple, it would be would five pages long. The new apple is only three pages because of the chemical farming, the pesticides, the herbicides, the soil, and the artificiality of it. Our food is lacking things. It's not just poisons, toxins, and contaminants—things are *lacking*. Essential fatty acids that we need are not in animals now, and enlightened people who can afford it, like myself, are frantically buying the right omega-3's to add to our diet.

But in the long term, what's going to happen to everyone? In my life, having raised three children who are each nine years apart. I believe I'm seeing changes in their brain that are more than cultural, that might very well have to do with their diets—what people are eating and not eating. It's easy to think of the nuclear winter and all that. But even before that, I could see in another fifty years, at the rate we're going, the average IQ is going to be around 60, and people won't even know it.

DAVID: Assuming that we do survive, how do you envision the future evolution of the human race?

CANDACE: If we're going to survive, there has to be (*laughter*) the dawning of the Age of Aquarius. People have to become much more changing of their nature. All people have multiple personalities. Everyone of us is capable of being very selfish, as well being very loving and feeling very much part of a group. We're just going to have to keep reinforcing the second part. Somehow people are going to have get back to feeling less alienated and being parts of local units. Everything that's fallen apart—organized religion, small towns, the things that made us part of a small group—has got to come back together again, somehow, if we're going to survive.

DAVID: You mention Aldous Huxley's book *Doors of Perception* in *Molecules of Emotion*. I'm curious: Have you ever had a psychedelic experience, and if so, how has it influenced your perspective on science and life?

CANDACE: I can say that I've had some unusual experiences. I basically missed the '60s, and even the '70s in terms of experimenting with drugs at the normal time, because I was a young mother, and I was always in a very responsible authority figure role from a very young age. But later on I experimented with marijuana and some of the psychedelics. I think the biggest influence was marijuana, which I didn't even try until I was like thirty-five years old. I think that had an impact on me, because it erases boundaries and gets you into interesting altered states. I've experimented with that, and less with some of the psychedelics. Has this influenced me? Sure. Spending time in an alternative reality, which is noncompetitive and loving, must have taken away my East Coast competitive nature. Of course, now I am convinced that marijuana should be avoided since it wreaks havoc with one's endocannabinoids.

DAVID: What type of potential do you see for new types of psychoactive drugs in the future?

CANDACE: I'm never moving in that direction. In my book I talked about not using drugs with an almost puritanical insistence. This is at least where I am now—that we're at our best when we have our natural drugs. It's like our own natural chemicals, unadulterated, are just totally amazing. But this a great ideal. I mean, I'm a major user of supplements, vitamins and things like that.

DAVID: I thought the primary point that you were making in your book was that using any type of psychoactive drug on a regular basis will cause the brain to compensate for the drug's continued presence by reducing the number of receptors that bind to it.

CANDACE: Exactly. Anything you take changes your brain, because there's a law that a natural system will always compensate when you perturb it. So in some very romantic idealized way I see our perfection is like, let it all hang out. Let it be what it is. But yet that's an ideal. I smashed my arm playing on the ski slopes four weeks ago, and I'm now taking Vicodin for my broken arm. I'm trying not to take it. But, heck, it helped me, and it's okay.

DAVID: A few scientists that I've spoken with told me that they don't think that the HIV virus is responsible for causing AIDS. What do you think about this idea?

CANDACE: I can be a lot more definitive on this than I can on some of the other questions you asked me. These people are nuts. The evidence is clear, and it's the most elegant scientific story. There was a movement against HIV research, and the main champion was Peter Duesberg. There was some personal animosities against the power and the money that the early AIDS researchers got, and there's a lot of political aspects to this. But beyond a shadow of a doubt— and I'm speaking as somebody who studies data in the lab—there is just no doubt about the fact that HIV is the cause of AIDS. There's just so much elegant science behind it. Just let me cite one little tidbit that tells you how clean the whole thing is. There's two primary receptors that the AIDS virus uses to enter and infect cells. One of them, which I mentioned earlier, is called CCR-5. It turns out that a small percentage Caucasian Europeans don't have that receptor. They have a genetic mutation where the receptor should be, and it's missing a major chunk of it in the middle. Now, those people who have that mutation, no matter what risky behavior they indulge in, they do not get HIV disease. Isn't that interesting?

DAVID: Extremely. I didn't know that.

CANDACE: Then, of course, you can show clearly in the test tube that you can artificially make cells that have this receptor and they will become readily infected with the viruses that use this receptor. And if the cells don't have the receptor, then they don't. That's summarizing like hundreds and hundreds of papers that elegantly address this, so there's no doubt that HIV causes AIDS. Duesberg may not like some of the HIV virologists, and their style and all, but it's just so silly. And it's sad, because they've created a movement that's been very destructive. My understanding is that out in California, some of these people are like Luddites. Some of the activists—not all of them, but some small percentage—have gotten this into their head and have stormed research labs. They've gotten very angry and very crazy, and it's complete rubbish. I have no doubt in my mind. I'm 100 percent sure about this.

DAVID: Why do you think its important to question authority?

CANDACE: Because the experts are usually wrong (*laughter*)—often they're wrong—at least experts on disease, because if the experts knew so much about the disease, then the disease would be cured. But, by definition, the experts are the guardians. They become the gatekeepers on what kind of research goes on and what kind ideas are right and wrong about a disease. What I've experienced and observed is the longer that a disease has been around, been studied, and had money thrown at it, the more hardened and more difficult it is to get any kind of novel idea in there. This is the case for a lot of the neurological diseases, and there's all these mythologies. There's all kinds of data, but people keep studying the same systems. So you should question authority because the experts aren't always right.

DAVID: What are you currently working on?

CANDACE: I'm currently working on the AIDS drug that I invented with Michael Ruff in 1986. We have recently published the results from a small clinical trial in the journal *Peptides*, in which we observed the amazing result that the drug dramatically reduced the amount of virus-forming potential, viruses hiding inside the cellular reservoirs in the blood. It's been known that even the state-of-the-art therapy, which greatly reduces the amount of virus that's loose in the blood, doesn't touch this reservoir. So, basically, we are now in the process of organizing new trials to replicate this finding in a large double-blind, placebo-controlled trial.

DAVID: That's really exciting.

CANDACE: Yeah, so we're on this, man. I finish everything I start, and if God gave me this unbelievable gift, we will finish it. Then we're also exploring other aspects of the drug. I mentioned that it turns out that chemokines and chemokine receptors have an important role to play in the normal and inflamed brain, so there's all kinds of spin-offs into the possibility of treating neurological disease like Alzheimer's disease and others with Peptide T or analogs of Peptide T.

So it's weird. I've actually gone back into straight science. This year I've been to all the major neuroscience meetings that I used to go to years ago, and yet I'm somehow fusing that with my—I want to say my "New Age persona," or my "new paradigm-thinking" person. It's like I'm starting to feel more and more okay about doing both and being both.

DAVID: I think what you're doing is extraordinary. It's truly amazing the way you've been able to bridge those two worlds. When I studied neuroscience in graduate school, we couldn't even talk about consciousness. It was completely taboo—unless one was referring to an animal being "conscious" or "unconscious." I'm really in awe of what you've been able to accomplish.

CANDACE: Yeah, but it's exhausting and weird. Like this broken-arm thing is weird. It really slowed me down. I think I was vibrating too fast, and I was about to fly off. (*laughter*)

DAVID: Do you mean off the ski slopes or off the planet? (*laughter*) My friend John Lilly used to warn me about the dangers of evolving too quickly. He said that I had to be careful not evolve too much faster than the evolutionary speed limit, or I might get busted by the evolution cops.

CANDACE: Oh, that's interesting. It's like you can't go too fast. Simmer down here.

DAVID: John Lilly was big fan of your work. That's how I first found out about you actually. He used to talk about you a lot.

CANDACE: I have pictures of him and me. He came to the National Cathedral. He was wonderful. God, that's such a shame when people have to die. I've had people close to me die, and sometimes I think there are some amazing communications and synchronicities, where you think that they are trying to communicate, or some aspect of what has survived is coming back. There's some amazing stories, with things like doors slamming. I've had a few things happen at funerals. I've been through quite a few funerals in the last few years, and have seen things like leaves swirling at critical moments in the burial ceremony. There's stuff that seems kind of amazing. (*laughter*)

DAVID: Yeah, it definitely seems like there's much more going on than conventional understanding would lead us to believe.

CANDACE: Right. I was just thinking about blending the new paradigm perspective and straight science, melding the two. It's almost like my ongoing, I hate to call it a struggle—but it's getting easier, I think.

DAVID: Do you think that's because there's more receptivity to it now in conventional science?

CANDACE: I don't know. But no, I never cared about what other people thought. That's never been my thing. In fact, as part of my transformation, I've had to learn to be sensitive to what other people think. But it's like talking out of both sides of your mouth. The new paradigm is so different from the left-brain way that I was raised. It's just been personally difficult to go both ways at once.

DAVID: When you say the "new paradigm," you mean the idea that consciousness creates reality, rather than vice versa.

CANDACE: Yeah, that whole idea. Right. But I think that the new neurons—neurogenesis—is the key to this, which could be why people are resisting it so much. (laughter)

DAVID: Is there anything that we haven't spoke that you would like to add?

CANDACE: I'm getting up in years—oh, I'm not that old, and hopefully I'll work things out and live really old. My ancestors all lived pretty old. But now the challenge is how do I take what I've experienced and boil it down into something that I could give to other people? This is all great and inspiring, and I'm like this just weird person out there, but how do I create something that could actually help people—and, I mean, people who are not Ph.D.'s in neuropharmacology.

So I'm very excited about this new project that I'm working on right now. It's actually going to start to come into reality a lot this week—like starting on Friday. What I've come up with is this—I'm producing my own CD. The CD is going to be a musically excellent series, but I don't want to call it anything that already exists. On one level you could call it a relaxation tape, but it's basically something that's going to put into action the sound scientific principles of learning with relaxation, things that I've experienced over the years, workshops that I've done, and make something that might be really helpful for people's personal healing, progress, and transformation. It's helping me a lot to do it (laughter), so that must mean I'm on the right track.

DAVID: It sounds like something I'd be very interested in hearing. I think there was quite a bit of insight and wisdom in your book *Molecules of Emotion* actually.

CANDACE: A lot of people liked the book. They write me and all. I'm glad it inspired people, but it's a book, and it takes a long time to read. What if there was something that people could listen to every day, for a brief period of time, and it could really help them? I think we're there. I think that by having lived on both sides of the paradigm, maybe I can make something that would really be practical and useful. Since I am a scientist, the other idea is that after we make it, I think we could test it and see if it really does help in this and that way by having some actual rigorous, controlled scientific testing. Then it's like an experiment. We could continue to optimize it, make new versions, and make it better and better. It wouldn't take a lot of effort, or a lot of my time, and it's also a way to not spend all my life force like on the Peptide T project.

My work used to have a very exhausting struggle struggle struggle quality to it, but I'm now starting to laugh at it and see how easy it is. Today was great day at the NIH. There were people who had once been staunch enemies of the drug who couldn't believe it. Now they got to hear a talk by another scientist who's saying, we're all looking for a drug, and there's people in this room who have a drug that acts just this way—and he looks over at Mike and me, and everyone knows exactly what he's talking about. Afterward everyone is smiling at us and shaking our hand. It was unbelievable, and we don't have to try too hard. All we have to do is not be negative and not trip over ourselves at the end of the day. It comes down to your own feelings about yourself, how we relate to ourselves. It's like the last line of that episode of *Sex in the City*, "the most important relationship we have is with ourselves." The way we relate to ourselves has this eerie way of expanding wildly all over, because it's also the way we relate to the world.

DAVID: Yeah, it really is uncanny isn't it?

CANDACE: It's spooky as hell. So it's like every stupid thing I ever did keeps coming back to haunt me until I heal it. Then I can like laugh at it—and then whoosh—that's gone. Each day these things are coming at me, and I'm quite sure now that it won't be a struggle if I can just really walk the talk, and not be a bossy overbearing shrew (*laughter*)—which I can be—and truly kick some joy into what's going on. And take some delight in the way that this drug has just popped out, and realize—eeehhh—it's not me. I don't have to have so much ego tied up in it. It's truly a miraculous creation, and it's fallen into my lap. And, hey, at least one other person—Mike—is responsible for at least 51 percent of it. So it's a little more generosity, a little more humility, and I'll be a saint by the end of this. (*laughter*) Stay tuned.

From Outer Space to Inner Space and Beyond

An Interview with Edgar D. Mitchell

Edgar Dean Mitchell—the lunar module pilot for NASA's Apollo 14 space mission in 1971—was the sixth man to walk on the moon. In addition to his historical achievements as an astronaut, naval officer, and test pilot, Dr. Mitchell has also made important contributions as a research scientist, author, and lecturer. He has spent the last thirty years studying human consciousness in search of a common ground between science and spirit. Dr. Mitchell founded the Institute of Noetic Sciences to sponsor systematic research into of the nature of consciousness, especially in regard to how it relates to psychic phenomena and alternative healing techniques. The institute has grown into one of the world's largest research groups studying the unexplained powers of the mind. Dr. Mitchell received his Sc.D. in Aeronautics and Astronautics from the Massachusetts Institute of Technology, and has received many distinguished awards and

honors, including the Presidential Medal of Freedom. He is the coauthor of Psychic Exploration: A Challenge for Science *and* The Way of the Explorer.

* * *

DAVID: Can you briefly describe the mystical experience that you had when you viewed the Earth from space, and how did that experience effect your perspective on science and spirituality?

EDGAR: Sure. Okay, let's set the stage for that a little bit. Remember, my job was lunar module pilot. That meant that I was primarily responsible for the lunar spacecraft and the lunar surface activities, which I took the lead role in for this mission. Alan Shepard was our commander, of both spacecrafts. Stuart Roosa was the expert in the command module. I was presumably the expert in piloting the lunar module and on the surface activities. So when that was complete, and we were on the way home, it kind of relieved me of responsibility, after having completed my task successfully.

Like other lunar module pilots, I had the opportunity to be a little bit more of a tourist on the way home, with a well-functioning spacecraft, and a chance to look at the heavens—the Earth, the Sun, the Moon, and galaxies. And you have to realize that we were oriented perpendicular to the plane of the ecliptic—the plane which contains the the Earth, the Sun, and the Moon—and we were rotating in order to equalize the thermal balance on the spacecraft. In other words, we were flying one direction, and our spacecraft was oriented perpendicular to that direction in what's called barbecue model, so that it continues rotation. And every couple of minutes you'd get to see the Sun, the Earth, the Moon, the heavens, and that was a pretty wild experience.

When I earned my Ph.D. I studied star formation and, presumably, how galaxies formed, as we understood it at that time back in the sixties. I suddenly realized that the molecules of my body, the molecules of the spacecraft, and those of my partners had been prototyped in some ancient generation of stars. And, okay, that was nice intellectual knowledge, but all of a sudden it hit me at the gut, and—wow—*those are my molecules*. It became personal.

I could see the stars, see the separateness of things, but felt an inner connectedness of everything. It was personal. It was wild. It was ecstatic. And it made me ask myself, well, what kind of a brain–mind–body is this that reacts to this vision, this sighting? What is this? What's going on here? Well, it took awhile to figure that out after I got back, but essentially that was the insight. And it made me realize that our story of ourselves as told by science was probably incomplete, and maybe flawed. And that our story of ourselves as told by cultural cosmology, rooted in religion, was archaic and certainly flawed—particularly since each culture had its own story for a different cosmology.

It occurred to me that the difference between a scientific cosmology and our cultural cosmology was because we really didn't understand what consciousness is. We hadn't really answered the question: Who are we, and how did we get here? And that, as a new, budding ET civilization, maybe we needed to ask that question again. Even though every culture, every generation since the beginning of time, has pondered that issue. But now we're a spacefaring civilization, maybe we need to relook at it.

So that was the event. That was the circumstance. That was the challenge. And this feeling of bliss, ecstasy, and insight continued when I wasn't working, which was a good portion of the time on the way home. Even though we had a few experiments to perform and a few things to do, it was mostly just riding home in a well-functioning spacecraft. So there was plenty of time to be touristy. That was the experience, and that's the background. When I came back I started doing research, even though I had to finish my duty with *Apollo 16*. I was then rotated to backup crew on *Apollo 16*, and I had to go through that cycle. But in the meantime I was doing research and trying to understand what this experience in space was.

It took me a long time. I couldn't find anything in the scientific literature pertaining to it, so I started delving into the mystical literature on consciousness. Very shortly thereafter I found—in the Sanskrit of ancient India, and rooted both in Hinduism and Buddhism—the concept called "samadhi." And a particular type of samadhi, Savikalpa-samadhi, which is where you see things in their separateness, and experience them viscerally, and inwardly, in their unity. The sense of unity of all things, accompanied by an ecstasy or bliss. And I realized that was precisely the description of what had happened to me in space. I continued to do further research, and realized that, in one form or another, these types of transcendent experiences are described and present in the mystical tradition of every culture. From the Aboriginal cultures of the Bushmen in Africa, and the South American peoples, to the shamans of Tibet, and throughout the world, there's something akin to what we're describing in the literature or in the folklore.

We call that type of experience the "esoteric" experience. It's tough describing it. It's almost indescribable. It's an ineffable experience. But, nevertheless, we try to describe it. We explain it to our friends and to writers who are requesting it, like yourself. And let's call that the "exoteric." The explanation of the esoteric we call the exoteric, and the exoteric equates to religion. In other words, all of our religions are based on such insightful, esoteric experiences by great people in history—Jesus, Buddha, some would say Zoraster, Moses perhaps. And in those traditions you'd describe that experience as a mystical experience, touching the face of God, and so forth. Being more of a philosopher-scientist, I asked the question: What's going on here? And I realized that we couldn't answer that question until we really understood the answer to the question: What is consciousness? Why is it here? How is it here? Where did it come from?

So my approach for thirty years has been to work on what is the cosmology of consciousness, with the notion that our cosmology, our description of ourselves, will forever remain incomplete until we answer that question. And that's what I've been about for thirty years with the Institute of Noetic Sciences. We founded it around that to investigate that question. And for most of those years I've believed that when we really bring principles of quantum entanglement to bear on the issue, we'll make progress. And that's what I've been doing in recent years.

DAVID: What type of relationship do you see between gravity and consciousness?

EDGAR: Well, you've touched on something that seems to be very important, and may be the connecting link here. There's other people pushing on that too. I didn't know that until recently. Brendan O'Regan (who was an aide to Buckminster Fuller shortly before I met him) and I were discussing precisely that issue of pushing to understand consciousness. And we both agreed that, probably, when we understand gravitation, we will understand consciousness and vice versa. I think the major connection that we can point to right now is that both seem to be nonlocal phenomena. That's the obvious one.

And this is problematic, since, according to Einstein's Special Relativity, presumably, signals or influences cannot travel faster than than the speed of light. But all of the evidence for gravitation, or perhaps thought, seems to suggest that isn't true. What other influences of nature respond nonlocally? That remains to be seen, but certainly these two are problematic. I have a whole thick book here of essays on instantaneous action at a distance—pros and cons—and, I mean, we still haven't resolved that issue in physics. We haven't found the graviton, that is presumably the mediator for gravitation. And there's a number of writers that insist that evidence shows that planets instantaneously know the presence of other matter, but we don't know how that propagates. It's hard to understand, and it seems likely to involve quantum resonance— resonance at the quantum level—which is right on the frontier of our research.

DAVID: Have you ever been in one of John Lilly's isolation tanks?

EDGAR: Yes. Not necessarily any one created by John Lilly, but I've been in isolation tanks, and it's a wonderful experience.

DAVID: Was the shift in consciousness that you experienced floating in the isolation tank in any way similar to what you experienced being in the weight-lessness of space?

EDGAR: I don't find it particularly different. I mean, I don't need that to get into this state of consciousness, but you can. That's a good tool. Since my initial experience in space, I have recreated the Savikalpa-samadhi experience many, many times. I've reached the point of where I can almost do it at will.

DAVID: How did you become interested in the scientific study of psychic phenomena?

EDGAR: Quite a few years ago, back in the sixties, I got introduced to J. B. Rhine's work over at Duke University, and I became interested in the whole field of so-called paranormal phenomena. By the way, I hate the word "para." I've come to realize there's nothing "para" about it. It's very normal stuff. So I studied Rhine's work, as well as the research of quite a few others in the field—who had worked a great deal at it—and I came to realize that the evidence was very strong. Dean Radin and a number of research people have compiled a metastatistics on all sorts of paranormal phenomena, and it's very clear that it's real. It's there, and it's working, in spite of the fact that science didn't believe it can, or as the dogma of science says no, it can't be. And that is because they didn't have a mechanism. Well, we now seem to have a mechanism, so it cuts the legs out from under any scientific objections that come from classical thinkers. Because it is quite true—there isn't an explanation in classical science. It appears to require quantum science to be able to explain the nonlocal aspect of the so-called psychic information transfers. The nonlocal information transfer is clearly a quantum phenomena.

DAVID: Why do you think that so many scientists have difficulty accepting the evidence for psychic phenomena?

EDGAR: It's not hard at all to understand. Let's go back to Newton. Even before Newton, a few years back to René Descartes. Are you familiar with Descartes' work?

DAVID: Sure. I read his *Discourse on Method* in college.

EDGAR: Okay, so you know about that the Cartesian duality that René Descartes pronounced—the separation of body–mind, physicality–spirituality. He essentially declared two realms of existence—the material realm and the supernatural realm—and that has been dogma in the Western world for almost four hundred years now, because what it did was it freed intellectuals to pursue an understanding of nature without oversight by the Inquisition. It prevented them from being burned at the stake, tortured, and the things that went on with Galileo and Bruno, et cetera. But somehow or another it has become a part of the dogma that science doesn't look at things like consciousness—that that is the realm of theology. So it also deeply engendered this notion of a material, atomistic world, a deterministic world, where, if you knew the state vectors of atoms and molecules at any point in time, then, in principle, you could compute them forever after. And it suggests that consciousness is simply an epiphenomena of the classical material world, a by-product of these collisions of atoms and molecules.

Well, that was true until quantum physics came along in the early twentieth century. The formulation of the early quantum principles immediately suggested how mind–matter interact. As a matter of fact, the earliest formulations required the observation of the system to collapse the state vector, or the wave function, in order to make a measurement. So there is directly an interaction of mind–matter. But, basically, virtually all physicists, after touching that subject and examining it a little bit, run like hell. They refuse to look at it. And it's because of this ages-old Cartesian tradition that says that this is getting into theology, and science isn't about theology. And it's become entrenched in our academic systems for four hundred years. That's the only explanation I can give you. It's been enculturated, and it's just damn wrong. It's just wrong, that's all.

DAVID: Do you think that being in a gravity-free environment might enhance the capacity for psychic phenomena?

EDGAR: I'm not sure that being in a reduced gravitational environment has much to do with it, but I suppose it could. We don't know. We haven't done any studies on that, and we can't do studies on that very handily, so there's nothing that's that systematic about it.

DAVID: What do you think happens to consciousness after death?

EDGAR: All I can do is state the evidence. Let me give you my position, and my approach to this, because it's very important and germane. My take is that the universe is natural. It's a natural universe, and therefore knowable. If Descartes was right, then the supernatural aspect of the universe is not knowable by humans; it's only knowable by God, if you will. Well, I reject that postulate. I'm a positivist, in the sense of Karl Popper's investigation. We may not be able to prove things, but we have to advance by creating hypotheses and then try to falsify them. So I have made the single assumption in my work that the universe is natural, and proceed, therefore, to try to understand consciousness in terms of that. That means it's knowable, and if we push on it, we can gain understanding and data.

Now, essentially, we have two major philosophies—science and theology. There's the materialist philosophy, which is science. Classic Newtonian physics believes that everything is based upon matter, and the interaction of molecules is deterministic. The other philosophy is the Idealist, which is the basis of theology, and that believes that everything is consciousness, and that consciousness is independent of matter. If that is so, then it's assumed that the universe is unknowable. So I simply make the unitary assumption that the universe is knowable and natural, and to pursue and extend our science, of course, we have to look at subjective phenomena. Then we will eventually get to the answer. And so far I haven't been wrong. Everything we approach seems to be right.

Now, to answer your question, does consciousness survive death? The modeling we can do so far does not accommodate that idea. It doesn't point in that direction. The most advanced modeling we can do at the moment, I believe, is called quantum holography—which I've been very forward in working with and pushing. Essentially it says that the historical events of all matter are preserved in its quantum holographic record, and it's preserved nonlocally, which means it is useful or usable by future generations. Now, there's a lot of ifs, ands, and buts that go with this, but this is the sound-byte version.

So this supports the idea that there is information available to us at the psychic or subjective level, and it's rooted in this quantum holographic phenomena. But this does not suggest that consciousness can exist independently of the living system. It merely says the information is available to the living system. So there's a whole host of ramifications to this. It seems that this quantum holographic phenomenon is a mechanism for nonlocal information in nature. I've written a paper on this subject called "Nature's Mind: The Quantum Holograph."

Others have picked up on it, and we're pushing it very hard. It seems to be responsible not only for psychic abilities, as we understand them, but also the basis of why we have perception at all. So the modeling, so far, suggests that information about existence is preserved following life. We haven't yet been able to account for discarnate consciousness. I don't know how to account for that, or how to model that. That is an article of faith among a lot of religious people, but as a scientist I can't model that yet. Although I think we've made enormous progress in modeling much of psychic stuff, we haven't been able to model life after death.

DAVID: What is your concept of God, and do you see any teleology in evolution?

EDGAR: Again, look for the evidence. The holographic model suggests that matter is necessary for consciousness to exist, that it is a phenomenon of complexity, but rooted in the quantum principles of entanglement, coherence, and nonlocality. The model also suggests that nature is a learning organism, or a learning system—as opposed to the classical notion of evolution being an accidental mutation and natural adaptation. This mechanism suggests that nature is a learning system, all the way down to the subatomic level, and that's quite a different take. We're currently working very hard on a quantum cosmology, because if what we're saying is correct, it's very likely that the Big Bang is wrong. And there's a lot of people starting to jump on that bandwagon—that the Big Bang is not the right answer. But we'll see. It's going to take some time.

For me, the mystical experience, as the basis of religion, is probably a quantum event, and it can probably be explained in terms of quantum mechanics. Now, I won't state that with a great deal of certainty. I will say that if that isn't true, then we still have to get through and understand quantum phenomenon before we can get beyond it. So there may be more to it, but we're not at that yet, and we're going to have to wring out this area of quantum physics, which say for seventy-five years since the beginning of quantum physics, the particle physicists, the quantum guys, had said this does not pertain to macroscale, to biology. It doesn't pertain to our scale size of objects. And that is dogma that is just dead wrong. We're now showing that that's wrong.

The quantum hologram is a quantum aspect of biology, and we've got more and more biologists and microbiologists starting to jump on this bandwagon. We're creating a field of quantum biology, and I think we've got that one through to its limits before we can even get close to answering the question Does consciousness survive death? There's such a host of problems attendant to the survival issue, the way it is classically modeled and thought about. I would have to ask the question, What is the difference in that regard— survival regard of our life—and every insect, every worm, and every bit of other life species that are alive and around? I can't say that there should be any difference there. With the quantum holographic model there is none, and all matter emits a quantum hologram. But if you're going to say that conscious- ness, as we experience it as living beings, survives death, then it must be the same for all types of living species, and that hardly makes sense. But we'll just have to see where it goes.

Let me be clear, I don't close my mind to this at all. I merely say it's a work in progress, and we're still a pretty ignorant species. We think we know a lot, but we don't. There are so many unanswered questions in all of this, and sci- ence is the only way we will eventually answer them. And what do I mean by science? That means the protocol of investigation, creating hypothesis, doing experimental work, validating or invalidating hypotheses, and taking the next step. It's the Hegelian process of thesis, antithesis, synthesis, and starting all over again.

DAVID: Have you ever had a psychedelic experience?

EDGAR: Yes.

DAVID: How does it compare with the mystical experience that you had while you were in space? Is there any similarity?

EDGAR: Well, it can. What you're really doing here is opening channels in the brain to more perception. If you've studied any of Charlie Tart's work, you know that there are many, many states of consciousness, and if you use psyche- delics, that is just a different state of consciousness. So what you're perceiving is different bits of information, and giving different meanings or attachments to it. I think a fundamental contribution that I have made to this field is what I call the Dyadic Model, and that's been published. It still hasn't been picked up on by a lot of people, but it will be eventually, I believe, because it's correct. Let me give you a thumbnail sketch.

If we start with the quantum physical principle of Special Relativity $e = mc^2$, there is an energy equivalent to all matter. So matter is simply com- pressed, or condensed, frozen energy. It is energy in a state of existence. So we explain existence based upon an energy model—the structuring of energy—but we live in a universe in which we know it knows itself, in some sense. How does it know? Because we, nature, manages information, utilizes information. We know anything at all because we can utilize and process information.

What is information? Information is basically patterns of energy. So instead of the Cartesian dualism, of things being separate, we have both our existence and our knowing based in energy. And we've learned how to model energy in nature better and better. That's what quantum physics is about.

That's what physics is about in general—how do you take the natural aspects of our universe and create models of them, so we can understand it? So here we're modeling, instead of dualism, two different things—energy as a dyad. It has two faces of the same thing. It has the face we call "matter," and the face we call "information." They work together to help us exist and to know we exist. What we're doing is building upon that model, and quantum information is really fairly new on the scene.

We've talked about information in general. Electromagnetic information, the print media, the television media—those are all forms of information. But only recently, as we've broken away from the dogma that quantum physics only pertains to subatomic particles, we've learned that there is a basis in quantum information. That's what the quantum hologram is, and it is now being used to create technologies, so we know we're correct. It's improved MRI machines. It's been used in face-recognition technologies. There's a whole host areas now that we're using quantum technology and quantum information systems.

My group and I are using this to try to develop more on how the mind works. Thirty years ago Karl Pribram very clearly pointed out that the brain stores information holographically—that we perceive holographically, and that's how information is stored in our brain. And recently Stuart Hameroff at the University of Tucson and Roger Penrose at Oxford have been working on microtubules of the brain, as the mechanism that allows information to be processed—and that is totally consistent with our quantum holographic modeling that we're seeing.

DAVID: Do you think that the human species will survive the next hundred years, or do you think that we're in danger of extinction?

EDGAR: I think we're in danger of extinction. Whether we survive or not depends upon whether or not we get smart and start to take responsibility for what we're doing to the planet. It doesn't take a great deal of smarts to see this, and the evidence is all around us. Any measure of human activity you make—whether it's the number of television sets or automobiles produced, the number of people—is on an exponential growth curve throughout history, with a very sharp upturn around the beginning of the twentieth century. With our new technologies and our population growth at the beginning of the twentieth century, we see exponential growth.

Our technologies have produced more and more of everything—from information to whatever you name. And it is rather clear that you cannot have exponential growth in a finite space. I mean, it doesn't take a great mathematician to realize that. So we're outgrowing ourselves, and we're outrunning our feeding grounds. We're demolishing our natural resources. We're using up all the petroleum, and there's global warming. We all know what the problems are. They're around us, but the political system isn't taking it seriously. So, yes, we could indeed destroy ourselves sometime in the next century or so. We might just eat ourselves out of house and home. If we tear up the planet, ignore global warming, species extinction, and deforestation, it'll bite us in the butt. Or we can get smart and do something about it. If we are going to follow Illya Prigogine's concept of dissipative structures and chaotic systems, then we must consider our social system as a nonlinear chaotic system. That means that we're now headed for a bifurcation point. Some of us have been saying this for thirty years, and watching it happen.

What's a bifurcation point? When a dissipative system is chaotic and non-linear, and far from equilibrium, it comes to a point where it bifurcates, or splits and branches into new states. And that's exactly where our social system is right now—far from equilibrium. It's like water rushing down a rapids and over a waterfall, trying to get to a more calm place below. What we're rushing toward is the bifurcation point. Our civilization is in that rapid stage about to go over a waterfall, and what's going to come out below, who knows? But it's a bifurcation point, and we don't really know which way it's going to be pushed. We'd like to think it's going to be pushed to a more benign, sustainable civilization. That's what we'd all like to see happen. Whether it happens or not depends on how smart we get. Not only how smart, but how deep and sincere we get. We have to learn to take responsibility for ourselves.

DAVID: Assuming that we do get smart enough in time, and we do survive, how do you envision the future evolution of the human species?

EDGAR: It obviously has to involve sustainability. We have to bring this consumption and exploitation to an end so that we are living in harmony. Now, the main message here that comes out of what my work has been is what the mystic has forever been telling us. It's at the heart of traditional systems. I don't want to use religious notions, but I'll use a spiritual notion. We are a brotherhood of humans. We're all interconnected. In the mystical tradition that's basic, that everything is interconnected. Well, that is precisely what quantum nonlocality shows us. So we're finally discovering in science, at the basis of physics, the interconnectedness that the mystic has talked about forever.

Now, the mystic didn't know how to express it, and we've expressed it in different ways. But here science now has a way to express it. We call it quantum nonlocality, and it's exactly pushing on that concept, to show how we're integrated. And we can utilize this understanding to better improve our value systems and our behavior, and to help ourselves reach sustainability. This is what my group and my understandings are all about. Now, how exactly are we going to get there? We're going to live more simply. We're going to treat each other more kindly. We're going forgo killing each other at the drop of a hat, in the name of my god is better than your god, and my ideas are better than your ideas. We're going to learn how to solve our issues, short of conflict, violence, and the way we've been doing it forever—the law of the jungle.

Experiments That Could Change the World

An Interview with Rupert Sheldrake

Rupert Sheldrake is a biologist whose research strongly challenges the paradigms of conventional science. He is the author of more than fifty scientific papers and six popular books, including Seven Experiments That Could Change the World *and* Dogs That Know When Their Owners Are Coming Home. *His research and books are based on his controversial hypothesis regarding how morphic fields organize the ways that forms occur in nature, and they document his groundbreaking research into mysterious phenomena that traditional science has great difficulty explaining. Dr. Sheldrake received his Ph.D. in biochemistry at Cambridge and became a Fellow of Glare College, Cambridge, where he was the Director of Studies in biochemistry and cell biology. He is a Fellow of the Institute of Noetic Sciences in San Francisco.*

* * *

DAVID: How did you become interested in the unexplained powers of animals?
RUPERT: My interest in the unexplained powers of animals goes right back to my childhood . . . and my interest in homing pigeons. This was really the first area that I started investigating. When I was at Cambridge working on plants I was still very interested in animals, and I used to ask people about homing pigeons. I found that my colleagues in animal behavior really just didn't know how pigeons found their way home. They didn't know how navigation occurred in animals. Then, when I was thinking about it, I had the idea that maybe the pigeons were linked to their home in some way through a field, a kind of morphic field. That led me to think of an experiment which is the opposite of the normal experiments with pigeons. The normal experiments involve taking the pigeon from the home. My experiment was the opposite—taking the home from the pigeon. So even while I was at Cambridge doing work on plants, I actually started a project on homing pigeons. I set up a homing pigeon project with a mobile loft in 1973 on a friend's estate in Ireland.

So I started working on this unexplained aspect of animal behavior right then. This got me into the whole subject of other unexplained aspects of animal behavior. The more I asked people, the more I thought about it, the more such examples came to mind—including the phenomenon of animals knowing when their owners are coming home. So that became the basis really for my investigations that I set forth in my book *Seven Experiments That Could Change the World*, published in 1994, in which three unexplained areas of animal behavior are three of the seven experiments—dogs that know when their owners are come home, homing pigeons, and the social behavior of termites. That started me off on a whole new phase of research looking experimentally into these unexplained animal abilities.

DAVID: Why do you think studying the human–animal pet bond is particularly important?
RUPERT: Because there's a lot we don't understand about animal behavior, and the animals we know best are the pets that we keep in our houses. There's a huge amount of information available on these pets from people who keep them. We know far more about them than we do about wild animals—which, after all, we don't watch that much—or laboratory animals, which are kept under extremely artificial conditions. The behavior of laboratory animals is usually not really observed very closely, and their behavior is always very constrained by the cages they're kept in and the artificial situations they live in. Domestic animals are the animals we know best, and which have most to teach us I think.

They also form bonds with their owners, which mean that people are not just external observers, they interact with their animals. This interaction is very interesting to people. It's one reason they keep pets. After all, they want to have interactions with their animals, and they're interested in it. So this provides a huge amount of potential material for research. By working with pets, and the bonds between people and pets, we can find out a great deal just by asking people what they've noticed. I have a huge database with now more than five thousand cases of unexplained behavior in pets and other domestic animals, and this information really is the starting point for my natural history of unexplained abilities. In cases where it's possible to test what people observe about their animals and their behavior, we then move on to do experiments.

DAVID: Can you talk a little bit about some of the latest developments in your research with the unexplained powers of animals?

RUPERT: I summarized the main phase of my research in my book *Dogs That Know When Their Owners Are Coming Home* in 1999. Since then I've gone on working with animals, most particularly with parrots, and in particular with the parrot Nkisi, belonging to Aimee Morgona in New York. This parrot turns out to be one of the most remarkable animals in the world. He's an African gray that now has a vocabulary of more than 950 words, which is a world record, and he speaks in sentences. He's used at least 7,000 different sentences, and he uses language creatively. He also seems to have a concept of self; he uses the word "I."

So this a completely astonishing situation, of an animal that talks and uses language in a meaningful way—better than chimps or gorillas that have been taught to use language through American Sign Language. He does it in English. You can hear what he says. All this is in itself totally amazing and mind-boggling, but most amazing of all is that he picks up what his owner's thinking telepathically and comments on her thoughts and intentions—even on her dreams. Sometimes he wakes her up from her sleep by commenting on her dreams. She noticed this and got in touch with me in 2000, and of course I went to visit her as soon as I could in Manhattan to see for myself. And sure enough, what she told me seemed to be true.

We set up a whole series of controlled tests to see if he really could pick up what she was thinking. In these tests we filmed the parrot continuously in one room, and she was in another room—with all the doors closed, on another floor of the house, so there was no sound transmission possible. She looked at a series of photographs that she hadn't seen before, which were in sealed randomized envelopes. In each trial, she was filmed as she opened an envelope and looked at the picture in it for two minutes. She didn't say anything. Then we had independent transcription of what the parrot said. Three independent people transcribed it, blind, not knowing what was going on. We then saw whether the words the parrot said matched the picture she was looking at. In some tests the parrot didn't say anything. But when he did, we could check and see if the words corresponded—and in an astonishingly significant way they did.

In some trials, for example, she was looking at a picture of a man on a phone, and the parrot said, "What'cha doing on the phone?" In other trials she was looking at pictures of flowers, and the parrot said, "Those are flowers. It's a pic of flies," and went on talking about flowers. In other trials she was looking at water, and he said the word "water." When you see the videos it's pretty obvious that something really astonishing is happening, but of course we had to have them evaluated in an objective way. All the statistics were evaluated independently by a professor of statistics in Amsterdam, and, sure enough, the whole thing is a hugely significant statistically. A paper on this research was published in January 2004 in the *Journal of Scientific Exploration*, and the text is available on my Web site for anyone interested in the details.

DAVID: Could you explain the model that you use to understand telepathy and other unexplained phenomena?

RUPERT: The model I have is that members of a social group are linked to each other through a morphic field. Members of a flock of birds or a school of fish are like cells within a larger organism. The whole flock, or the school, is like an organism, and they're like parts of it. I think there's a field for the whole flock or school. If some members of the group go away, the field isn't broken—it stretches. So, for example, if a dog forms a bond to a human being, they're part of a social field. The human being's an honorary member of the dog's pack, as it were.

If the person goes away the field linking them doesn't break, it stretches. I think that stretched field—like an invisible band which continues to connect them—is the channel through which telepathic communication can take place. Interestingly, telepathy typically happens at a distance between members of social groups, people who know each other well, or animals who know each other well. It doesn't typically occur between strangers. If you look at human telepathy, most of it occurs between best friends, parents and children, twins, brothers and sisters—people who know each other very well, or have emotional bonds. So I think that telepathy is a reflection of these morphic fields that link together members of the group, even when they're at a distance.

DAVID: A number of scientists that I've interviewed have told me that they didn't think that there was any scientific evidence for psychic phenomena. What would you say to these scientists about research in psychic phenomena?

RUPERT: I'd ask them if they'd actually looked at the evidence. It's a common assumption in the scientific world that there is no evidence for psychic phenomena. But all the people that I've met who say that are unbelievably ignorant of the evidence. Most of them have never read a book or any of the papers in journals on the subject. One or two of them, when I pressed them, have said, Oh well, they vaguely remembered having read a paper about thirty years ago on an analysis of Rhine's experiments at Duke in the 1930s and thought there might be something wrong with the statistics. It's that kind of level of information that I encounter.

This was thrown into sharp relief in January 2004 when I held a debate with Professor Lewis Walpert, who is one of the pillars of the science establishment in England. Until recently he was chairman on the Committee on the Public Understanding of Science, which was set up by the Royal Society. And for twenty years he's been making statements to the media, saying there's not a shred of evidence for telepathy and so forth. He's often given statements to the press. For example, with my parrot research, when there was a report on television about this research—which had taken us two years to do, and a great deal of detailed analysis—he appeared on the same television program saying it was all rubbish, there was not a shred of evidence that parrots or any other animal could be telepathic.

The program makers at the television company told me they were astonished that he said this. They offered to show him the film of the experiments, and he said he didn't need to see the evidence because he knew it wasn't valid. So his comments were based simply on prejudice and not on information. Well, I challenged him to a public debate that was held in London at the Royal Society of Arts, and the position that many scientists have in more or less strong forms was actually thrown into sharp relief. In this debate he was invited to speak for half an hour, to put forward his case. Then I had half an hour. There was a high court judge in the chair to ensure a level playing field and a fair debate.

But, the fact was, he couldn't speak for half an hour. At first he said he'd only speak for a quarter of an hour, and, in the end, he only spoke for ten minutes. The reason is, he hadn't read any of the evidence for telepathy. He was totally ignorant of it. Really, apart from just saying over and over again, "There's no evidence," "It doesn't exist," "It's impossible," and that "anyone who believes in this must have something wrong with their heads," he hadn't really got anything else to say.

I then put forward the evidence. I summarized hundreds of published papers on card-guessing tests, dozens of papers on dream telepathy tests carried out in the '60s, twenty-five years of ganzfeld experiments with dozens of published papers, all with meta-analyses, published in proper scientific journals. I summarized my own papers, based hundreds on trials for telepathy in dogs and cats, and my own data on hundreds of trials on telephone and e-mail telepathy. I presented a huge amount of evidence, none of which he'd ever read or heard about. And the fact is that his case simply imploded. It ended up with virtually the entire audience coming to the conclusion that telepathy did exist, and his position collapsed. This debate was written up in *Nature*. The report in *Nature*, published on January 22, 2004, is on my Web site in the full text version.

DAVID: Why do you think so many scientists have difficulty accepting the evidence for psychic phenomena?

RUPERT: I think it's a very deep-seated, kind of knee-jerk prejudice, and there's nothing new about it. The same kind of prejudice was more or less in place at least a hundred years ago. If you read the kinds of comments that scientists made about some of the early psychical research in 1880s and '90s, it was just as ignorant, with almost the same words as they use today. I think, firstly, the reason is ideological. A lot of scientists are committed to a materialist ideology. They think that the mind and the brain are the same thing. The mind is nothing but the brain, or the activity of the brain, so therefore it's all inside the head. So anything like telepathy that suggests that there might be mental inferences working beyond the brain simply doesn't fit into that view of the world, and therefore it has to be rejected.

It's just like the cardinals at the time of Galileo, who didn't believe there could be craters on the Moon, so they just didn't want to look through his telescopes which showed that there were. And in the nineteenth century people who didn't want to believe in evolution had to explain away the fossils as being, in the most extreme case, put there by God to try our faith. This attempt to explain away, ignore, or reject things that don't fit into a world view is a very well known human tendency. It's happened over and over again in the history of science. In the end the evidence wins out, but in the case of psychical phenomena, this denial is still quite strong. So I think that it's essentially ideological. It's based on a particularly limited worldview—a worldview that was developed in the late eighteenth century, before we knew anything much about electricity and magnetism, and certainly before quantum theory and quantum nonlocality was known about. It's really Enlightenment rationalism of the sort of 1790s variety.

The Enlightenment rationalists believed that science and reason should sweep away religion, dogma, and superstition, and this was an ideological and social agenda. In many ways this was liberating and important. We're all the beneficiaries of this, but it's become a restrictive dogmatism now, and science has moved on a long way since the late eighteenth century. Field phenomena were unknown then. I think a lot of these phenomena that were classified as superstition, like psychic phenomena really do exist, and they can be explained in terms of fields. But many scientists are locked into a worldview that says they're impossible and fear that if you allow them to exist, the whole of reason and science will be undermined. This leads to an irrational attitude of denial, and a refusal to look at the evidence.

I think telepathy is a normal biological function present in many animal species, a means by which social animals keep in touch with each other at a distance. It's evolved under natural selection. It's part of animal nature and human nature. I think its explanation in terms of morphic fields involves extending science as we know it, but it doesn't involve overthrowing science, abandoning the scientific method, the whole of civilization crumbling and being overwhelmed by superstition and irrationalism. On the contrary, I think it's the best way to pursue a scientific agenda—whereas to deny the evidence, and to close one's eyes to it, is profoundly unscientific, and I think actually holds back research and gives science a bad name.

DAVID: When I interviewed Clifford Pickover for this book, I asked him what he thought about your research into psychic phenomena. He replied, "At heart, I'm a skeptic and demand very strong evidence for claims of the paranormal. . . . What I would really love to see is Dean and Rupert draft a precise paranormal claim and a means for testing the claim—followed by a letter to CSICOP [the Committee for the Scientific Investigation of Claims of the Paranormal], James Randi, and Robert Todd Carroll . . . asking if they would accept the 'new' test as a valid test for a claim of the paranormal . . . and agree to participate in Randi's one-million-dollar prize offer to anyone who can show, under proper observing conditions, evidence of any paranormal, supernatural, or occult power or event." How would you respond to Cliff?

RUPERT: I'm surprised Cliff takes Randi and these dogmatic skeptics seriously. Randi is a showman with no scientific credentials whose main claim to fame is the claim that he has money to offer as a "prize." This is not a serious scientific project but a publicity stunt—see the analysis on www.skepticalinvestigations. org. In particular he excludes statistical evidence. His Rule 4 states: "Tests will be designed in such a way that no 'judging' procedure is required. Results will be self-evident to any observer." Most scientific research, including research in particle physics, clinical medicine, and conventional psychology, depends on statistical results that need to be analyzed by experts to judge the significance of what has happened. Practically all serious scientific research would fail to qualify for the Randi prize. In any case, even if someone were to win it, it would be scientifically irrelevant, as Randi's fellow skeptic Ray Hyman has pointed out: "Scientists don't settle issues with a single test, so even if someone does win a big cash prize in a demonstration, this isn't going to convince anyone. Proof in science happens through replication, not through single experiments."

Randi is scientifically naive. . . . I think it's pathetic that people want media personalities like Randi to give them permission to believe things rather than reading the evidence and making up their own minds. In any case, I'm sure Cliff wouldn't think that evolution would only be credible if leading creationists could be persuaded of the evidence. They always find ways of dismissing what doesn't fit into their belief system, and I'm afraid dogmatic skeptics are the same. My own method of research is to set up hypotheses, test them, and submit papers on this research to peer-reviewed scientific journals, where they are evaluated by professional scientists and experts following the normal procedures of science.

DAVID: What is your concept of God, and do you see any teleology in evolution?

RUPERT: I think that God is an organism, rather than a sort of huge disembodied mind or an old man in the sky. My concept of God is influenced by the Hindu and the Christian traditions, both of which see the ultimate reality as being a trinitarian, or threefold. The Hindus have the trinity of gods: Brahma, who's the ultimate creator; Shiva, who's the energy principle, the change principle; and Vishnu, who's the preserver of form and the formative principle. In the Christian trinity you have God the father, who's the source of all things, a kind of primordial consciousness. You have the Logos, or the word, which is the formative principle in nature. And you have the spirit, which is the divine breath or energy, which gives the movement and change in all things.

So I think, in fact, these are reflected in the physical world, as we understand it, through modern physics and the principles that underlie all matter in the universe, which are the formative aspect of fields. Everything is shaped through fields. The gravitational field shapes the whole universe. Quantum fields shape atoms, and electromagnetic fields shape molecules. And morphic fields shape organisms, the arrangement of social groups, and so forth. There are all these fields that give form and order to nature, and there's energy, which is the moving principle of nature. It's what makes things happen, change, alter. It's the principle of activity. So I think these are both ultimately derived from the divine source of the universe, and they're reflections of the divine nature, the ways in which the universe is within God and God is in the universe. I think we can know about the consciousness of God directly through mystical experience. I think all religions are based on mystical experience, where people directly contact a form of consciousness or intelligence, or sometimes many forms of consciousness and intelligence beyond the human level. All religions are based on that experience. So it's an experience rather than dogma, which I think underlies this perception.

I think the evolutionary process involves the dynamic principle of change that comes through the spirit, or the energy principle, in its biggest sense. This works through the expansion of the universe. Unless the universe were expanding nothing would change. At the moment of the Big Bang, the universe was less than the size of the head of a pin. It's been expanding ever since, and as it does so, there's a kind of driving force. There's an arrow of time that makes things change. Nothing can remain the same indefinitely. The whole universe is in this state of development, because it's growing like an organism. And this change principle is one that's always creative. But then as things change, there's a possibility for new forms to appear. And when new forms appear—like new ideas in the human realm—they just spring into being. We don't know where they come from. When people have new ideas they just say, "It came to me," or "I suddenly saw something," or "It happened in flash." And if you ask, "Where did it come from?," the answer is they don't know. We don't even understand human creativity.

I think there's something in the universe that, on the one hand, promotes change, and causes creativity to occur, and there's something else, a formative principle, that gives rise to new forms. Often there's a tremendous proliferation of new forms, as I said earlier. Human beings have lots of new ideas. They're not all good ideas. So there's a tremendous fertility and creativity of forms in universe, but then they all have to be winnowed and selected through natural selection, and the viable ones survive. So I think that divine creativity works in two ways—one through this creative production of new forms, and the other through the driving principle, the dynamic principle of energy or spirit, which makes sure there's always change. This ensures that nothing can ever just settle into repetitive habit, because the universe doesn't settle down into repetitive habits. It's always growing, expanding, and changing.

DAVID: Do you think it's possible for consciousness to exist independently of a physical structure like the brain, and what do you think happens to consciousness after death?

RUPERT: For me the best starting point for this question is experience. We all have the experience of a kind of alternative body when we dream. Everyone in their dreams has the experience of doing things that their physical body is not doing. When I dream I might be walking around, talking to people, even flying, yet these activities in my dreams, which happen in a body, are happening my dream body. They're not happening in my physical body, because my physical body's lying down asleep in bed. So we all have a kind parallel body in our dreams. Now, where exactly that's happening, what kind of space our dreams are happening in, is another question. It's obviously a space to do with the mind or consciousness, but we can't take for granted that that space is confined to the inside of the head. Normally people assume it must be, but they assume that all our consciousness is in our heads, and I don't agree with that assumption. I think our minds extend beyond our brains in every act of vision, something I discuss in my book *The Sense of Being Stared At, and Other Aspects of the Extended Mind.*

So I think this then relates to out-of-the-body experiences, where people feel themselves floating out of their body and see themselves from outside, or lucid dreams, where people in their dreams become aware they're dreaming, and can will themselves to go to particular places by gaining control of their dream. These are, as it were, extensions of the dream body. Now, when we die, it's possible, to my way of thinking, that it may be rather like being in a dream from which we can't wake up. This realm of consciousness that we experience in our dreams may exist independent of the brain, because it's not really a physical realm. It's a realm of possibility or imagination. It's a realm of the mind. It's possible that we could go on living in a kind of dream world, changing and developing in that world, in a way that's not confined to the physical body.

Now, whether that happens or not is another question, but it seems to me possible. The out-of-body experiences, and the near-death experiences, may suggest that's indeed what's going to happen to us when we die. But the fact is that we're not really going to find out until we do die, and what happens then may indeed depend on our expectations. It may be that materialists and atheists who think death will just be a blank would actually experience a blank. It may be that their expectations will affect what actually happens. It may be that people who think they'll go to a heavenly realm of palm oases and almond-eyed dancing girls really will. It may be that the afterlife is heavily conditioned by our expectations and beliefs, just as our dreams are.

DAVID: And just as our lives are. Rupert, you just touched upon what I wanted to ask you about next. You mentioned to me that you think that people can sense being stared at because, in looking at someone, a part of the observer is, in a sense, reaching out to touch the person being observed in some way. I'm curious as to whether you think this is true in other states of consciousness, where the person that one is observing is not in consensus or material reality. For example, in lucid dreams, DMT-induced states of consciousness, or in a computer-simulated virtual reality, do you think that the act of looking at someone—or some being—in one of these alternative realities is actually expanding a part of that person's mind into another dimension of sorts, or do you think this might be an illusion that's just in the mind?

RUPERT: I think these things are in the mind, but I don't think the mind is in the brain. I think in an ordinary act of vision, when we look at something, the mind extends beyond our brain. If I look out of my window now and see a tree, I don't think that image of the tree is inside my head. I think the image is where it seems to be. I think it's projected out. Vision involves a two-way process: light moving in, changes in the brain, and then projection out of images. And oddly enough, when you think about the conventional theory, that it's all in the brain, it leads to very peculiar consequences. I'm looking up at the sky now, and according to the conventional view, my image of the sky, what I'm seeing in front of me, is actually inside my head. That means that my skull must be beyond the sky. When you look up at the sky, your skull's beyond the sky. Now, this is absurd really, and yet that's what the conventional view is telling us, and most people take it for granted, without realizing how very counterintuitive and very peculiar this speculative theory is. So I think that we go beyond our brain in the simplest act of vision, and I think that many of these other experiences also involve going beyond the brain. I don't think the mind is confined to the brain. So it may be true to say that near-death experiences, visionary experiences, and DMT trips are all in the mind, but that doesn't mean to say they're all in the brain.

DAVID: What sort of relationship do you see between your concept of a morphic field and the theological concept of a soul?

RUPERT: There may be a relationship. I think it might be better to use the phrase "philosophical idea of a soul." In the Middle Ages, it was generally taken for granted that all plants and animals have souls. The reason animals are called animals is because the word "animal" comes from the Latin word *anima*, meaning "soul." So, what the soul did, according Aristotle and St. Thomas Aquinas—who were the main authorities for the medieval view—was to act first as the form of the body, to shape the developing organism as it grew. In animals the soul also underlaid the instincts, the movements, and the organization of the sensations and behavior. In human beings the soul also included the intellect, the rational mind, the conscious mind.

So the human soul had three levels, or layers. One was the conscious mind, second to the animal soul, which was largely unconscious, and we shared with animals. And thirdly there was the vegetative soul, or the nutritive soul, which shaped our bodies and gave rise to the form of our bodies, helped maintain them in health and in healing from injury and disease. Those ideas of the soul fit very well with what I mean by morphic fields. Interestingly, up until the seventeenth century, everyone thought that magnets had souls. The magnet was believed to have a soul, which was how it attracted and repelled other magnets at a distance. In fact, what's happened in science is the old idea of souls has been replaced by fields. The magnetic soul became the magnetic field. The formative soul of the animal or plant becomes the formative morphogenetic field. So in many ways the field concept has replaced the soul concept in modern science.

So I think many aspects of our minds can be understood in terms of fields. I think when we look at something, and our visual world is projected out around us, it's projected in the morphic fields that stretch out from our brains. I think our brains are the source. The morphic fields of perception and our behavior are rooted in our brains—just like magnetic fields are rooted in magnets, or the fields of cell phones are rooted inside cell phones—but nevertheless stretch out beyond their surface. I think our minds are rooted in our brains during our normal waking life, and stretch out beyond their surface though fields. So in that sense the field concept and the soul concept are indeed related.

DAVID: How has your experience with psychedelics influenced your perspective on science and life?

RUPERT: I think that psychedelics reveal dimensions of the mind and experience that most of us would otherwise not experience. They show us there's a lot more going on than we're led to believe through textbooks of psychology and the standard kind of scientific model of the brain. I think they show that there are realms of experience that transcend ordinary waking consciousness, and for many people, including myself, I think psychedelics can reveal a world of consciousness and interconnection that is akin to mystical experience, of the kind experienced in many religious traditions. So I think in that sense the psychedelic experience is akin to mysticism, indeed, is a kind of mysticism. And by mysticism I don't mean obscurantism. I mean direct conscious experience of expanded realms of consciousness, or other regions of consciousness, which go beyond those we normally experience in our everyday lives.

DAVID: Do you think that the human species will survive the next hundred years, or do you think that we're in danger of extinction?

RUPERT: Extinction might be putting it too strongly, but we could be in for some very nasty shocks. Very few species that are as numerous as ours become totally extinct. I think there could be catastrophes, population collapses, and so on, but I personally don't think the whole human species is likely to become extinct. The going could get very rough indeed if things go badly wrong, and they might well through our own actions. People who live in modern cities are extremely vulnerable. If the food supply, water supply, and electricity supply break down, how are 10 million people living a huge city going to survive?

But if you look at peasants in India or Africa—small farmers who are not part of a cash economy, who just grow their own crops and make their own houses—the situation appears different. If the whole of the urban system on which we all depend breaks down, their lives wouldn't be that much affected. They would just carry on. They're much more resilient and much more likely to survive than we are.

So I think that the most vulnerable part of humanity is modern urban industrial civilization. I think subsistence economies, which still survive in many parts of the world, might be much more resilient. I would expect, even if things go badly wrong, that there will be places where people survive more than others. I should think New Zealand, for example, would have a better chance of surviving pretty well intact than certain other places in the world. So I wouldn't take the total Doomsday, total extinction scenario. I think there might be very bad shocks, but total extinction, I don't think, is going to be one of them.

DAVID: Assuming that we do survive, how do you envision the future evolution of the future species?

RUPERT: Frankly I just don't know. I know enough about prophesies made by people in the past to realize this is a hazardous undertaking. I just hope and pray we'll survive, that sanity will prevail, that the worst excesses will be curbed, and the destruction of the environment will be greatly reduced. So I'm a kind of optimist, but I wouldn't like to make any detailed predictions.

DAVID: Where do you think the human race should be focusing its scientific efforts right now?

RUPERT: I don't have a master plan for scientific research, but I think we need to basically move to a more holistic way of studying nature and a more ecological way of looking at things. There are certain areas where it's obvious what we ought to be doing. We ought to be developing much more sustainable uses of energy—wind power, wave power, solar power, and so forth. Those are already done to some extent. I think in medicine we ought to be looking at alternative and holistic therapies, as well as high-tech medicine, and trying to develop preventative medicine systems that lead to better health, rather than expensive fixes for problems.

I think in biology we should be looking at a field approach and studying things much more holistically. I think in fundamental physics we should be looking at the evolution of the laws of nature, and the memory of nature, and how this fits in with what we know about quantum theory and relativity theory. I think in cosmology and astronomy we should be looking at the possibility of consciousness within the universe—either in the whole universe or associated with stars and galaxies. I don't mean just looking for little green men on other planets. I mean considering the possibility the Sun and the entire galaxy might be conscious—that the whole solar system might be a living organism, and the Sun might be like it's brain. I think these are some of the areas of science where a different approach could be extremely revealing, and lead to a completely different view of ourselves and our place in nature.

Science and Psychic Phenomena

An Interview with Dean Radin

Dean Radin is a psychologist and engineer who has specialized in the study of anomalies associated with human consciousness, principally so-called psychic (psi) phenomena. He has investigated telepathy, psychokinesis, and precognition at Princeton University, the University of Edinburgh, Bell Laboratories, SRI International, and as part of a classified program for the U.S. government, and he was president of the Parapsychological Association affiliated with the American Association for the Advancement of Science. Dr. Radin earned his Ph.D. in psychology and M.S. in engineering, respectively, at the University of Illinois, Champaign. His research awards include the Parapsychological Association's 1996 Outstanding Achievement Award and the 1996 Rhine Research Center's Alexander Imich Award for advances in experimental parapsychology. Dr. Radin is Senior Scientist at the Institute of Noetic Sciences. He is also the author or coauthor of over two hundred scientific papers and popular articles as well as one of

the most popular scientific books on psi research: The Conscious Universe: The
Scientific Truth of Psychic Phenomena.

* * *

DAVID: A number of scientists that I've interviewed have told me that they
didn't think that there was any scientific evidence for psychic phenomena.
What would you say to these scientists about research in psychic phenomena?
DEAN: The usual reason for such comments is that these folks are simply
telling the truth. They are not aware of the evidence. That's an expression of
ignorance, which is fine. We're all ignorant about lots of things. But the fact is
that there is an enormous amount of evidence for anyone who wishes to go
looking for it.

Here's one way of thinking about this. Rupert Sheldrake was visiting here
[the Institute of Noetic Sciences] this week. Last week he was involved in a
debate on the evidence for telepathy at the Royal Society of Arts in London.
His opponent was a biologist named Lewis Wolpert, who is a well-known skeptic and promoter of science in England. In the debate Rupert was presenting
the experimental evidence for telepathy, and Wolpert acted as the devil's advo-
cate. Wolpert's position was that telepathy doesn't exist because we know it
doesn't exist, and anyway there's no evidence that it exists. If you expand those
words to twenty minutes of repetition around the same theme, then that was
his position.

Rupert, on the other hand, presented one study after the other—showing
here's some evidence, here's some more, and here's some more, and so on.
The debate was cast in terms of a scientific court, where the members of the
audience—about a hundred people—were the jury, and there was a judge
that would rule on the case. Well, 80 percent of the people agreed with Rupert.
The overwhelming majority was such a shock to the reporters present that a
few days later it appeared as a news item in the journal *Nature* with the title,
"Telepathic Charm Seduces Audience at Paranormal Debate." The article
reported that the debate had won hands down in favor of telepathy. So, this is
just a microcosm of what goes on all the time. Many scientists are unaware of
the evidence because they either wish to not pay attention to it or because it just
isn't visible in their orbit.

There's another aspect to this, which occurs when you discuss taboo topics.
There's a big difference about whether something will be mentioned in private
or in public. Rupert and I were comparing notes on this. We both found that,
in private, most people—including the vast majority of scientists—will admit
that, even though they may not know the literature very well, they've had personal experiences, or someone that they know and trust has reported things
that do not seem like they can be accounted for by the usual explanations, like

coincidence or wishful thinking. So, privately, many people are willing to admit that there's something interesting going on, far more than publicly. As soon as you are going to commit something to paper, or to the press in some way, you become more circumspect about what you're going to say. It's a lot easier to then act the role of the skeptical scientist and say, Well, I don't know of any evidence, which is portrayed as a dismissal of the topic rather than what it really is, an admission of ignorance.

Many of these scientists are not aware of my book, or any of the other books written on this topic, which as you know show in great gory detail that we do have ways of studying these things. We may not have very good theoretical explanations for them yet, but the fact is, for over a century, we've had empirical ways of studying psi. And if we believe in empiricism as reflecting something about what's really going on out there, then there's very little doubt that these phenomena do exist.

DAVID: It really is interesting how strangely taboo this particular research topic is. Most scientists that I talk to are either unaware of this research, or they immediately dismiss it.

DEAN: It's partially because there's kind of an understanding that if experiments of this type were really true, then they should have already appeared in *Nature* or *Science* because it's truly revolutionary. But what many scientists working in the mainstream don't appreciate is that there are publication biases that prevent certain topics from appearing in the mainstream scientific press. Of course, anyone who's been working in a controversial field knows this immediately, that certain things simply cannot make it to press. But if you haven't worked in an area of high controversy you would never have any reason to suspect this. You'd have no reason to guess that prejudice exists in science like it does anywhere else. So it's frustrating, of course. Rupert and I have talked about this extensively, and we're trying to crack this nut, but it's a slow process. It's like affirmative action: Prejudice carries enormous inertia, and it will not go away unless an affirmative stance is taken to counter it. Unfortunately, in science, there is no equivalent of affirmative action. So it can take a very very long time, as history has shown, for unpopular ideas to finally make it though. As Max Planck said, "Science progresses by funerals."

. . .

DAVID: Why do you think the various psychic abilities that humans are capable of evolved to begin with?

DEAN: That's a good question. It's not clear to me at all that it evolved, because I think we're dealing with something which is before evolution in a sense. It's part of the fabric of the universe. It has to be, because if it was something that evolved, it would suggest that we have created ways of transcending space and time, which doesn't make sense. How can we create something which, from a conventional point of view, would be a violation of "laws of science"? It can't be that way.

So, another way of thinking of it is that we make the presumption—and one that most scientists have faith in—that the universe was here before people showed up, that we didn't create it as a fact of thinking about it, and suddenly it all fell into place. In fact, we have to take that faith, otherwise science would stop, because it becomes a solipsistic universe, and anything we wish to be true would be true. So you start from the assumption that the world is given in some way and that we're evolving in it. And if there's any evolution at all, it's the evolution of a realization that the fabric of the universe is not the way that Newton saw it. Or actually it is in his mystical sense, but not in the classical physics sense of the Newtonian-Cartesian world.

DAVID: So you see it as being an inherent part of the basic structure of the universe?

DEAN: Yes, there's some aspects of the world for which we now have the term "nonlocality," which nobody understands very well, but seems to be a fundamental, underlying aspect of the universe. If that is in fact the case, as it seems it must be, given theory and experiments, then in many ways psychic phenomena is something you would be compelled to predict. You would predict that occasionally people would have some sense or experience of this kind of interconnectedness.

. . .

DAVID: What are some of the practical applications of parapsychological research?

DEAN: Well, realistically we don't know. Any time science stumbles across some new understanding of the world, it typically gets spun out into a few novel applications at the time when the invention or the discovery was made. But no one had any idea what would happen down the line. Could Madame Curie have imagined that her experiments with radium would lead to the atomic bomb, or that atomic energy would someday drive megawatt electrical generation plants or drive starships to other galaxies? I doubt it. I mean, it's very difficult to know how a new discovery will be used, or its political, societal, or environmental consequences. So the easiest, and maybe the only, way to answer your question now is to say what psi is being used for already. It's being used for medical diagnosis, for detective work, for making better decisions, to enhance psychotherapy, a lot more than people probably know. I mean, privately psychotherapists sometimes will admit that they use this stuff.

. . .

DAVID: Tell me about your research at Bell Labs with regards to developing a psi-based technology.

DEAN: First of all, we don't really understand how any of this stuff works yet. We have working models, like how you can focus your attention on one thing versus another. But a big mystery all along has been why there's extremely good evidence for psi perception, but the evidence for psi action is not anywhere near as good. In other words, if we're passive we can perceive all kinds of interesting things. But if we try to make something happen, it's not so clear that that is in fact what's happening, because there are lots of ways of appearing to make something happen, if you have the right knowledge.

DAVID: It's difficult to differentiate between what's action and what's perception?

DEAN: Not for ordinary phenomena, but for mind–matter interactions, yes. Perception and action seem to be like two sides of the same coin. They are not identical, but they do seem to be complementary in a way that is difficult to disentangle. We're working on experiments now that may be able to turn perception into action. Could you make a garage door opener out of this, where you think about it opening and it does? Probably, and it may not be distinguishable from the person's point of view as to whether they're imagining that the door opened in the future, and the door actually opens at that time, or if it's because one has actually created a causal loop with the object in the future. There might be clever ways of making these things occur.

DAVID: Or making it seem like they occur.

DEAN: No, it really will occur. We think that some things may be "caused" to happen as a result of a perception of the future. I should preface this by pointing out that ordinary, commonsense language is not really adequate in discussing these sorts of ideas, much in the way that Einstein's theory of relativity is extremely precise mathematically, but our minds go agog when we try to think about the consequence of space–time bending.

That said, once you can take advantage of a phenomenon that is no longer bound by time's arrow flying in only one direction, then somewhere between "all hell breaks loose" and "anything is possible" is in the offing.

. . .

DAVID: What do you think are some of the most important implications of parapsychological research?

DEAN: The history of science shows that for a long time scientists develop a good sense of what they think the world is like, and then somebody comes up with a nutty idea and revolutionizes everything. Then there's great chaos, and then it settles back down. It goes through these cycles over and over again, and the speed with which those cycles are changing is getting shorter. What used to take centuries became decades, and now takes six months.

The direction that science in general seems to be moving is perfectly compatible with the idea that there is some kind deep interconnection between things. One time I gave a talk where I was suggesting the topic of psychic phenomena as the middle ground between science and religion. This was because it addresses a lot of the phenomena that give religion its power—namely things that look supernatural, and therefore must be from some higher place or something. Yet all our research suggests that we are at the center of these phenomena. It's not disembodied entities doing it; it's us.

If you follow the logic out—especially with Eastern ideas, and even some Western notions about how reality is created—and if it truly is the result of an interaction between observation and some formless stuff out there, then psi phenomena are just the tip of the iceberg. The evidence almost suggests that a quasi-solipsistic view of the world may be right, and that we are engaged in continuous creation by virtue of our observation.

. . .

DAVID: What sort of relationship do you see between psychic phenomena and altered states of consciousness?

DEAN: I believe that our ordinary state of awareness evolved in a direction where it has become extremely good at excluding psychic or mystical awareness, and this evolution makes a certain sense. Let's say that the primordial state is awareness of everything. So now you're an organism in which there are tigers around trying to eat you. If you sustained that mystical sense of awareness of everything, then you're not going to live very long. If you want to survive, then it would behoove you to pay much more attention to what is going on right here and now, i.e., the tiger in front of you, rather than what was happening on Mars 50 millennia ago.

If you go through enough generations of that kind of evolutionary pressure, then you're going to get really good at not being psychic. You'll have a sense that our world is in very sharp focus around us, which is exactly the way we perceive it. Yet, under the right conditions, either through brain damage, or through drugs, drumming, or high emotions, or a natural talent, you can push somebody slightly out of that ordinary state, and suddenly that larger awareness creeps in.

DAVID: That's very similar to what Aldous Huxley said in *Doors of Perception* about Big Mind and Little Mind. Are you familiar with any research that studied the relationship between the psychedelic experience and psychic phenomena?

DEAN: There's some interesting new experimental evidence developing right now, actually. This research is not being done in the United States, because you can't do it legally here, at least not very easily. But I have a colleague in Amsterdam who has been running telepathy studies using psilocybin, with amazing results.

DAVID: What kind of studies?

DEAN: These are the ganzfeld experiments, like I describe in my book. Since basically drugs of any type are freely available in Holland, they went to find volunteers that were willing to do a Ganzfeld experiment under the influence of psilocybin. I forget whether they provided it, or they asked to bring their own, but they had some way of standardizing the measures of how much psilocybin they were getting. So the person who was the receiver in the experiment was the one under the influence. And they got exceptionally high hit rates. Then the next stage, which was started last year, was similar, only this time both the sender and receiver are under the influence of psilocybin. We don't know what will happen, so we'll see.

. . .

DAVID: Has anyone else done anything like that? I think I heard of a telepathy study done in the '50s with mescaline.

DEAN: There were some studies done with LSD as well, before it became Schedule 1. And lots of informal studies with marijuana, occasionally with ayahuasca. I guess ayahuasca is the main one because one of the psychoactive components—harmaline—in particular seems to be an interesting component.

It's too bad that most of the psychoactive drug research was shut down. I think there is a likelihood that we would have learned by now that some areas of the brain can be activated to open the doors of perception, but also keep ordinary focus high. If you just opened those doors without any controls, you'd become psychotic instead of psychic.

But if you can still focus, then you have a chance of creating a superpsychic for a short period of time. I think that something like that actually does occur. But since most of the recreational use of drugs is generally done under conditions where when you're under the influence, you're no longer thinking about trying an experiment, and it's even harder to set the experiment up in advance.

. . .

I was interested in the use of ecstasy or MDMA and its supersensory enhancement, because you still feel tranquil and you can retain good focus. It sounds like it would be a good drug to use in these experiments, and it's probably misnamed. It should be called empathy, not ecstasy. Well, that sounds a lot like telepathy, so let's do experiments. It would be interesting to bring people in a lab, or at least under conditions where somebody else is actually controlling what's happening, because otherwise it may become too recreational and people won't want to do it.

DAVID: I know somebody who was on MDMA when they took part in one of Rupert Sheldrake's staring experiments. He was the recipient of the staring in the experiment, and he was right about 85 percent of the time, which is a very high hit rate.

DEAN: Yes, that makes sense to me. If we could do those studies legally here, I think we would make much faster progress. The other approach, though, which is actually happening, is to find people with natural talent—because there are folks out there whose brains are wired just slightly differently, and they can do this all the time—and do brain scanning, PET studies, functional MRI, and maybe EEG topological mapping to find out what in fact is going on in their head, which is different than ordinary people. Or different in their head when they're highly psychic versus not.

DAVID: Has there been anything like that done?

DEAN: There have been some EEG studies and a few functional MRI studies. They're providing promising results, and much more needs to be done.

DAVID: Have you ever had a psychedelic experience, and if so, how has it affected your view of science and life?

DEAN: I've had hallucinatory experiences as the result of drugs, only twice, each time in the process of waking up from an operation. They were both very funny experiences, so I wouldn't say it changed my views much. It just was, I imagine, a peculiarity of my brain trying to figure out the strange state it was in. So, no, I haven't had the designer chemicals or the plants that would cause one to have a hallucination. My body is pretty sensitive to drugs, so I tend to stay away from things that I know are going to push me too hard. Also I never felt I needed to perceive reality in a different way to know that there are many ways of seeing reality. So it's just not something I've been attracted to.

I am interested in psychedelics from an experimental point of view. With many of them—including concoctions like ayahausca or psilocybin—people often report transpersonal experiences, and we have now pretty good ways of testing for transpersonal experiences in the laboratory. So I am interested in seeing whether we can objectify those experiences. For example, I'd like to see if the ego-dissolving experience between two people is in fact verifiable.

DAVID: What do you think happens to consciousness after death?

DEAN: I expect that what we think of as ourselves—which is primarily personality, personal history, personality traits, and that sort of thing—goes away, because most of that information is probably contained in some way in the body itself. But as to some kind of a primal awareness, I think it probably continues, because it's not clear to me that that's produced by the body. In fact, I think that elementary awareness may be prior to matter. So when you go into a deep meditation and you lose your sense of personality, that's may be similar to what it might like to be dead.

On the other hand, if you're not practiced at being in that deep state, or don't know how to pay attention to subtle variations in what might at first appear to be nothingness, it's not clear that your consciousness would stay around very long. In other words, you might have a momentary time when you have this sense of awareness, and then it just dissolves. It goes back and becomes part of the rest of everything. So it's like a drop that settles into the ocean and disappears into it. On the other hand, some people, who either spend a lifetime preparing in meditation or who are naturally adept, may be able to sustain being a drop. They may be able to settle into that ocean and still have a sense of their "dropness," even though they're also now part of the ocean.

Then maybe one's sense of awareness would expand dramatically, and yet still have a sense of unity. I imagine that all this probably occurs in a state that is not bound by space and time as we normally think about it. So, presumably, you would have access to everything, everywhere. I imagine that something like that is the reason why ideas of reincarnation have come about, because people remember something about it. They may even remember something about the process of coming out of this ocean into a drop, into a particular incarnation, because a drop is embodied in a sense.

DAVID: So you're of the opinion that it's possible that not the same thing happens to everyone after they die. Perhaps some people merge back into everything, and some people are able to maintain some element of their individuality.

DEAN: If there's anything that psychology teaches, it's that people are different. So I imagine that there may as many ways of experiencing after-death as there are people to experience it. And no one explanation is the "correct" one.

. . .

DAVID: What is your perspective on the concept of God, and do you see any teleology in evolution?

DEAN: I'm not a fan of the image of a large white man with a beard sitting in the clouds. In other words, I think that a being projected in our image is awfully limiting, as human beings are collectively just one small step out of the monkey tribe, as evidenced by watching the nightly news on TV. But in the sense of a larger scale of intelligence I do think there is a role for a teleological presence that some might call spiritual. It is conceivable that there's something much bigger than us, not in terms of size but in scope, and not in terms of a "thing" or being, as a principle. Whatever it is I imagine it is impersonal, in the sense that we might have an ant farm where we probably don't care much about each individual ant, but we may care deeply about the collective. I should add that I am agnostic when it comes to religion. I prefer to question rather than blindly accept anything based only on faith. And I especially distrust anyone who claims to know the truth based solely on faith or, worse, personal revelation. History and the nightly news shows that this sort of certainty has been one of the most destructive social forces ever created.

In terms of teleology, I think it is clear that evolution has a certain degree of random pushing. It pushes itself randomly into the future, and natural selection does an excellent job—but I'm not convinced that this can account for everything that we see. And, especially because of my work in parapsychology, I have a sense that it is possible that causation is not constrained to flow in only one direction, and in particular that there are retrocausal influences. That being the case, then we would experience a retrocausal influence from the future as a teleological pull. In fact, I've just finished a series of experiments looking at that very issue. Under the right circumstances it looks very much like the future can "pull" us into itself. So could there be teleological pulls into the future on very large scales? Perhaps. We, meaning civilization, might be pulling ourselves into the future.

DAVID: Do you ever entertain the idea that there might be any type of intelligent design in the evolutionary process?

DEAN: I would put that in the same category as teleology. Something is pulling us, whether something is pulling us intelligently or not, I don't know. But, I mean, I should also add that intelligent design is the new, slightly more sophisticated version of creationism. From that point of view I don't agree with the use of a veneer of mathematics to hide what might amount to a religious ideology. But, in the same breath, is it conceivable that there is a teleological pull from somewhere and some-when? I think yes, and not as part of a religious agenda, simply as part of my interpretation of the empirical evidence suggests.

DAVID: Do you think that the human species will survive the next hundred years, or do you think we're in danger of extinction?

DEAN: We are always in danger of extinction—not always just because of us. An asteroid could hit us. A virus could mutate. There are plenty of reasons why we could be wiped out. So there's always that probability. The question is, how big is the probability, and how does it change over time? I tend to be an optimist, so I presume that we will survive. We have a very strong imperative to survive, so I think that if things got dicey politically, at some point our collective urge to survive as a species will take over. At least I hope so. On the other hand, we live in times when a few insane individuals can wipe out large sections of the planet, and that's a troubling thought.

DAVID: Assuming that we do survive, how do you envision the future evolution of the human species?

DEAN: I would say that we have an enormous amount of inertia, so we're unlikely to change very much in the short term. On the other hand, there's also a lot of new evolutionary pressures—environmental changes, demands on our intellect because of the rise of information, and new advances in science and technology. Any one of those can spawn unattended consequences that might force a very fast physical or mental change. A hundred years might seem too short a time to see much happening, but you never know. A human mutation could be born tomorrow which turns out to be a lot better than what we currently are. After a couple of dozen generations that new species could significantly change the world. In fact, ultimately a single powerful mutation, especially a human with highly enhanced psychic abilities, could completely transform the entire world in twenty to thirty years. One hopes that such a mutation would be kindly and compassionate, but the universe has room for many variations, and one never knows. Also, a compassionate act from one person's perspective might seem cruel and unjust to another.

DAVID: Can you talk a little about the "presentiment" research?

DEAN: "Presentiment" is the term I use for unconscious precognition. This is an experiment that I talk about in my book. The idea is we're testing the notion that intuitive hunches are sometimes caused by perception of your future, something, usually of an emotional nature, that's about to occur to you.

In my version of the experiment a person is wired up to measure their skin conductance, and it's recorded continuously. They sit in front of a computer screen, and they're asked to press a button, whenever they wish. They press a button, and the screen is black. Five seconds later an image appears. The image is randomly selected from either a pool of calm images, like a tree or a cup, or emotional images, like either a violent or a sexual scene. That image stays on screen for three seconds. Then the image goes away, and they get a chance to cool down for at least ten seconds. Then, whenever they wish, they can press a button and the trial begins again with a new randomly selected picture. The hypothesis is that, if we are affected by our immediate future—in this a case a future five seconds down the line—then skin conductance should begin to rise before an emotional picture but not before a calm picture. And that is what we see.

Since I conducted my first experiments looking at this effect, about six other groups have successfully replicated it. The most recent replication, by Ed May and James Spottiswoode, used an audio version of the test that I did, and they got incredibly good results. Their overall statistical result was millions to one against chance, using a simpler method of analysis and a more rigorous design in many ways. So it's encouraging because it means that not only can the effect be replicated, but ways have been found to make it even stronger.

So that's one development which is somewhat new. The other one is that about a year ago a short article came out in *Neuroscience Letters*, which is a mainstream journal for short reports in neuroscience. The article talked about an experiment looking at correlations in the EEGs of isolated people, where one person gets a stimulus, like a light flash, and then you look in the brain of a distant person to see whether there's a corresponding response.

DAVID: What's the connection between the two people? Do they know each other?

DEAN: Yes, like two friends who come together, and they're told to "feel the presence" of the other person. They meditate for a short while beforehand to intensify that feeling, and then they're separated. Assuming some form of interconnectedness exists, then you would expect that if you poke one person, that the other person will go "ouch!" What you actually look for is evoked potentials in the brains of the two people. So this was a study published in *Neuroscience Letters*, and it was significant. I know the people who did the study, and they're very rigorous about what they do.

The night after reading the article I had a dream that if I ran a similar study, in a certain way, and if I could finish the entire experiment from beginning to end in three weeks, then I would be able to significantly replicate that study. So I woke up in the morning with that dream in my mind feeling a certain pressure, especially since the dream had a sense of urgency in it. I felt compelled to go ahead and do this. So I did it, and it did work. Since then I've expanded the study. To date we've run thirty pairs of people, and we get very significant evidence of a brain-to-brain correlations, which presumably also means a mind-to-mind connection between two people who are isolated.

So I started looking at the literature, and it turns out that there's about a dozen articles like this that have been published, and one of the interesting things about it is that most of these articles have been published in mainstream journals. They're not hidden away in the parapsychology journals like a lot of psi research. It includes *Science, Nature, Physics Essays*, the *International Journal of Neuroscience*, and so on. My study is coming out in the *Journal of Alternative and Complementary Medicine* shortly.

So, this is not really new because the studies go back to the mid-'60s. But it's new in the sense that there's been a new rush of interest and this work is starting to appear in mainstream journals. As far as I can tell, with only one exception every group that has tried to replicate this effect has been successful, and that's remarkable.

Alien Encounter Therapy

An Interview with John E. Mack

John E. Mack, M.D., is a Pulitzer Prize-winning author and a professor of psychiatry at Harvard Medical School. He is the founder of the Department of Psychiatry at the Cambridge Hospital and the founding director of the Center for Psychology and Social Change. He is also the author or coauthor of 11 books and more than 150 scholarly articles that explore how our perceptions shape our relationship with each other and with the world. In 1977 Dr. Mack won the Pulitzer Prize for his biography of T. E. Lawrence (Lawrence of Arabia)—A Prince of Our Disorder—but he is probably best known for his two bestselling books on the alien abduction phenomenon, Abduction *(1995) and* Passport to the Cosmos: Human Transformation and Alien Encounters *(1999). He earned his medical degree at Harvard Medical School, and he is a graduate of the Boston Psychoanalytic Society and Institute.*

* * *

DAVID: What do you think is the most compelling evidence for the existence of the abduction phenomenon?

JOHN: That's a good question. It depends what compels you, I suppose. For me, the most compelling evidence is the powerful, consistent accounts of these extraordinary experiences from people that are altogether believable. Now, there are some good photographs and videos of UFOs. There are some implants that have been studied. But it is the accounts themselves that for me carry the most weight. The thing that makes this all so difficult is that the abduction phenomenon is so elusive. I'm not persuaded myself that all of this is to be taken totally literally. The fact that something is experientially so deep, real, and powerful does not mean that you are dealing principally with advanced types of metals or vehicles, or that other people will necessarily always be able to observe that a person is missing, although some abductees are observed to be missing during these times. But some are not, and I just don't know in what reality this occurs. To the experiencers their bodies were taken, they're up there, and it's real. But it's tricky in that sense.

DAVID: Why do you think it is that no hard evidence of alien abduction has ever been encountered?

JOHN: I've been reading a book by Patrick Harpur called *Daimonic Reality*. "Daimonic" means "unseen agency," and it refers to the invisible world that—although immeasurable—may, in fact, be more real than the material world of appearance. If all this is maya, then the daimonic world is the source of reality in a deeper sense. This is the world from which telekinesis, crop formations, and near-death experiences originate. If you study any of these phenomena—poltergeists, apparitions, the huge variety of psi phenomena that have been looked at, or the massive flood of synchronicities that come upon people when they're spiritually opening—you discover that none of these phenomena provide the kind of hard material evidence that would satisfy a scientist who is exclusively oriented in a materialist's worldview.

There's always the tease, the trick, the tantalization. They're giving you just enough so you know there's something real going on, but not enough to satisfy proof. Proof in the classic scientific method is best adapted to an entirely material universe. It doesn't do very well in working with the subtleties of the crossover phenomena that enter the physical world from some other realm.

DAVID: What do you personally believe is really going on?

JOHN: That they are being abducted, in a sense. Abduction is a bad word. Something very powerful is happening to them. Sometimes they experience that their physical bodies appear to be taken. There are witnesses who report that people are missing. The abductees will report as altogether real that they have been floated through walls, taken up into a spacecraft, subjected to all of these physical, ecological and spiritually related experiences. It's totally real. At the same time, I'm not sure how it's real—in other words, in what dimension it's occurring. And again, what's happened to me has required that I, in a certain sense, suspend my literal notions of reality, because reality in this sense is not limited to the physical world. People may, in fact, be taken physically, but it's going to be very hard to prove. I don't think it should be looked upon so literally. I think that there are some kinds of energies, entities, and daimonic agents that our culture is unaware of.

If you were in an African society you'd have a whole different perspective on this. I've worked with African medicine men who have a whole classification of beings that their people encounter. And the beings are completely real in their experience, but they wouldn't be real to our culture, because we don't have the senses anymore to know them. As the poet Rilke said, by daily parrying we have cut off our connection. The senses by which we can know the spirit world have atrophied. I wasn't prepared for this when I first got started. When people say that I've been converted to something, they don't know that I'm the last person in a certain way that would be converted. I was raised in a very secular, rational, empirical, materialist—whatever you want to call it—view, and the only thing that led me to take this seriously is I just couldn't place it clinically. It just didn't fall into anything. It acted like it was real, but if this was real, then—good heavens—what's going on?

. . .

DAVID: What type of relationship do you see between the abduction experience and altered states of consciousness?

JOHN: For reasons that are interesting, but not altogether clear, people in altered states of consciousness seem to be able to access these experiences more easily. But sometimes the experiences occur and create an altered state of consciousness. Someone will be in bed, and then there will be a blue light or a humming, and they will suddenly find themselves in a new reality, as one man put it. It's like this reality is a kind of theater screen, and the beings come through, and they experience a new reality—an underlying or a different reality, which is just as real as the one they were already experiencing before, but it's another one. Now, you can say they're in an altered state at that point, because they're experiencing another reality.

DAVID: Do you think that there is any relationship between the abduction phenomenon and the extraterrestrial contact that some people—like Terence McKenna and John Lilly—have written about in regard to their experience with psychedelic drugs or shamanic plants?

JOHN: I find that interesting. It's very mysterious. I've seen this too, and it does seem that when some people take psychedelics, they may open themselves up to something that seems similar. Terence McKenna talks about taking DMT and then suddenly finding all kinds of alien beings around him. What does this mean? Obviously it didn't cause something to materialize physically, so it suggests that, in a certain sense, the person has become proactive in discovering another realm. Those cases may be experienced quite similarly to the cases where there's actual physical evidence that some material UFO has actually appeared in somebody's backyard, but that doesn't help me with the situation I face. I have cases where a neighbor or the media report a UFO close to somebody's home, or where they were driving their car, and independently the person will tell me about a UFO abduction experience. They don't know that the media has tracked the UFO. So there is a physical dimension to this. And it's that aspect of it that has created so much distress in the Western culture, because we felt we were safely cornered off in our material sanctity.

The idea that some kind of entities, beings, or energies from some other dimension can cross over and find us here, in a way that no missile defense is going to help, is—I guess—scary to most people. It doesn't scare me particularly. But I guess that's scary if you've been raised with the notion that we're the preeminent bosses of the cosmos, and nobody can get us, and all we have to do is create better technologically controlled atmospheres, astrodomes, and that kind of thing, and no one will ever reach us. I mean, think about what the military's Star Wars project is. The Strategic Defense Initiative is part of that kind of effort that is based upon the belief that somehow technology can make us secure and inviolate from ourselves and the powers and energies of the cosmos. I've read most of Terence McKenna's books, and I find they're very compatible with what I'm about. But I don't think he quite realizes how robust the abduction phenomenon itself is because his access to it has been so much through psychedelics. I don't think he realizes how powerful these crossover experiences are in a material sense.

DAVID: Are there any people among the sample that you've worked with who have had both a classic alien abduction experience and a psychedelic experience with a hallucinogenic drug or plant?

JOHN: I know people who've relived alien encounter experiences, or lived alien encounter experiences, under psychedelics.

DAVID: Has anyone ever had the classic alien abduction experience while they were tripping on LSD or a psychedelic plant?

JOHN: Pretty much so. You might want to take a look at Rick Strassman's book.

DAVID: You mean *DMT: The Spirit Molecule?*

JOHN: Yes. He has a whole section in there where he compares the DMT experiences and my cases. Some of the similarities are quite striking.

DAVID: I understand that there's a lot of similarities, but has anybody ever had the classic abduction experience while they were tripping?

JOHN: Pretty close to it.

DAVID: Really? Of going up in a beam of light, being in the ship, that whole scenario?

JOHN: Yeah, and again, how literally do you take it? The experience can be very real, but you're not going get what Budd Hopkins had, which is where you have a physically objectifiable event happening, like people on the Brooklyn Bridge outside the buildings seeing a person accompanied by little beings going out a window. A full-fledged alien encounter experience under psychedelics (which I have seen, maybe not exactly the same, but pretty close to it) can be very much like the actual experience where there might be something observable, like a person actually floating out a window, or with marks on their bodies. It's interesting that they can be so similar in one way yet not another. I mean, obviously the person wasn't taken anyplace in the physical literal sense, except in consciousness, and in the other situation they may well have been physically moved. And yet the experience so similar. I find that interesting.

DAVID: Have you personally ever had a psychedelic experience, and if so, how has it influenced your perspective on science and life?

JOHN: Yeah, I've had psychedelic experiences, as have many people who don't necessarily want to talk about it. What psychedelic experiences do is remove the veil. They remove the barrier between yourself and the surround, so that you experience a much more powerful vibrational connection with the world around you. You experience something like, I guess, what people call the divine, or a basic creative force. It opens you to that. Many people who have moved into what is called the new paradigm, or the new worldview, have, at some point, been jump-started by psychedelic experiences. I mean, you could do a study of that if you wanted. I think the resistance to psychedelics in the culture is not because they're medically threatening so much—I guess people could have bad trips—but because, by taking away the veil of socialization that lies on top of our true selves, people then become open-hearted, open-minded, think for themselves, and are less likely to be programmable by the conventional media or the socioeconomic system we live in.

It isn't like a conspiracy, but there's an intuition in the established collective that psychedelics are threatening to it, because, as I say, people that have opened their hearts, minds and souls through that means—or any other means that undoes the programming that we've all taken in—begin to question, think for themselves, don't accept the political lies or the inequalities that exist. Or they feel more connected with the environment, so they find viscerally abhorrent the whole deterioration of the environment and the commercial callousness that is at the root of that. So I think they're very threatening. I don't work in this area, but I'm interested in the resistance to psychedelics as a cultural or political phenomenon. And, at this point, I'm persuaded of their power.

DAVID: Have you personally ever had any kind of encounter with a being that you believed to be from another world?

JOHN: No.

DAVID: How can the abduction experience be part of a larger psychologically or spiritually transformative process?

JOHN: In a certain sense, it becomes clear if you turn it around. In other words, it's a kind of constricting hubris to have come to the place where all that exists is a material world. It is our birthright to know something beyond the material world. We've treated the universe like it was just dead material—you know, matter and energy. If these beings do reflect some kind of intelligence in another dimension, then when they show up for people, the people don't have any choice but to acknowledge their reality. This then begins a very powerful psychological opening process for them so that they then come to realize that we are connected with much more—not just with these beings, but other energies, other entities. And it begins a kind of enlightenment process which can be very disturbing, but they come to realize that the universe is an intelligent realm, not just a physical fact.

DAVID: What are some of the common psychological and spiritual features that you've noticed in how the abduction phenomenon appears to transform people over time?

JOHN: When I first began to work with people who'd had the encounter experiences, my focus was on how remarkable this was that people were being seemingly contacted by strange beings, or at least so it seemed. So there was kind of a "Isn't this amazing?" factor. But then, as I got more deeply into it, and began to meet with medicine men and other people from indigenous cultures and other parts of the world, I began to realize that this was only a gee-whiz matter in terms of the Western scientific worldview, and that other cultures have known of this phenomenon throughout time.

The reason that we don't know about it has to do with, possibly, the way we structure perception, or what our worldview allows us to perceive. I'm not sure. But as I spent more time with it—and had done so before writing *Passport to the Cosmos*—it became increasingly clear that the debate about Is it real? Is it not real? Can we prove it? Can we not prove it? is a very narrow element, and restricts the conversation entirely to a purely materialist question, the literal physical reality of it or not. And although a lot of energy is spent inside and outside the UFO community on that question—which is certainly intriguing for a lot of people, and perhaps needs to be pursued—the more interesting question is: What is the impact of this on human beings, and on the culture?

Now, this is not necessarily the majority view among people in the UFO field. But the literal reality about UFOs—isn't this the greatest story ever, and so forth—has become of less interest to me then the matter of what is the effect of this? What is the impact of this on human lives? And at first that may seem discouraging, 'cause, gosh—aren't we going to try to explain it and understand it? You know, box it and put a ribbon on it. And find out what it is, where the aliens are coming from, who are they, what's behind it all, and so forth—all legitimate questions, certainly. Yet there are elements of life which really don't lend themselves to explanation.

For instance, take people who have had near-death experiences. Neal Grossman—a philosopher at University of Illinois in Chicago—has worked with many people who have had near-death experiences. And once these people have the experience, the question of What is its literalness? or What is its physicality as reality? is not important to them. What's important is the experience itself. In other words, what it's opening them to? The cosmic reality or dimension of being it opens them to is far more important to them. So this drone that we get from Carl Sagan on down, of Where's the proof? Where's the physical evidence? is an attempt to move the conversation on to their rather narrow turf and then battle it on that level. And I think that's a useless exercise.

The fact of the matter is that the UFO encounter experiences, like other transpersonal experiences—such as near-death experiences, kundalini awakenings, spontaneous spiritual epiphanies, psychedelic experiences, and others—crack this, I would say, meticulously constructed and somewhat artificial programming of the Western mind that's gone on over several centuries to separate us from the divine, so we can declare arrogantly and confidently that God is dead. It strips away this programming, and it opens people to this connection with the numinous, with the transcendent, higher consciousness, creative principle, God—whatever you want to call it. And that becomes a living reality for people who have this kind of trial by fire that the so-called alien abduction experience—or near-death experiences and similar overwhelming confrontations with these kind of forces—can do.

This is not to say that these experiences can't be traumatic. They can be traumatic by the very intensity of them, or the seeming lack of consideration for human sensibilities that the so-called aliens may exhibit. So the traumas are very real. But I think to stay at that level, and not go on into the resource that these experiences represent for possibilities of transformation—for individuals, and from the worldview standpoint, for our whole culture—we'd be missing a great opportunity. So this transformation does occur in case after case. However, if you don't get beyond the point of the person who's had this overwhelming experience, and they're traumatized by it, they may stay stuck in a kind of victim place. This happens to many experiencers, so we become sympathetic healers.

. . .

DAVID: You mentioned in your book *Abduction* that the abduction phenomena has important philosophical, spiritual, and social implications. Can you explain what you mean by this?

JOHN: This has to do with the notion that the whole Western scientific, philosophical, and religious enterprise has been to eliminate unseen agency from the cosmos, to deny it, to isolate ourselves in what Tulane philosophy professor Michael Zimmerman called anthropocentric humanism—meaning that we think we're the center of the intellectual cosmos.

That's actually a terribly painful place to be. Maybe there's a certain narcissistic pleasure in thinking you're the top of the hierarchy in a Godless universe. This self-inflated, technologically oriented culture that we're in can provide a kind of egoistic pleasure, but at the same time it's a terribly false and isolating state of mind to be in. So there's a natural appetite—what Jung called a spiritual hunger—to feel some real connection with something beyond our material surroundings. So anything that suggests this will be attractive, particularly in a case with this much evidence, because it's not just what somebody is saying in church—there's actually something that frames itself at least in part materially.

This is very exciting, because it says that we are not alone. I mean, just look at all the excitement around this possibility of some sort of microorganisms from Mars. Stephen Jay Gould said that the leap from there to sophisticated complex beings like us is a vast one. Well, it's also a pretty great leap from beings like us to the kind of things that I talk about, and yet there is some kind of psychological connection. I think that the excitement around all this is that it does hint that there is some kind of other intelligence. It reanimates the universe. It reconnects us to the divine, and potentially it may bridge us back to the daimonic world. There's a deep hunger to be reconnected with what my abductees call "Home" or "Source."

This phenomenon appears to require that we acknowledge that, if the universe isn't intelligent in itself, it contains intelligences. Acknowledging that people's psyches are opened to a much wider universe is very exciting and powerfully transformative for many people, although it's a kind of shock at first. The whole Western scientific enterprise seems to be predicated on the notion that the material world is really all there is, and yet at some deep level that's so profoundly unsatisfying. So I think this raises a question about the whole matter of what is reality and what does exist. Where do we place phenomena that seem to come from some other dimension but manifest in our reality, and how do we understand that?

The major religions focus on particular spiritual entities—like Jesus, Allah, God, the Holy Spirit, or angels—so here we have some other entities, but these entities seem to enter into our material world. What are the theological implications of the introduction of these strange beings into our universe? They seem to create a bridge from the unseen into the material world. I think it raises important philosophical questions.

. . .

DAVID: Do other cultures report the phenomenon as often?

JOHN: In different forms, and not always in the literal physical way that our classic abduction cases here are. Sometimes they're quite physical, and sometimes they're less. Often the beings will communicate to people that they're not really like how they appear, but they have to show up in a certain material form for us to perceive them. If they showed up as they really are, you'd either be disturbed or you couldn't recognize them.

If these beings actually are many thousands of years more advanced than ourselves, it's very possible that the way such entities would naturally appear would not be familiar to us. But these other cultures that have these cases don't find it as shocking to their worldview as we do. This is because they haven't set up this dichotomy to the same degree as us between the material world and unseen realms, and that there shouldn't be any crossover between them.

In the nineteenth century there was this fad of mediumship and access to other realms by different seers. In particular, there was a renowned spirualist named Home, and the British Academy set out, as they would, to debunk him. They sent a leading scientist by the name of Sir William Crookes to visit Home and to look into all these claims of visitations from the other world, et cetera. So Crookes soaked himself in this and came to the conclusion that it was real, that he couldn't debunk it. He couldn't show it all to be fraudulent. So he came back to the Academy and reported what he had found. Needless to say they were quite irate, and they said to him that it is not possible, and he said, "I never said it was possible, I just said it was true."

DAVID: How has your study of shamanism helped to shed light on the alien abduction phenomenon?

JOHN: I noticed two things. As I worked with the experiencers in this country and in Western cultures, they seemed to be personally drawn to shamanism. The reason for that has to do with the fact that many of the animal forces that they encounter and many other aspects of the experience seem to them to have similarities to shamanic initiation and journeys—such as the representations of beings in animal form, and the initiatory aspect of it. So they become interested in this. The other aspect of this has to do with the work I was talking about earlier that I'd done with indigenous people, especially medicine people, who very often, if not virtually always, can report some kind of encounter with strange beings, or with what we call UFOs. So I saw this from both directions. It seemed to me that the consciousness that is associated with the shamanic education, shall we say, admits of the phenomenon and it's part of that consciousness. So one is naturally led into that world. Sue Jamieson and I wrote an article that appeared in the magazine *Shamanism* in the last year or so, where we compared UFO encounters and shamanic initiations and journeys as two ways to enter into a nonordinary state of consciousness.

DAVID: What is your perspective on psychic phenomena like telepathy, and why do you think so many scientists have a hard time accepting the evidence for it?

JOHN: It has to do with the nature of the universe. As scientists focused on so-called physical or material science, their approach influenced the universe that they discovered. In other words, they've concentrated on the universe's material and energetic properties, the four basic kinds of energy and matter itself. And in situations where, apparently, there is a connection, without an identifiable physical mechanism—like electrical impulses, electromagnetism, or something that can indicate a passage of something in the matter–energy realm—then the mainstream scientists say it can't be.

It's a worldview that says that it can't be. This includes all these phenomena, like telepathy, remote viewing, clairvoyance, and all the other psi phenomena— like the work at Princeton, which shows the effect of emotionally charged collective events on random number generating. This research demonstrates a relationship between world events and what happens in the computer, and because it is identifiable without a physical mechanism, it's challenging to the whole scientific edifice, and therefore tends to be dismissed, except by certain open-minded scientists.

A number of people—Edgar Mitchell, Larry Dossey, Russell Targ, with his work on remote viewing, and others—have shown that, in a sense, we live in a kind of hologram. In other words, there is already connection between us. The universe is a seamless web of connectedness. Therefore, for one mind to be discovered to connect with another communicatively is consistent with the whole notion of nonlocality, but since there's no obvious mechanism for this, many scientists find this, again, a challenge to a purely materialist worldview. Are you following me?

DAVID: Yes. I interviewed Dean Radin for this book, so I'm pretty familiar with the scope of psi research.

JOHN: Yeah, he's a very good example of someone who's done an absolutely incontrovertible summary of the various research that's been done, and yet he'll still run into people who say that there's no real evidence. Well, they just don't want it to be true.

DAVID: I also worked with Rupert Sheldrake for three years. I did the California-based research for his books *Dogs That Know When Their Owners Are Coming Home* and *The Sense of Being Stared At*.

JOHN: Well, there you go. Then you know all about this. All those dog experiments with morphogenetic fields demonstrate that there can be information picked up or gained without any obvious, familiar, electronic communication element. And, God, I mean, what does that do to our scientific edifice?

DAVID: Consciousness seems to be a particularly thorny subject for a lot of scientists.

JOHN: Take a reductionist neuroscientist like Francis Crick, who has this book on consciousness where he reduces it the firing of brain cells. Crick is a archetypal figure because he won the Nobel Prize with Watson around DNA, and that reductionist orientation is still, I think, the dominant one.

So if I say to someone like Crick, what does that have to do with consciousness? He'll say, Consciousness is what's happening in the brain. Well, no it isn't. Consciousness is the experience of being conscious. He would repeat his reductionist statement, and I'll keep asking that question, What does it have to do with consciousness? Consciousness is the inner experience of knowing what is around. And he'd say, Okay, but that's just the firing of nerve cells.

Well, what does the firing of nerve cells have to do with consciousness? You can go back and forth like that, on and on, and you're just butting paradigmatic heads against each other. He says there's no soul because all there is is nerves firing. Well, how does he know? What gives him the right to conclude about something that's just so intersubjective and luminous from an objectification of nerve cells? How does anyone get away with that anymore? That's why the scientific community, by my definition of science, is unscientific. They try to reduce science to this very narrow framework.

DAVID: Do you think that the human species will survive the next hundred years, or do you think that we're in any danger of extinction?

JOHN: Well, I don't live in the negativity that we won't. I mean, I can only live in commitment to the possibility that we will, and what might bring that about. I sometimes think that the present administration in the United States has been given to us as a challenge, to see if we really have the will to survive and to live—because there's continuous destruction of the environment, and an escalation of wars and weaponry in this not terribly mindful way, which is obviously heading toward Armageddon. But I think there is a counterforce, an awakening of consciousness that is occurring, that realizes we just can't continue this way, and we won't survive if we do. There's a lot of opening to other possibilities now.

So it's not so much pessimism or optimism, as my contribution can only be if I live in the possibility that we will survive—what that will require, and what the future will be like. I'm actually working with Trish Pfeiffer now on a book called something like *The End of Materialism and the Primacy of Consciousness*, which is aimed at your question. We asked leading thinkers in the area of consciousness—physicists, philosophers, psychologists—if the paradigm that the universe is intelligent—that there is consciousness that permeates the all that is, as the creative force—were accepted as truth throughout the world, what would be different in the way we would treat one another and the Earth. So we have marvelous material about that, which is really directed aimed at your question.

DAVID: Assuming that we do survive, how do you envision the future evolution of the human race?

JOHN: I think that I only want to say one thing to this, because this is too huge a question, and it's too easy to get foolish about it. But the major shift I see that would happen would be a shift from the focus on the material world of technology to a focus on self-understanding, knowing who we are, what we are as a species, which will lead us into a spiritual renaissance. I had a phrase for this, something like, Can we afford to put billions of dollars into the physical world and ignore the inner world? But that's what I see happening, a shift to awareness, and then, as that occurs, the much more harmonious evolution of relationships to one another, and to the Earth, can occur. But it starts with this progression of this revolution of consciousness, which is now taking place all around us. Whether it'll happen in time, I don't know. But I certainly would work toward that.

DAVID: What do you think happens to consciousness after death?

JOHN: The honest answer is, of course, I don't know. There are various reasons to believe that there is some continuation of consciousness after death from research that's been done on near-death experiences and from certain people who, seemingly, have the capacity to enter into that realm and return—to live in both the realm where spirits reside and this realm, and report upon it. I myself am involved in research that has to do with a colleague and friend who died a year and a half ago. She has been communicating with her husband, friends, and patients in ways that leave, in my mind, little doubt it is she. In other words, there's information being communicated that only she had.

Then there's a whole body of research, which I've been brought in connection with, like the work of Frederic Myers. He talks about the continuation of consciousness after death, and actually did the rather classic experiment in which he communicated from the other side. There are books about this, recording this experiment, where he gave information to four different people, none of which made sense by itself. But when they put the pieces of it together, it was an intelligible communication. So that was an experiment from the other side that has become kind of a classic. Then there's all the work on spiritism. It's not proof, but there does seem to be something to it. Then there's the work on reincarnation, such as Ian Stevenson's research, work that's been done with people who report past-life experiences. You probably know a lot of that.

DAVID: I know Ian Stevenson's book *Twenty Cases Suggestive of Reincarnation*.

JOHN: He's got several books, but that's one of them. There's a body of material that is developing that suggests that there is some form of consciousness, that is associated with a particular person, that continues. I mean, we're not talking about the question Is there consciousness in the universe? We're talking about a particular individual's consciousness continuing. Then there's Gary Schwartz's controlled studies with mediums, in which he shows that information was coming that the mediums didn't know and, apparently, could only have come from the relative on the other side. In other words, I can't say I know from my own experience, but I'm becoming familiar with literature from a number of different directions which support this. That's what you're asking, right?

DAVID: Yeah, and how all that research affects what you personally think.

JOHN: But opinion is so a matter of opinion. (*laughter*) It's in that area that has to do with experience as evidence, and we don't generally accept experience as evidence. Therefore this huge body of material tends to not be taken seriously because it can't be proven in physicalistic or scientistic terms. But, evidently, it seems to be the case that there is some form of consciousness after the body dies. Then you have all of the spirit visitations from the so-called ghosts, some of which have been anchored in quite good research. So I don't know, I think the burden of proof has shifted in the direction of those that would deny it.

DAVID: What is your perspective on the concept of God?

JOHN: Well, as soon as you say a "concept," there are two questions here. One is the concept of God, which is one idea. The other is the experience of the divine, and I don't know which you mean exactly.

DAVID: I'm just curious what the word means to you, how you interpret it.

JOHN: The word "God" has become the shortcut term for what has historically been applied to the overarching or the ultimate creative principle in the universe, that is sometimes experienced in humanlike terms—because I think that our psyche can grasp things if we anthropomorphize them—but, in its essence, is mysterious, luminous, numinous, and overwhelming in its sense of presence when one is open to it. The problem is its all concept now, mostly, because the actual experience of the divine has been pretty well eradicated from the Western psyche by what Rilke called "daily parrying," so that, as he put it, the senses by which we can know the spirit world have atrophied. So you can only know it experientially, and people that know it experientially are not very good at describing it in a way that's going to create the experience for somebody else. Therefore, somebody who hasn't had the experience, or whose senses aren't open, will say, well, you haven't convinced me, because I haven't had the experience. So that's usually where the conversation ends.

DAVID: So you see God as something like a state of consciousness.

JOHN: As an experience of the divine. God as a separate entity, a theistic notion of a being that is separate from us—no, I don't have any sense of that. I have a sense of being part of some infinite spirit wisdom, or spirit intelligence, that is sometimes present, real, and alive to me. But I'm indwelling in it, and it in me. There's no separate thing like churches sometimes try to make of it.

DAVID: Do you see any teleology in evolution?

JOHN: No, I think the future is up for grabs.

DAVID: But you do see an intelligence inherent in nature?

JOHN: That's what I was saying, yes.

DAVID: Do you think that intelligence is helping to guide the evolutionary process, or do you see any type of design crafted into how evolution progresses?

JOHN: A guiding process? Sometimes it seems like it.

DAVID: I guess what I mean is, do you see the evolutionary process as working entirely through blind chance, random mutation, and natural selection, or do you think that there's some type of intelligence inherent in the process—an intelligence that is, perhaps, groping toward something?

JOHN: Yeah, I think that there is some type of intelligence, but we're part of it. In other words, the thing is that most of us are kind of saying, well, I don't see any intelligence out there. Or I'm waiting for it to show up. Or why doesn't it speak to me? Whereas, in fact, we are cocreating the divine. The intelligence is expressed in higher or lower forms through the choices we make. So if we make a choice, say, to demonize the Other, that's an expression of God at a very low level. Or if we experience a sense of love that transcends any individual differences, then we're expressing our participation in the divine in a higher vibrational sense. But it's all participation in what people call God.

Designing Higher Intelligence

An Interview with Ray Kurzweil

Ray Kurzweil is a computer scientist, software developer, inventor, entrepreneur, and philosopher. He is a leading expert in speech and pattern recognition, and he invented a vast array of computer marvels. He was the principal developer of some of the first optical character and speech recognition systems, the first print-to-speech reading machine for the blind, the first Charge Coupled Device flat-bed scanner, the first text-to-speech synthesizer, and the first music synthesizer capable of re-creating the grand piano and other orchestral instruments. Dr. Kurzweil successfully founded and developed nine businesses in speech recognition, reading technology, music synthesis, virtual reality, financial investment, medical simulation, and cybernetic art. In 2002 he was inducted into the U.S. Patent Office's National Inventors Hall of Fame, and he received the Lemelson-MIT Prize, the nation's highest award in invention and innovation. He also received the 1999 National Medal of Technology, the nation's highest

honor in technology, from President Clinton in a White House ceremony, and has received eleven honorary doctorates and honors from three U.S. presidents. Dr. Kurzweil has also written several popular books on the evolution of artificial intelligence, including The Age of Intelligent Machines *and* The Age of Spiritual Machines.

* * *

DAVID: What kind of potential do you think there is to develop new technologies, such as neural implants, that enhance the abilities of the human mind?

RAY: If you ask, What is a human being? I think the response is the fundamental attribute of human beings is that we seek to expand our horizons. Biological evolution, which defines us as some specific niche, is not only limited, but is really missing the whole point of what human beings are. Evolution works through indirection. It creates something in that new capability creates the next stages. At one point, biological evolution created a technology-creating species, and then the cutting-edge of evolution since that time has been human cultural and technological evolution. We didn't stay on the ground. We didn't stay on the planet. We're not staying with the limitations of our biology, and we're already greatly extended the reach of our bodies and our minds through our technology.

The Age of Neural Implants, which is really only one of quite a few revolutionary technologies that are in their early stages, has already started. There are quite a few people walking around who are cyborgs. These people have computers in their brains that are hooked up to their biological neurons, where the electronics works seamlessly with the biological circuitry. We've started by using these computer implants to help with specific medical conditions and disabilities. For example, we have cochlear implants for the deaf and deep-brain stimulation implants for people with Parkinson's disease. In the Parkinson's case, the new-generation devices actually have downloadable software, where you can download new software from outside the patient for the device. In the first ones the software was hard-wired in the device.

These little computers interact with biological neurons and replace the function of the corpus of cells that are destroyed by Parkinson's. In the early demonstrations of this system, the French doctor Dr. A. L. Benebid had people come in, and he had the device turned off. He could turn it on or off from outside the patient. They were in advanced stages of Parkinson's with very rigid motor movements. And when he would then flip the device on, it was as if these patients came alive. They were then able to move and act normally. This has been approved by the FDA in the past year, and it's now being looked at for other neurological conditions.

There are retinal implants that are being prepared, which are experimental, and there are experimental implants for a wide range of other conditions.

Today neural implants have two limitations. One is they have to be surgically implanted. So people are not going to use them unless they have a very compelling reason. Having advanced Parkinson's is such a compelling reason. And it can only be placed in a very small number of places, generally just one place.

However, both of those limitations will be overcome when we have full-scale nanotechnology, and, specifically, nanobots—nanoscale robots, the size of blood cells—that can go through our capillaries, and into the brain, noninvasively. That's not as futuristic as it sounds. In fact, there's already four major conferences today on something called Bio-MEMS [Biological Micro-Electronic Mechanical Systems], which are organized to develop the first generation of little devices that would go inside the bloodstream, for a wide range of diagnostic and therapeutic purposes.

For example, something that actually works today is a little device that's actually nano-engineered, with seven-nanometer pores. It's a little capsule that lets insulin out and blocks antibodies. It has actually cured Type 1 diabetes in rats. Since the mechanism of Type 1 diabetes is the same in rats and humans, there's no reason why this kind of device, once fully perfected, shouldn't also work in humans.

Now, this is the first generation. I think it's important to understand—which, actually, very few observers really do understand fully—that these technologies are growing, not linearly, but exponentially. Not only is the power of these technologies roughly doubling every year, but we're actually doubling the rate of progress every decade. That's probably an important point we should come back to. But if you look at the trends in the exponential growth of computation and the exponential shrinking of technology, you'll see that we're shrinking both electronic and mechanical technology at a rate of 5.6 per linear dimension per decade. Look at the exponential growth in communication technologies.

Then there's the exponential growth and the knowledge of the human brain. We're reverse-engineering the brain, understanding how it works, and getting more and more detailed information about the brain. We're doubling the amount of knowledge we have about how the brain works every year. It's conservative to say that by the late 2020s we will have the following. We'll have really completed a very detailed reverse-engineering of the human brain. We'll have blood cell–size robotic devices that have considerable intelligence, that communicate with each other and with our biological neurons noninvasively.

So we could then have the following scenario. We can send millions, or billions, of nanobots noninvasively through the bloodstream by injecting them, or swallowing them, and they'll make their way into the brain, without surgery, through the capillaries of the brain. The capillaries go to every single spot in the brain, so these nanobots can be widely distributed, and this limitation that I mentioned before, of only being able to put it in one place, will be overcome.

They could be in billions of places. They could be introduced noninvasively, and they will communicate with each other. They'll be on a wireless local area network, that could communicate with the Internet, which can communicate noninvasively with our biological neurons. All of these capabilities have already been demonstrated on small scales. We can't build these devices small enough yet to put billions of them in the bloodstream. But that's a conservative scenario based on what I call the Law of Accelerating Returns—which is the exponential shrinking of the size of these technologies and the ongoing exponential growth in computational capacities, which is the power of these underlying technologies.

We then have a number of scenarios that would follow from that. For example, we could have full-immersion virtual reality, where the nanobots can shut down the signals coming from our real senses and replace them with the signals that your brain would be receiving if you were in the virtual environment. Then your brain would feel like it's in that virtual environment, and these can be as realistic, detailed, and compelling as real reality.

You could go there by yourself, or with other people, and have any kind of experience with anyone in these virtual environments. Some of these virtual environments can be realistic re-creations of earthly places, like taking a walk with someone on a Mediterranean beach. Some can be fantastic imaginary environments that don't exist on Earth, and couldn't exist. They may not follow the laws of physics. Designing new environments, just like designing new game environments today, will be a new art form. You can incorporate all five of our senses in these virtual environments. They can also include the neurological correlates of our emotions. So that's one application.

Another application, really the most profound one, is to extend human pattern recognition and cognitive ability. Even though we're constantly rewiring our brain, and we grow new connections all the time, it has a fixed architecture. Rewiring our brain is part of the basic method we use to learn, and using our brain is the best way to keep it healthy, but we're limited to a fixed architecture, on the order of a 100 trillion connections. While that might sound like a big number, human bandwidth is pretty limited.

For one thing, those connections are very very slow. Electrochemical signaling takes place, which is a little bit different than a digital calculation. It's really a digital-controlled analog transaction, but it's 200 calculations per second, and that's about 100 million times slower than today's electronic systems and close to a billion times slower than would feasible with nanotube-based circuitry. A one-inch cube of nanotube circuitry would a million times more capable than the 100 trillion connections in the human brain.

So we will be able to expand the human bandwidth by intimately interfacing with these nanobot-based computational systems. We'll be able to add new connections. Instead of having 100 trillion connections, you could multiply that. You could run these new virtual connections faster. You could interface with nonbiological forms of intelligence, have direct brain-to-brain communication and download knowledge. That's one thing the machines can do even today—simply share their knowledge bases—whereas I can't download my knowledge of French, or my knowledge of the novel *War and Peace*, to you. I can communicate with you. I can share knowledge using language, which is very very slow, but I can't just download my pattern of neurotransmitter concentrations and interneuronal connections to you, whereas machines can do that.

These are scenarios that will begin to be feasible in the late 2020s. I believe that 2029 is a reasonably conservative target date for machines being able to pass the Turing Test and achieving human levels of intelligence. They'll then be able to combine those benefits with advantages that machines already have, in terms of speed, memory capacity, knowledge sharing and so on.

. . .

DAVID: How long do you think it will be before computers exceed human intelligence, and how do you think human life will change after we have computers that are smarter than people?

RAY: There's two parts to achieving machines that will match human intelligence. One is the hardware requirement, and the other is the software. In my book four years ago, *The Age of Spiritual Machines*, I said we'd have the requisite hardware capability by 2019 in a personal computer, or at least in $1,000 of computation. Then people went around saying, Well, Ray Kurzweil says that when we have machines where the hardware capacity matches the human brain, we'll just automatically have human-level intelligence, and that's never been my position. That's only one part of the equation, although even that part, the hardware part, was controversial four years. I would say there's been real sea change in attitude about the hardware.

Now, generally, the mainstream opinion is Oh, of course we'll have the hardware. That's very obvious. There's been enough progress in three-dimensional molecular computing over the last four years, and there's a great deal of confidence we'll have three-dimensional molecular circuits before Bor's Law runs out with regard to two-dimensional circuits. The controversy has now shifted to the software question. Okay, we'll have these very powerful machines, but will they just be extremely fast calculators, or will they be intelligent? There's more to human intelligence than just the fact we have 100 trillion interneuronal connections that could compete simultaneously. The way they're organized, and the whole paradigm of their operation, is very important.

There's many different ways in which we might achieve the software intelligence. One's through our own continued experimentation, and developing,

I think, in particular, pattern recognition algorithms, which are getting more and more powerful. But the most important project is the project to understand the human brain itself and to reverse-engineer its principles of operation. And it's not hidden from us. Brain scanning is growing exponentially. It's doubling in resolution, price, performance, and bandwidth every year. We are getting more and more detailed models of the brain every year. Already there have been detailed mathematical models of a couple dozen regions of the brain, and those have been replicated in software. Those software systems have been administered psycho-acoustic tests—because these are replications of acoustic areas of the brain, parts of the brain that deal with acoustic information—and they performed similarly to the actual brain circuits.

We've shown that it's feasible to develop these mathematical models. For years some scientists, like, for example, Doug Hofstadter, wondered, Are we inherently intelligent enough to understand our own intelligence? Maybe our own intelligence is below the threshold needed to understand our intelligence? Is the way our intelligence works so complicated and profound that it's beyond human intelligence to understand it? What we're finding is that it's really not at all the case that the brain is, first of all, just one big information processing organ. That's like saying the body is one organ. If you want to understand how the body works, you have to break it down—into the heart, the liver, the lungs, and then you can begin to understand each region separately, because they each use different principles of operation. The brain is several hundred different regions, and each one actually works quite differently. It represents information differently. It transforms it differently and uses a different principle of operation. But we're finding that we can actually model these quite precisely.

We haven't done this with the vast majority of brain regions, but we're showing that the process is feasible, and we're getting more and more powerful tools. The tools to do this with are themselves growing exponentially in power. It's very comparable to where the Genome Project was maybe ten years ago. At that time mainstream scientists were saying Oh, it's going to be hundreds of years before we are able to sequence the whole genome, because, at the speed we're going, we can only do one-ten thousandth of the job in a year. But there also, the bandwidth, the speed, the price performance doubled every year. So most of the project was done in the last couple years of the project. We'll see a similar process with reverse-engineering the brain. So we will understand the brain and have detailed models of the several hundred regions in the 2020s. These will provide us with the ideas, the templates of intelligence. We'll modify them. We'll reengineer them.

One thing we discover when we start to understand how natural systems work is that very often they're very inefficient. I mentioned already that our internal, interneuronal connections computed two hundred calculations per second, using a very very complex, cumbersome electrochemical system. We already have circuitry that can operate many millions of times faster. So as we reengineer it, we can greatly improve its performance. So I believe we'll have the hardware and the software by the late 2020s. I've said 2029 as a reasonable date, at which point I think machines will match the subtlety and range of human pattern recognition and human intelligence in general. And once a machine achieves human levels of intelligence, it will necessarily soar past it, because it'll be able to combine the subtlety and flexibility of human intelligence with the ways in which machines are inherently superior—being able to share knowledge, operate a lot faster, always perform at peak performance, master billions and trillions of facts accurately. They'll be able to go out on the Web and read and master essentially all of the human-machine civilization's knowledge.

I think the primary impact is going to be, not a set of alien machines that come from over the horizon to compete with us, but we're going to merge with our machines. There's not going to be a clear distinction between human and machine. This issue we talked about before of neural implants—I think that will become quite ubiquitous. And it's not going to be some computer we stick in one place in our brains, but, rather, we'll have really pervasive computering that we interact with in our biological brains. If you talk to somebody in 2035, you'll going to be talking to somebody that really is a hybrid of biological and nonbiological intelligence.

So we're going to augment our own intelligence. We'll be able to think faster, think more deeply, develop more profound skills in creating knowledge of everything from music to science, and, basically, become smarter by merging with our technology. One thing to realize is that once nonbiological intelligence gets a foothold in our brains, it'll grow exponentially, because that's the nature of nonbiological intelligence. It doubles every year. That's what it's been doing. It's actually going faster than that. But there's a second level of exponential growth. There's exponential growth, and the rate of exponential growth.

In comparison, our biological intelligence is not growing at all, although biological evolution is still operating. It's operating on a time scale that's so slow as to be effectively zero. So right now, today, we have 10^{26} [ten to the twenty-sixth power] calculations per second in our biological brains, in our 6 billion humans. Fifty years from now that figure will still be ten to the twenty-sixth power for biological intelligence. Today nonbiological intelligence is a good deal less than that by a factor of millions. But since it's more than doubling every year, as we get to the 2020s it'll cross over. And, as we get to the 2030s, in the bulk of human-machine civilizations, intelligence will be nonbiological.

DAVID: Do you think that a computer, or a nonbiological form of intelligence, can develop consciousness?

RAY: People use the term "consciousness" and "self-awareness" in a very ambiguous way. If we're talking about something that we can observe—as in a third party looking at another entity, and asking Gee, does that entity have a concept of itself?—that's an objective observation, and certainly these machines will do that, because they're going to do everything that humans do. They'll understand themselves actually better than we understand ourselves. I mean, how well do we understand how our own intelligence works? We actually don't understand it very well. These machines will understand themselves very well. They'll understand how humans work very well. So, in that sense, their self-awareness will be much greater than human self-awareness is today.

But that's not actually dealing with what David Chalmers calls the "hard question of consciousness," which is this first-person sense we have of actually experiencing the world in our subjective states. It's a first-person phenomena, and it's not a scientific question. There's no scientific test you can administer to an object where you can have some green light go on that means Okay, this entity's conscious. Or: No, this one's not conscious. There's no consciousness detector you can create that doesn't have some philosophical assumptions built into it.

I'm aware of my own consciousness, but beyond that I can only make assumptions. I assume that other humans who seem to be conscious are conscious, but that's an assumption on my part. Other human beings seem to be making a similar assumption. That shared human consensus breaks down as you go outside of human experience. Human beings don't agree if animals are conscious. Some human beings say that the higher-order animals are conscious, that their pets are conscious. Other human beings say, No, animals operate by instinct, which is some kind of primitive machinelike reaction. They're not really conscious. That's the whole issue underlying the animal rights and animal suffering issue. And we're going to have that controversy with nonbiological intelligence.

But right now, when a machine claims to be conscious, or to have feelings, it's not very convincing. There are machines that do that. If you go to your kid's video games, they'll be virtual creatures there that claim to be angry, happy, or whatever. They're not very convincing today because they don't have all the subtle features, reactions, and understanding of language that we associate with really having those feelings. But when we get out to 2030, we're going to be encountering completely nonbiological entities that do have the subtlety of humans, that really are convincing. And it's going to be a philosophical debate as to whether or not that's just a really convincing simulation of an entity that is consciousness, or if it's really a conscious entity. Or if there's a difference between the two. Now, some people say, Since it's not a scientific question, therefore it's just an illusion, and we're wasting our time to talk about it.

My own view disagrees with that. The reason that there's room for philosophy is because the question is not scientific. Science can't answer every question, and it's really the ultimate ontological question. It's also extremely important for our whole system of morality and our legal system. Our whole legal system is based on the idea of suffering. If you cause suffering to someone by assaulting them, that's a serious crime. If you end their consciousness by murdering them, that's a serious crime. It's okay to destroy property if it belongs to you, provided society doesn't have some interest in it, like it's not a historical house or something. But I can't go and destroy your property—not because of the suffering I'm causing the property—because of the suffering I'm causing you, as the owner of that property. But it's all based on there being a conscious entity who has the potential for suffering, and if the entity's conscious experience is affected by these actions, there'll come a point where that question will arise with regard to machines. It's arising already with regard to animals.

DAVID: How do you think consciousness evolved on this planet in the first place?

RAY: Well, again, the problem with that question is deciding what consciousness is. Let's take the obvious behavioral phenomenologically perspective—that entities are conscious if they appear to be acting in a self-aware way. This is to say that consciousness follows from sufficiently intelligent behavior, the ability to behave in an intelligent way, which we associate with higher-order animals, and particularly with human beings. Now, if that's the assumption that we make about consciousness—and that's the common wisdom assumption—then consciousness evolved with intelligence.

But again, I have to point out that there's a big philosophical leap there. If we make that assumption, then it evolved with intelligence, and intelligence evolved because of its survival benefits. Evolution moves toward higher-order systems that are more capable of solving problems, and it has moved toward more intelligent organisms. It finally created a species that not only was intelligent, but could manipulate the environment because of its opposable appendage, the thumb. So we've created technology, and the technology has become increasingly intelligent. Ultimately we're going to use our technology to amplify our own intelligence.

DAVID: What role do you see technology playing in the evolution of life on this planet?

RAY: As I've said, we're going to reverse-engineer our own intelligence and understand in detail how it works. We're going to re-create it then in our technology. We will, in the process of doing that, greatly amplify it and merge with it. We will basically re-create who we are—both our bodies and our brains—through nanotechnology, artificial intelligence, and vastly expand human intelligence. And that's inherently who human beings are. We are that species that seeks to extend our own horizons, not only physically, but intellectually. So we will merge with our technology and vastly expand our horizons.

DAVID: What is your perspective on God, and do you see any teleology in evolution?

RAY: I see evolution as a spiritual process, because it moves toward greater and greater qualities that we associate with God. I mean, "God" is a word. What do people mean when they say the word "God," or any of the synonyms that we have for it? If you look at all the different religious literature, the real common theme is that God is infinitely intelligent, all-knowing, infinitely beautiful, infinitely creative, and infinitely loving.

I think that most people of different religious faiths would find some agreement with that kind of description. Very few people would be offended by that. If you say God is all-loving, all-knowing, and infinitely creative, generally religious people would find that to be satisfactory. Okay, now what do we see in evolution? We see that evolution creates entities that become—not infinitely creative or intelligent—but more creative and intelligent over time. Mammals are more intelligent than lizards, and we're more intelligent than the other mammals. We're more creative. We're able to create technology. We're more knowledgeable.

Evolution works exponentially. An exponential starts out very slow, but then it kind of explodes. And we're actually getting to that point now in the twenty-first century where technological evolution, which has taken over from biological evolution, is exploding. It will explode in the twenty-first century, into vastly accelerating levels of intelligence, creativity, higher-order emotions such as love and, in my view, beauty. Now, even an exploding exponential doesn't become infinite, but it's moving very rapidly in that direction.

So, although evolution never achieves an infinite level—which is to say, it doesn't absolutely become God—it's moving in that direction of becoming more God-like. And it's doing this at an explosive speed, as the exponential moves beyond what I call the "knee of the curve." Biological evolution has really been eclipsed now by technological evolution, and technological evolution is going to explode as we get to the really powerful parts of the exponential growth of technology in this coming century.

DAVID: Do you think that there's any type of organizing intelligence inherent in nature, or do you think that evolution is purely a random process?

RAY: I think nature has the potential for what I'm talking about, but I believe the universe, right now, is basically what I call "dumb matter." It's operating by these primitive machinelike forces. But our technology is going to saturate the matter and energy in our vicinity of the universe with our human-derived intelligence, and then it's going to spread out throughout the universe. Ultimately, the entire universe will be part of our exponentially spreading human-machine civilization, and, as a result, the universe will wake up. It will become sublimely intelligent.

If you read the various debates of the cosmologists as to what the universe will do billions of years from now, you'll see that they ask questions like Will it all go back to a Big Crunch and then another Big Bang? Or will it expand forever, and all the stars will burn out? Never does it enter into any of their discussions as to the role of intelligence. Intelligence plays no role in any of those discussions. It's as if intelligence is just a little bit of froth that has no bearing on these grand celestial machinelike, clocklike forces. But that's not my view. In fact, if you do the calculations, it's actually a very short period of time— measured in centuries—that our intelligence can spread (at the speed of light, and possibly even faster through wormholes) through the universe. Ultimately the entire universe will be suffused with our human-derived intelligence.

And intelligence can trump these natural forces. It doesn't exactly repeal the forces of nature, but it can manipulate them with such powerful and subtle engineering that it can overcome them. If the universe, on its own, might expand forever, or contract, this now-intelligent universe can decide to do something else. It's going to be a conscious intelligent decision that we're going to make as to the destiny of the universe, not this mindless grinding of these big forces like gravity and antigravity.

DAVID: When I spoke with Noam Chomsky a few weeks ago, he told me that he believed that military technologies were putting our species' survival at serious risk and that he thought there was a high probability that we might actually drive ourselves into extinction. How likely do you think it is that the human species is going to survive the next century?

RAY: There's the potential to destroy ourselves. I mean, it could happen tomorrow, because we have enough nuclear weapons to destroy all mammalian life on the planet. Even though we're no longer in the Cold War with the Soviet Union, those weapons have not been destroyed. They still exist. So that kind of existential risk to the entire human civilization is something we've lived with now for close to half a century. But up until the middle of the twentieth century, there weren't existential risks to the survival of our civilization. So we did introduce an existential risk, and there will be new ones with twenty-first century technology. There are superweapons, that one can describe conceptually using nanotechnology, that are even more powerful than nuclear annihilation.

We're really in the early stages now of the potential for biotechnology. I don't mean just biological weapons like smallpox, but modified viruses that could spread easily, have a long incubation period so they couldn't be detected, and could be very deadly. These could be engineered. And then nanotechnology and artificial intelligence could become a runaway phenomenon. Let's say you have malevolent machines that actually go and design a new generation on their own. They create more powerful machines that then go and create even more powerful machines that are not under control of responsible forces. I mean, there's many different scenarios one can imagine that are destructive.

I'm more optimistic now than I was. I've actually been thinking about it for quite some time. I think if one really understands these technologies, there are three phases that one goes through with them. I know I did. The first phase is a tremendous awe at the power of these technologies to solve human problems—to overcome disease, extend human longevity, clean up the environment, and solve age-old problems that we've been struggling with for thousands of years. Then the next stage is to discover—oh no, wait a minute—these technologies, like nanotechnology, could have a profound downside of enormous destructive potential, and to become potentially overwhelmed with that specter. I think the third stage in this is to begin to understand that this dual nature of technology—the promise and peril—has been a dual nature of technology ever since there was technology, and that we do have means to overcome these problems, despite the very chaotic world we live in.

Let's consider nuclear weapons. When they were exploded in the 1940s, who would have predicted that, nearly sixty years later, not a single other atomic weapon would have been used in anger? We live in a really chaotic world. There's a lot of things that we don't like about human behavior, and yet we have actually been successful in not only not destroying the world, but in not even having a single weapon go off. Now, we can't say, okay, we solved that problem, because we still have the enormous danger. But that does give us some cause for optimism.

I like to point to software viruses as a test case. With each successive generation we see more and more sophisticated pathogens, as well as more and more sophisticated defenses. Irresponsible engineers are continually creating more and more sophisticated software viruses, and yet our defensive systems, our antiviral programs and the technological protections we've created, have been able to keep pace with it. We haven't eliminated the problem completely. We still worry about it. But, so far, software viruses have been kept to a relative nuisance level, and no one would say let's get rid of the Internet because software viruses are such a big problem. The benefit we get from the Internet and other communication computational resources is far greater than the damage.

I take some measure of comfort from how we've dealt with the SARS virus. There's a virus that was fairly deadly, looks like about 20 percent die. It spreads pretty easily, through the air and through contact, and the virus can live outside the human body for quite a few hours. It has a lot characteristics of a really bad virus; it spreads easily and is deadly. And through a combination of high-tech and low-tech means we were able to avoid an epidemic. High tech being the fact that we sequenced the virus's genome in a matter of days, whereas the AIDS virus took years to sequence. So we could develop a test very quickly. And with the Internet we were able to communicate and coordinate our activities very quickly. And we combined this with an old-tech, the old-fashioned means of quarantine.

So despite what seems like a lot of chaos in the world, through this really unprecedented level of international cooperation, we've been able to keep the SARS virus from becoming an epidemic. There was tremendous cooperation, despite the original hesitation by the Chinese to communicate about it. I don't think we can declare victory yet, but it certainly looks like we're winning against the SARS virus. It's very encouraging that we could actually organize like that, very quickly, and suppress a virus that could have spread around the whole world and become like a flu killing millions of people, because it certainly seemed to have that potential.

I think ultimately nanotechnology will overcome the dangers of biotechnology and that artificial intelligence ultimately will overcome the problems of nanotechnology. There's actually no ultimate protection against malevolent artificial intelligence. I think there's some possibility we'll destroy ourselves. I would not put the probability well under 50 percent, but I think it is the biggest issue or challenge that human civilization has in the next century. I don't think we have any choice, though, but to face the challenge. Some people say, Well, even if the risk is one in ten, that's much too high, and we shouldn't take that risk. So let's just stop technology. But I don't think that's a viable choice. In order to do that we have to have a Brave New World type of totalitarian government that completely banned what is now totally ubiquitous, the pervasive phenomena of human progress in science and technology.

Some people say, Okay, let's keep the good technologies. Bill Joy actually said this in his *Wired* cover story. He said, I, Bill Joy am not antitechnology. Let's keep the good technologies. But those dangerous ones that could potentially could destroy, like nanotechnology, let's just not do those. I pointed out that those destructive technologies are the same technologies that are the helpful ones. The same technology that's going to save millions of people from cancer and other diseases utilize the exact same tools that a bioterrorist could use to create a destructive pathogen. The same nanotechnology that's going to help overcome poverty, clean up the environment, and improve human longevity and health is the same nanotechnology that can be destructive.

Nanotechnology doesn't come about because one laboratory is working on it, or ten laboratories. It's the pervasive end result of hundreds of benign steps. Each step is small and conservative. Texas Instruments creates a higher-resolution computer projector. That doesn't sound like a particularly dangerous technology, but that's a step toward nanotechnology—because they created millions of little mirrors that are much smaller than we used before. In the process of doing that we've learned how to make things smaller. It's hundreds of steps like that that get us from here to these very powerful technologies. The only way to stop it would be stop all technology, and I don't even think that would work.

That would just drive it underground. It would actually create a much more dangerous situation, which would be less stable, because the responsible engineers wouldn't have access to the tools to create the defenses, and the irresponsible practitioners would be experimenting with it in secret. I think that actually would be more dangerous, and it would also prevent us from getting the benefits of these technologies. I don't think we have any choice but to really confront the problem and develop these technologies in a way that emphasizes the benefits while we try to control dangers. And I do think we need to increase the priority of dealing with the dangers.

DAVID: What do you think is the biggest threat to the human species?

RAY: We're not yet on the threshold of these existential dangers from nanotechnology and artificial intelligence. We are on the threshold, though, of profound dangers from biotechnology. I think we should be spending hundreds of billions a year specifically to develop more powerful protective technologies, such as antiviral technologies, which are just beginning to emerge. But we really need to accelerate that, because it's really race between the destructive possibilities and our defensive technologies. We need to give a little bit faster course to the defensive technologies.

DAVID: What do you think happens to consciousness after death?

RAY: That's a question that really is beyond our current understanding. I do talk about some dilemmas in our understanding of consciousness. For example, is there a continuity of consciousness even in biological human life that continues? Am I the same consciousness that Ray Kurzweil was a year ago? And you say, Well, Ray, you're the same stuff. It's the same arm and the same face. But actually, no, I'm completely different particles than I was a year ago. Virtually all of my cells have been replaced. Now you say, Well, okay, but, Ray, most of your neurons haven't been replaced. Some of them have, but neurons tend to last longer than most of the other cells, which get turned over. But even those neurons that existed a year ago actually were made of different particles. The actual physical atoms and molecules making them up have been replaced, so nothing is the same as it was a year ago. Actually the only thing that's the same is the pattern.

There's a certain continuity of pattern, of how all these atoms and molecules are put together, that does have a continuity between myself today and myself a year ago. So that means what we are is a pattern, and the pattern persists. I draw an analogy to the pattern that water makes in a stream, as it, say, darts around some rocks. If you look at a stream going around some rocks, you see a certain pattern, and that pattern can look very stable. It can stay the same for hours or even years. But the actual water molecules making up the pattern changes in a fraction of a second, because water's flowing by. So it's completely different stuff every fraction of a second. But the pattern stays the same. And we're really pretty much like that pattern of water, because this stuff is flowing through us, and we're not the same particles at all. So if you hold your arm and say, Well, this is me, it's not.

We're just a pattern. And what is a pattern? A pattern is information. It's knowledge. I think that there's a great loss of pattern in death, a great loss of knowledge and information. I think death is a tragedy. And I think that, because we've had no alternative up until now, people have gone to great lengths to rationalize death—saying, Oh, well, death really isn't such a bad thing, and death's really a wonderful thing. It's really elevating and we transcend. We've gone to tremendous efforts to rationalize what's obviously a terrible thing, and a profound loss, so that we think it's really a good thing. Well, I don't think it's a good thing. I think death is a tragedy. I think it's a tragedy at the age of ninety just as much as if it's at the age of ten or twenty. And I think we're now reaching a point where we can do something about it. We don't have the technologies in hand at this moment to, say, just do X, Y, and Z, and you can live indefinitely, but we do have technologies in health understanding that can keep us healthy until we get the next bridge, which is the full flowering of the biotechnology revolution. This will not allow us to live forever, but will be a bridge to the next revolution, which is the full flowering of the nanotechnology revolution, and that will allow us to live indefinitely by being able to really rebuild our bodies and brains using much more durable technologies.

So we actually do have a path, which I call a bridge to a bridge to a bridge, that can give us virtual immortality. My children's generation actually doesn't have to do a lot to take advantage of that, barring an unusual premature death. But by the time kids today who are twenty become forty, these technologies will be at a fairly mature level. This is a message though for the Baby Boomer generation. I'm fifty-five, and my contemporaries, if they really go to the edge of what's known today in terms of health and medical knowledge, can stay alive and healthy until the full flowering of the biotechnology revolution, which will then keep them going longer till the flowering of the nanotechnology revolution. But I would say that 99.99 percent of my contemporaries are completely oblivious to this fact and are planning to just live and die the old-fashioned way. And they will be essentially the last generation to die in the normal course. Radical life extension is another one of the profound transformations that lies ahead.

. . .

DAVID: What gives you hope?
RAY: I find these profound transformations that lie ahead, through all of these different technological revolutions, very hopeful—because we will have the means to overcome disease, death, suffering, poverty, pollution, and really transform the world in profound ways. There's also some profound dangers along the way. I think we have to face up to them, and not try to stick our heads in the sand by trying to relinquish our way out of them, because that's not going to work. But I do find the ability to amplify human potential and creativity very hopeful.

Robots and Children of the Mind

An Interview with Hans Moravec

Hans Moravec is one of the world's leading experts in robotics. He is a Research Professor in the Robotics Institute at Carnegie Mellon University, where he founded the Mobile Robot Laboratory and directs the world's largest robotics research program. Dr. Moravec is the author of two of the most popular books on the subject of robots and the implications of evolving robot intelligence, Mind Children: The Future of Robot and Human Intelligence *and* Robot: Mere Machine to Transcendent Mind, *which renowned science-fiction writer Arthur C. Clarke described as "the most awesome work of controlled imagination I have ever encountered." Dr. Moravec has also published many papers and articles about robotics, computer graphics, multiprocessors, space travel, and other speculative areas. He received his Ph.D. from Stanford*

University and cofounded the SEEGRID Corporation, which promises commercial free-ranging mobile robots within a decade.

*   *   *

DAVID: Do you think that we will ever have a true scientific measurement of consciousness?

HANS: The position I take in the new book [*Robot: Mere Machine to Transcendent Mind*] is that consciousness is not really an objective property—though ultimately I decide *nothing* is an objective property. Existence itself is subjective. But before you get to that stage, you can look at an entity like a robot that maybe exhibits behavior that could be interpreted as conscious. But you can look at it in a strictly mechanical way if you want, especially if you understand enough of the details of the internal mechanism. You might be able to fully explain its behavior in purely mechanical terms, such as cause A produces effect B, which produces internal cause C, which produces D, and so on. Just a chain of simple causes and effects, and that explains everything about the robot.

So some people look at machines and say that's all they are, and therefore they can't be conscious, because they're just mechanical. But I answer that you can also look at a human being that way if you understood them well enough. Neural signal A causes electrochemical events B, and so on, and just a chain that way. I even imagine that some day there will be entities able to process vastly more data than we can, and they could be intelligent enough to look at us exactly that way, as if we were just these clockwork mechanisms. They could interact with us on that basis without ever forming an interpretation about our thoughts or feelings or so on. We're just causes and effects.

Interacting with such a thing would be interesting, because, probably, most of the time, it wouldn't be that different from interacting with a person. If that supersmart entity wanted you to do something, he would calculate what mechanical things they should do to you to cause you to do that thing. But probably the easiest mechanical things they could do to you is make certain certain sounds at you, such as please pick up that thing. Then calculating the effect in the long run they would probably also say thank you afterward. (*laughter*) In their minds that would just be a string of craftily constructed sounds, right? That wouldn't have the psychological implications that we put on it, but yet it doesn't really matter does it? Their interaction with us would be effective.

The only reason it would be strange is because sometimes they would be able to figure out something to do to us that's not the usual kind of interaction that our psychological models would suggest. So maybe there's a certain song that—as far as we're concerned—they could sing, which has nothing to do with what we ended up doing in response to the song. It might seem like some kind of subtle mind control because that's another path that isn't contained in our psychological models of each other.

So, in the same way that you can look at a human being, either psychologically, as we're able to, or mechanically, as we're not quite up to yet, you should also be able to look at a robot in various ways—including the mechanical, as the engineer that built the robot probably would, or in the psychological way, as probably most people interacting with the robot on a casual day-to-day basis would. If the robot says, "My energy stores are low, and I'm really feeling down today. My servos on my right side are not functioning correctly, and I'm just not feeling well." Then, ultimately, it would take a very hard heart basically not to sympathize a little bit—especially if it does this consistently, and also asks you about your feelings (*laughter*), and responds to the answers you give in the appropriate ways.

I think that's completely reasonable. You can map psychological properties onto the behaviors of the robot regardless of the mechanism that causes them, because, really, who cares what the mechanism is? There is a mapping from the psychology to what it does that makes complete sense and is for us undoubtedly the most effective way of interacting with a machine. So I'm saying the psychological properties are not really an objective thing. They're a way of looking at something. Once you are open to that, you realize that you can actually look that way at lots of things, if you wish to. Sometimes it's not the most effective way.

Basically we have mental mechanisms for dealing with things in the world. We have one set of mechanisms for dealing with inanimate objects. They tell us how to pick up sticks, throw stones, put things together, make houses, and so on. But we have another set of mental mechanisms for dealing with the other people in our tribe. There we worry about whether they like us or don't like us. Or how we feel about them, and whether they're in pain. We feel for them when things like that happen. Or maybe we're angry at them, and we enjoy it when they get hurt, and so on.

Those are a different set of tools, and usually we keep them kind of separate. We're actually upset when somebody inappropriately uses the mechanical interpretations on us. One of the things you can do under the mechanical interpretations, and it's perfectly all right, is to hurt inanimate things, to break them, whereas when you do that to living things there are more serious consequences—because they might fight back, or their relatives might come and get you, or whatever.

So in day-to-day life it's often dangerous. In fact, if, because of some mental-brain defect, somebody tends to treat other human beings in this mechanical way, we usually call that psychosis. Those type of people can be dangerous because they have no feelings. So I think some of the natural defenses against such things in some people get called into play when people talk about building robots, and then interpret them in human ways. With a little bit of corollary you might be able to interpret humans in mechanical ways, and that could be a dangerous thing in society. We have instincts for that, because there are ways in which that could be done where it is indeed dangerous, things that have presumably come up regularly in our evolutionary history. So we have instincts that tend to make us defend ourselves against that kind of thing.

DAVID: How do you think the internal experience of consciousness is created?

HANS: Oh, there's another aspect to the interpretation of consciousness, of basically something having a mind, namely that it has beliefs and feelings. Those are also attributions. But one of the other things that you attribute to it is the ability to make such attributions. When you look at something in a psychological way, and it's something that you interpret as complex as a human being, then it can look at other things and basically project psychological properties on to them. That's part and parcel of the interpretation, that it's able to make those kinds of interpretations, and it's able to make those kind of interpretations about itself. Within the abstract interpretation of psychological properties is the ability to make abstract interpretations of psychological properties, and also of itself.

So you have this cycle where the being is itself believing itself to be conscious, and believing itself to have feelings, and feeling itself to have feelings. All right, so I think that's what it is, it's a way of looking at the world and a way of looking at ourselves, which includes, of course, looking at ourselves that we have the ability to look at things. So it's no more real and no less real than that, and you can have that in a program. In one way of looking at it, you can sort of prime the pump, in that you build a machine from the ground up, and it's all mechanical at first, because that's all you'd built.

You just build mechanisms that affect other mechanisms and act in a certain way. But you've built it in such a way that it's easy to make the interpretation that certain parts of this mechanism represent beliefs. Like there's a string of memory cells here, and you interpret them in whatever language is being used to store things as meaning something. Some of the meanings are "I believe this. I believe that A is B." Then other memory cells represent feelings. So if some number is zero I feel good, and if some number is large I feel bad. These are most natural if you have a framework in which there are certain kinds of actions that result from the states of the beliefs being such and such.

I describe that in chapter 4 of the new book: how to build up the right structure through a series of layers. The first-generation universal robot has basic functionality. The second generation has a conditioning system which causes certain events to reinforce behaviors that it did, and other kinds of events to prevent behaviors in the future that it did in the past. So you basically have a thing that you can interpret as desirable and undesirable, which shows up in a very clear way in the behavior. Then you have a third layer in which there is a simulation of the world, and you can look at the elements of the simulation as beliefs about the world. Then there's a fourth layer in which those beliefs are made even more explicit as in propositions, as things that are used to reason about.

DAVID: So you think consciousness occurs in the stage where the robot begins modeling the world?

HANS: Well, the third generation is the stage in which you can interact with the robot in such a way that it can actually describe how it feels, because it plays scenarios in its head. The scenarios produce conditioning effects from their second-generation conditioning system. If the appropriate words are attached in the obvious way to negative and positive conditioning, it can already tell you that it likes this and dislikes that. If the third generation of world models also includes psychological descriptions of actors in the world, then I think the model that the third-generation robot builds actually has three kinds of information about the world.

One is strictly physical. For instance, the robot can model if it drops something that it would fall, and if it spilled water that it would spread, and so on. Then there would be cultural information, which is the meaning and the use of various things in the world, so you don't use the fine china to empty the toilet and so on. Then there's the psychological description of the world, for things that are actors, primarily human beings and probably other robots of its kind, which is a shorthand way of describing how they behave, because the full description at the mechanical level just is much too complex.

So the robot can no more have a neural description of a human being than you or I could. But it could have a description which says John likes tea, and likes to sleep, and does not like red furniture, and so on. Also for psychological states the robot could infer things like John is happy right now, or John is angry. And those same psychological models could be applied, and probably tuned a little bit, to other robots, and even to the robot itself. So it could examine its own behavior using these psychological models and say, I don't like to fall down the stairs, or I like to please my owner, because that exactly summarizes the behavior that it has.

This means that you could have a conversation with it about what it likes, what it doesn't like, what you like, and what you don't like. It could also relate to you events in its past that illustrate these states of mind. I think it would be no trick at all to begin to empathize with it, and to say, well, this is actually an interesting person, and clearly conscious. It would take great mental effort to keep reminding yourself, well, this is not really consciousness. This is just the operation of this program behind it. In fact, it would make your interaction with the robot much less effective if you kept interrupting yourself with that kind of irrelevancy.

Now, the third-generation robot has only a very literal kind of knowledge about the world. Everything that it thinks about is in terms of concrete objects, specific cuts, specific tables, specific kinds of motion, and so on. So it'd be a little simpleminded when you were speaking with it. You couldn't talk to it about large generalities.

The fourth-generation robot adds real intelligence to that by having a layer in which things extracted from the simulator can be abstracted and reasoned about. Interesting interaction though between the reasoning system and the hard simulation, which is that sometimes when you go through an abstract reasoning, the main way you make the reasoning abstract is by leaving out certain details, and just using other aspects of the world situation and deriving results from there on the basis of rules of inference.

But sometimes you leave out the critical things, and it's not obvious at first that what you left out was important. So the intermediate results of chains of reasoning can be brought back and instantiated in the simulation of the world, to see if they actually make sense there. So if some chain of reasoning has led the robot to believe that you could support, let's say, a glass by standing it on a broom, then trying that in a simulation would show that in fact that doesn't work. The thing will always fall down. Each instance that's tried in the simulation wouldn't work, so the robot could then just disregard that particular chain of inference and save itself a lot of effort coming up with more derivations from it, that would be similarly nonsense.

There have been programs in the past, in the '60s, that were able to do things like that in much simpler domains. One of the best is the geometry theorem-proving program of Herbert Glanter. He wrote a program that did formal inference, going from Euclid's propositions and proving theorems. But as it did each step in such a proof, it also in parallel drew the equivalent of a diagram, actually using analytic geometry, representing points as two numbers, with XY coordinates, and lines as pairs of such points. Then testing whether two lines intersected by doing the appropriate kind of arithmetic with the coordinates of the end points, and seeing if these two lines have the same length by calculating the sum of the squares of the differences in X and Y.

If things that it was trying to prove—such as that line A equals line B in length—were actually true in the particular instances that it was drawing within its numerical accuracy checking system, and the drawings were all approximate, so that the numbers were not done to infinite precision, then if two lines were the same, they had to be the same within six decimal places or whatever. But if they were not, then it was still plausible to continue the proof, trying to prove that they were the same.

But if they were not the same in the diagram, then there's obviously no point in going on with that line, and that was extremely important. That's what made the system so good was that it was able to prune the vast majority of logical directions, because they didn't actually work in the specific examples. So obviously they were not true in general. So the fourth-generation robot,

I think, will work that way too, only reasoning, but much more complex things, like maybe the physical world around it.

DAVID: The idea that fascinated me the most in *Mind Children* was what you said was the inspiration for writing it. You discuss the possibility that, gradually, section by section, we may be able to download our personality, memories, and sense of self into a superior electronic computer.

HANS: Yeah, a lot of people like that. I'm actually a little off on that myself, in that it sort of strikes me now as building a car by starting with an ox cart. And the ox cart is us, the old design, back to the Stone Age. Then replacing the wheels with rubber tires, the ox with a motor, and the sideboards with sheet-metal panels. When you're all done, you have something better than [an] ox cart, but you still don't have a very good car. If you were to sit down instead with a fresh drafting board, or on a design screen and, using the best engineering knowledge you had available, design a car from the ground up, then you could build a much better car than replacing the ox cart.

DAVID: It wouldn't be a better design, but the idea is that we could transfer ourselves into it.

HANS: I think of that as kind of a frivolous thing to do. I mean, we'll do it probably, but it will be like a tourist thing. It'll be like a *Love Boat* cruise compared to real exploration. I think we'll do it for amusement, but it won't have a serious impact on the future.

DAVID: Another thought-provoking idea that you discuss in *Mind Children* is the possibility of completely scanning every aspect of someone's brain and body, and nanotechnologically composing an identical copy of that person. How do you think the original person and the copy would interact?

HANS: I don't think there's any problem there. Exactly what would happen is what you think would happen. There would be two of you that would both think they're you. There's no problem there. That's just the way that it would be, and you can imagine the same kind of scenario with other similar technologies, like the *Star Trek* transporter. What if you had two receivers? I see no reason why that's not possible, and you'd have a very identical twin initially.

DAVID: But we know from identical twins studies that the twins usually have very different personality types.

HANS: Well, the thing is that they were possibly identical when the ovum first split, but after that they had different histories. This copy that we're talking about would have the same history up until the point that the duplication process happened, and only then would they begin to diverge. So initially they'd be extremely similar, extremely identical, and it requires you to rethink or readjust your intuitions about what identity means. But that's all. I think the problems with your intuition is not with the scenario in any way.

DAVID: What do you think happens to human consciousness after the death?

HANS: In chapter 7 of *Robot* I develop some of what seem to be further consequences of my way of looking at consciousness. Basically I assume that a good simulation can be conscious just like we are. In fact, in some ways I look at ourselves as just a kind of simulation. We're a conscious being simulated on a bunch of neural hardware, and the conscious being is only found in an interpretation of things that go on in the neural hardware. It's not the actual chemical signals that are squirting around, it's a certain high-level interpretation of an aggregate of those signals, the only thing that makes consciousness different from other interpretations, like the value of a dollar bill.

It's not intrinsic in the dollar bill. It's an interpretation, an attribution that you make on to that. And that works because a lot of people make it so you're able to exchange the dollar bill as if it actually had any value. But there's nothing intrinsic in the twenty-dollar bill that makes it worth twenty times as much as the one-dollar bill. In some other society it could just be the other way around. They might treat the pattern that's on the one-dollar bill as being worth twenty times as much as the pattern that's on the twenty-dollar bill. It's an external attribution. And beauty, to give you another example, is in the eye of the beholder. The aliens from Rigel 4 might not find the Venus de Milo quite as beautiful as you do because they have sixteen tentacles. (*laughter*)

DAVID: Oh, so think of how repulsive she is with those missing arms? (*laughter*)

HANS: Right. Actually, what could be more horrible than that? (*laughter*) So I think consciousness is the same kind of thing. It's an attribution that we make on to—not so much the mechanism itself, because we didn't even know about those neurons until very recently—the behavior that we interact with. The only thing that's tricky, though, that somewhat makes consciousness different, is that it includes within that interpretation the ability to make interpretations. So the conscious being is able to interpret itself as conscious. It doesn't need people outside saying you're conscious. It can say to itself, I'm conscious. Of course, that's only meaningful under the right interpretation. (*laughter*)

If you look at that person saying I'm conscious, but you look at them in a strictly mechanical way, they're just making meaningless noises—a mechanism that's built to make noises like that. So you have this rather abstract property, and it really is an abstract property of consciousness. It's not the physical thing itself where the consciousness resides. It's in the abstract interpretation, which, in the case of consciousness, is self-closing. It is being made up by itself, as well as, presumably, by other beings.

I see no reason why you couldn't do exactly the same thing for a robot, or for an abstract simulation. So you have a person who's really just a simulation inside of a computer, but they interpret themselves as having thoughts, feelings, beliefs, and they feel themselves to be real and to experience their existence.

Now, if it's a simulated human being, then they probably wouldn't be very happy unless they also had a simulated body to go with it, so that they could feel their extremities, and sense things. Of course, in order to sense things, there has to be something to sense, and you also want a simulated world for them to live in. This whole scenario makes my point. So now if it's all done in one computer, you have a simulation of a person's mind, a person's body, and of a world for that body to live in. The whole computer can live inside of a featureless box.

A computer engineer who encounters this box without any special knowledge of how it got to be programmed the way it is wouldn't really see anything special there. He would look inside, perhaps, and see the program counter counting the memory locations that are happening, and where instructions are coming from. He would look at various portions of memory, and the numbers would be changing, just like they do in any program.

DAVID: Meanwhile, a whole lifetime of adventure is going on inside.

HANS: Right. There would be nothing notable. There would be no appreciation that there's a person in there suffering, or enjoying life immensely, having daily experiences of deep significance. Only those people with the interpretation, perhaps, that the original programmer had might be able to see that person in there. Of course, that person in there experiences their own existence regardless of what people outside are seeing or not seeing.

Now, to make this whole thing more explicit, imagine that there's a second computer which is able to interface with the first computer, through a network or something. The second computer has in it the means to take numbers from the first computer and interpret them in the way that the original programmer meant, so that it's able to produce a picture of the world inside the simulation. You can see the person living their life and experiencing things. You can hear them speak, possibly, and you could even listen in on their thoughts. So if you attach this device to the first box and look at the screen, there's the interpretation for you. So there's no doubt there's interesting things happening in there, and that there's really a person in there.

Now, imagine that you could change the representation for a simulation. The next step in the reasoning is just to pick a simpler example. Let's say in a simulation of fluid flow, you could have certain memory cells represent the pressure, the momentum, and the temperature of little bits of fluid. You have the way it's usually done, but there's other ways of doing it too. You could have variables instead represent the intensity and the phase of pressure winds throughout the whole liquid. If you have enough numbers representing all the possible pressure waves, then that's all you need. That can fully represent the fluid also. You don't need the original numbers that represented the localized pressures and temperatures.

So you can convert a simulation from the space domain into the frequency domain, and in doing so you'd utterly change the kinds of numbers that are being stored in the memory. You utterly change the way the program that changes those numbers looks. But, if you were clever, you still have a way of interpreting the result so that it looks just like the interpretation that you had of the original formulation.

So imagine that it's possible to do a mathematical transformation of the numbers changing in that first box containing the person to some entirely different set of numbers. But then you make the analogous mathematical transformation in the viewing box, with which you use to peek into that first box. Then the person's still in there, still undergoing their life, even though what the computer's actually doing is utterly different. Now there's no limit to what kinds of changes you can make to that first box and still retain your image of the person. One of the most general ways of showing that is to imagine that the interpretation box is made of a big look-up table.

A look-up table just says, if the first box has in all of its memory cells the following huge number, then it means this. If it has this other big huge number, then it means that. And so on. There's a huge table. It has an astronomical number of entries in it. So for every possible state of the memory cells in the first box there's a meaning, which ultimately translates into some picture on the screen with sounds and so on. By putting in the appropriate look-up table in the interpretation box, you can transform the simulation into anything. One extreme thing that you can transform it into is a simple counter—that just counts one, two, three, four, five, six.

But then in the interpretation box you have this giant look-up table that says One means the person is sitting down right now and they're sort of tired. Two means they're just starting to get up, and three means they're scratching their head and saying ouch, or whatever. I'm still claiming that you haven't lost the essence of the person, and that the person inside the box is still feeling real feelings, just like they always did. In fact, they're completely and utterly oblivious to the changes you're making in the representation, even when you go to the extreme of turning them into just a counter, because they really don't exist in the box at all. They exist in the interpretation, and the interpretation is not something that is in that external box. It's an abstract thing.

It's a mapping that anybody could have. Somebody from another planet could come up with another interpretation box with the right table in it and see that same person. It's not something that you create just by peeking, because anybody else can peek and see it, if they they just looked at the thing in the right way. So this leads me to the position that it isn't the viewers who are creating this person. The person exists independently. Inside of the box he's completely oblivious of these viewers. They're just living out the logic of the simulation, and they don't care if there are any viewers, if there's lots of viewers, or if the viewers are making mistakes. It doesn't change anything for them. Their existence is entirely tied up in the logic of the interpretation, regardless of who's doing the interpreting—even if nobody is.

So I can't but conclude from this way of thinking that existence is a platonic thing. It's not the simulation that created this person. The person existed within the logic of what was being simulated, and the simulation is just basically a way of peeking at them. But they already existed, as the logic of their existence is self-contained. Now, this has even further implications. Let's say you have a viewing box that looks at this simulation (whose importance I've greatly reduced now) and somebody else sees that particular person in there, but that person may have a viewing box with an entirely different look-up table and be able to see something completely different inside of the simulation that you've got.

There are many possible interpretations. In fact, there's an infinity of them. There are interpretations for all possible look-up tables of arbitrary events. So in this counter you can see any possible world. And any world that has an observer who's aware of their own existence in it exists for that observer regardless of whether or not somebody actually has that viewing box or not. So all possible worlds exist, period. In a platonic sense, that's really interesting, but there's no reason to add an extra hypothesis that the world we're living in is anything other than that. So now I'm starting to answer your question. I think this world that we inhabit is just one of those platonic worlds.

DAVID: It's just one interpretation of the infinite possibilities?

HANS: It's not just an interpretation. The interpretation was just the way that I got to this position that these wills that we're simulating already exist anyway. The simulation is just a way of connecting them to our perceptions. But actually a simulation doesn't create the world. The world exists by virtue of its own internal logic. The reason for believing that is that with the right interpretation, you can look at anything and see any particular world. I don't have to look at a computer. I don't have to look at a counter.

I can look at a rock where the particles in the rock are moving randomly because they're warm. Each state of motion of those particles of the rock can be mapped through some kind of look-up table into a state of some simulation. So you could see this person that we were talking about inside of that rock if you had the right interpretation. You could see them in anything. So what's the point of saying that the simulation created them? They're everywhere, and they don't care if it's a rock, a counter, or a computer that's simulating them in spatial detail. They don't feel the simulation at all. They only feel the internal logic of the simulation—the mathematical rules that define what's being simulated and how it's been simulated. So they just exist. This really is platonic existence.

So if our world exists platonically, but in a sea of other possibilities, you then have to ask the question: Why is our world so boring? In the space of all possible worlds, there's a world in which in the next second you sprout wings on your head and your nose grows into an elephant's trunk. There are worlds like that that exist in the space of all possible worlds. So why doesn't that really happen to us? Why does our world seem to be so boring, so tied to these simple physical laws that we're only recently starting to elucidate? I think there's answer to that, which is sort of based on simplicity.

First of all, you note that in some of those worlds you don't exist, and in some of them you do, but you will never find yourself in one of those worlds where you don't exist. So, for you, just because of the nature of your consciousness—the way you interpret and experience your own existence—you will only find yourself in that tiny tiny tiny subset of all the possible worlds in which you exist. But from the place you are right now, there are still an infinity of next possible worlds, next moments. Some of them have you with wings and a trunk, but those require a lot of coincidences—so that all that can happen, and your consciousness can still continue. You'll have be in one where your consciousness still continues.

Now, think of each of those coincidences that's required as a coin flip. So the more coincidences that are required, the more things have to be just so, and the lower the probability. The chance that you're going to find yourself in a place where a hundred coin flips come up just the right way is a lot less than a world where it only requires one coin flip or no coin flips. So new things have to be just so. The simplest world is probably the one that requires no changes at all, where things just keep going the way they are. Now, you have a history of going back to the beginning of the universe, where you have a structure that depends on the laws of physics working just so.

Your neurons wouldn't work if chemistry changed in some way. Your consciousness is an interpretation of the way your neurons work, and your connection with the world. A lot of your experiences depend on everything working just the way it does. If the speed of light were to change, certain chemical reactions would alter, and your consciousness would probably be gone. But pretty much if the laws of physics were altered in any way, your consciousness would no longer work the way that it does. In those other worlds, if that's all that happened, you would no longer exist. So you can't find yourself in those worlds. Maybe some other things could change that bring back your consciousness, but that would be like another coincidence that would have to happen. The odds of that happening are small.

So the most likely world that you will find yourself in in the next moment is one that's just a continuation of the world that you're in right now, because nothing has to change. The mechanism that you have all this investment in— this evolutionary and biological growth investment—just continues. The only other question is: Why are we in this kind of world in the first place? And again, now that we're in it, we're kind of stuck. Probably it is the case that this is the simplest world, the world that required the least number of coincidental starting positions to produce us.

If you look around, it's not immediately obvious that this world is simple. But if you believe the physicists, they're telling us that sooner or later we're going to find a theory of everything, which is some simple equation, that basically describes the underlying mechanism for the entire universe. The evolution of this equation produces everything, and really the world is simple. It's just that in order to have such a simple description produce us, you have to go through this long process of consequences from that simple starting point, which is the evolution of the universe, the expansion of space, the evolution of life, and on and on—all those 15 billion years' worth. Because, after all, we, as conscious beings of exactly the kinds we are, are pretty complicated.

We have hundreds of billions of neurons, and probably couldn't be as rich in our mental lives if we didn't have all of those. They have to be wired just so, and as a kind of a side effect of having to be just this way to be, and to have our sense of existence. The easiest way for that to happen was for the rest of the universe to happen too. (*laughter*) So all of this kind of holds us into being physical beings.

That's all true until the point where the physical existence is no longer working too well—basically the point where we die. Now, in the space of all possible worlds, there are certainly going to be continuations of consciousness in some of them, no matter what happens to us, because some of those possible worlds you can simulate. It's always possible when you have a simulation, and if something happens that you didn't like, to be able to make some change, and basically undo whatever that thing was that you didn't like, and have it continue.

So no matter how we die, in some possible world there's a way in which we, through some mechanism or other, continue on. And those are the only worlds which we're going to find ourselves. The others have zero probability for us personally, and this is sort of on an individual basis. Here really has different probabilities. I can find myself in a world in which you died pretty easily, and you can find yourself in a world in which I died, but I can never find myself in a world in which I died, and vice versa. Obviously, we don't really live in the world, we just have some momentary correlation.

So what does this continuation look like? Suppose you were hit by a truck, and you got flattened. What does the continuation look like? Well, I don't have great answers, but I can make up some things. What I can't tell you is which are the most probable, which are the ones that in a total sense require the least number of coincidences, and are thus the ones that you're most likely to find yourself in. Of course, they're all real, and they all exist. It's just that some of them are kind of the equivalent of winning a lottery. You'll probably never find yourself there.

One possibility that's kind of intriguing, and lets you do a personal experiment, predicts rather strange happenings for us individually. Maybe the easiest way for your consciousness to continue in the instance of the truck is that actually the truck noticed you, and blew its horn and you jumped back, and you didn't get hit after all. Then everything could still go on according to physical law, and just a few chance events had to be a little bit different than they were.

So maybe you will escape that truck, in your personal world, where you continue to exist, and maybe that's the easiest way for you to continue. Then the next time, maybe some cell that might have produced a cancer that killed you reverted back, because a cosmic ray hit it just the right way, or just some thermal event in the cell. So you escape that cancer. Then maybe some aging-related effect miraculously reversed because of some nutrient interaction. Maybe this goes on and on and on, and after a while, you find yourself the oldest living person (*laughter*) in the world, having miraculously escaped a number of close calls.

You don't even have to go through to this philosophical position where I am to have the idea of alternative universes, because the many-worlds interpretation of quantum mechanics is basically winning over the physics community. The many-worlds interpretation is kind of a microcosm of this, because in all those slices of the wave function, we still have basically the laws of physics as we know them. Whereas the worlds I'm talking about don't necessarily have the laws of physics as we know them. So it's a bigger set of possible worlds. But even in the many-worlds interpretation, indeed, there should be some in which for almost any event you manage to survive. Maybe eventually it gets too far-fetched for that to continue this way, although maybe not. All it really would take is for some aging processes to reverse themselves, which maybe isn't that big of deal. So that's one way.

Another way is, maybe you die. Suppose you were to explode in a hydrogen bomb, and you turned into high-speed plasma moving in all directions. Well, maybe it would be too far-fetched to continue you that way, as the probabilities required would just be too large. It'd be sort of like the probabilities that all the particles would reverse and reassemble you, just by chance. So maybe another alternative is that you find yourself knowing that this existence that you've been having isn't quite what you thought it was. What it really is is a simulation in somebody's computer, and when you die, they sort of pull you out of the simulation and reinstate you in slightly altered circumstances. Either they pull you out altogether into their world, or just into some other simulation. Something like that.

They continue you on. They have the power to do that if they're running the simulator. Or maybe you just find the logic of your consciousness continuing simply without the need for a bunch of neurons to kind of ape the structure of your thinking. And when we write artificial intelligence programs that are just plain reasoning programs, we don't simulate neurons or anything. We just simulate concepts, like beliefs and probabilities and so on. So there are just some numbers of strings. I would say that I think everything could be encoded that way a lot more simply than it is using all those neurons. Now, when we do it on the computer, of course, we have underneath those basic concepts.

We still have the computer, which is just as complicated as the neurons, but why can't those concepts just stand on their own in the appropriate abstract context? We need the computer to simulate the AI because we're still living in this physical world, so we have the physical substrate for the abstract concepts. But in all possible worlds there certainly will be some where those abstract concepts are all there. Then you could imagine an afterlife that's very much like the spiritual afterlife that a lot of religions imagine—where there is no physics. There's only psychology.

DAVID: It's all mind.

HANS: Right. I think all of these concepts here need further work. But note, all of this allows artificial intelligence. The robot minds are just as real as ours. None of this contradicts it. So those people who try to use this kind of thinking to rule out robots don't have a leg to stand on.

DAVID: Do you see any evidence for teleology in evolution?

HANS: No, not per se. On the other hand, in the scenario of all possible worlds, the one where the physical world is the only thing there is is an infinitesimal part. So we could be in a video game. We could be in somebody's imagination. In fact, there's reason to think that actually our existence is entirely platonic, and that we are just one universe out of a very high order of infinity of them. And the only reason we see this universe is because it provides the simplest explanation of us. There's a probability argument that the universe which provides the simplest explanation of us is the one that we're most likely to perceive, although we probably exist in a way that—from our personal perspective— we could not distinguish in many different universes.

DAVID: What is your perspective on the concept of God?

HANS: I don't even know what that means. Certainly in some of the video game universes there would things like gods, who are playing the game. (*laughter*) But no, I'm rather unimpressed with the traditional sort of tribal gods. (*laughter*)

DAVID: Do you think that the human species will survive the next hundred years, or do you think that we're in danger of extinction?

HANS: I think the whole concept of survival is not very well defined. I think we're on a road where we'll probably be transforming into something that will survive in the universe, as we currently conceive it. But I think we're going to grow into a form where our conception of what the universe is is going to change radically, so that the concept we currently have of survival is pretty parochial.

DAVID: How do you envision the future evolution of the human race?

HANS: I think we will be building successors that are vastly more capable than we are. Blind biological evolution kind of bootstrapped itself up to the point where we can now take the future into our own hands, however imperfectly at this stage, and sort of bootstrap ourselves further into a form where, naively speaking, we're smarter. Our descendants, anyway, will be much smarter than we are, and able to engineer their own further development even better. That's a positive feedback process that rapidly goes to a stage that we can't even imagine at this point.

DAVID: How long do you think it will be before computers exceed human intelligence?

HANS: I've been redoing and redoing that calculation since the '70s, and for the last twenty years the answer I've been coming up with is about the same—which is before 2050. At various times I throw in the numbers—the latest projections of computer power, and the latest estimate of how much computer power is needed to do various nervous system functions—and what I get is somewhere from 2020 to 2050.

Strange Brains and
Mathematical Games

An Interview with Clifford Pickover

Clifford Pickover is one of the most popular and prolific science writers in America. He is the author of over thirty popular science books and science-fiction novels that investigate a diverse range of mind-expanding topics, such as time travel, black holes, extraterrestrial biology, mathematics, creativity and computers. Some of Dr. Pickover's more popular books include Chaos in Wonderland, Surfing Through Hyperspace, Time: A Traveler's Guide, *and* The Paradox of God. *What all of his books share in common is a transcendence of the ordinary world and a fascination with the beyond. Dr. Pickover received his Ph.D. from Yale University's Department of Molecular Biophysics and Biochemistry. He is a Research Staff Member at the IBM T. J. Watson Research Center, where he has received over thirty-five invention achievement awards and three research division awards. Dr. Pickover is also the associate editor of* Computers and Graphics *magazine, and he holds over thirty U.S. patents for*

unusually innovative inventions, mostly in the field of computer hardware, software, and novel ways of interacting with computers.

*   *   *

DAVID: What is your perspective on research into psychic phenomena like telepathy and telekinesis?

CLIFFORD: At heart, I'm a skeptic and demand very strong evidence for claims of the paranormal. Readers may wish to refer to my May 2001 *Skeptical Inquirer* article, "The Antinoüs Prophecies: A Nostradamoid Project," in which I discuss my study of people who ascribe meaning to Nostradamus-like quatrains. I contend that Nostradamus's poems are verbal ink blots—not really foretelling anything but permitting people to fit future history to rather nebulous images. I discuss this further in my book *Dreaming the Future*, which also emphasizes the detailed historical meanings people ascribed to Nostradamus-like prophecies, which I randomly generated. In particular, I composed quatrains of gibberish just by letting my mind wander and writing the first images that came to my mind.

As far as I was concerned, they had no particular meaning or significance. After composing the quatrains, I asked people to match my quatrains with actual historical happenings. I called the quatrains the "quatrains of Antinoüs," which sounded suitably exotic. Amazingly, respondents found that my Antinoüs "predicted" such events as the 1989 Loma Prieta earthquake, the comet that wiped out the dinosaurs, the rise of Microsoft, the wreck of the *Titanic*, the American War of Independence, the Punic War, the Jewish Holocaust, the importance of Henry Ford, the Second Crusade, and much more. The famous Prophecies of Antinoüs are printed in entirety in my article and book.

Additionally, I've conducted a fake "ESP test" at www.Pickover.com in order to show how easily we can be fooled and how great our will is to believe in the spiritual, the paranormal, and phenomena beyond science. Give it a try. I receive more e-mail on this Web page than any other. My goal in conducting this little demonstration is to emphasize the need for skeptical thinking when evaluating claims of the paranormal. I believe the universe has facets we'll never truly understand—the universe is mysterious—but at heart I'm skeptical about ESP, telelepathy, precognition, haruspicy, cephalomancy, and other paranormal phenomena until we have very conclusive scientific results.

DAVID: But there actually has been quite a bit of serious research done attempting to measure unexplained phenomena like telepathy and precognition, with strong positive results. Are you familiar with the psi research that has been done by people like Dean Radin and Rupert Sheldrake?

CLIFFORD: Some components of their work appear to be quite interesting, and my goal is to become more familiar with their research. What I would really love to see is Dean and Rupert draft a precise paranormal claim and a means for testing the claim—followed by a letter to CSICOP [the Committee for the Scientific Investigation of Claims of the Paranormal], James Randi, and Robert Todd Carroll [author of *The Skeptic's Dictionary*], asking if they would accept the "new" test as a valid test for a claim of the paranormal.

Whatever differences Dean or Sheldrake may have had with James Randi in the past, perhaps there is a way to start fresh and agree to participate in Randi's one-million-dollar prize offer to anyone who can show, under proper observing conditions, evidence of any paranormal, supernatural, or occult power or event [www.randi.org/research/challenge.html].

So far no one has claimed the prize. If Dean or Rupert feel that they will not get a fair hearing from Randi, CSICOP or Carroll, then, in parallel, they send a letter to *Scientific American* and *Science*, asking if they would supervise the test. Whatever response Rupert and Dean receive from Randi, CSICOP, Carroll, *Scientific American*, or *Science* should be posted on the Web for all to view. In the meantime, people should type "Radin Randi" and "Sheldrake Randi" into the Google search engine and enjoy the remarkable Web pages that result.

DAVID: I don't think that either Dean or Rupert would refer to psi phenomena as "paranormal" or "supernatural," though, as they see these unexplained phenomena as part of the natural world. But Robert Anton Wilson once told me that he countered James Randi's offer by offering a million dollars to anyone who could demonstrate a completely "normal" event (i.e., statistically average in every way) in a controlled scientific experiment. In fact, he actually established CSICON [the Committee for the Surrealist Investigation of Claims of the Normal] to investigate claims of so-called normal events. [For more information, see www.rawilson.com/csicon.] According to Bob, no one has been able to demonstrate a "normal" event either.

CLIFFORD: Ha! I'd be happy to flip a penny a hundred times in a hundred trials to show that the penny behaves in a way you'd expect an unbiased penny to behave! Robert and I could agree ahead of time what this behavior would be and then start flipping. . . . Instead of paying me a million dollars when I win, all Robert needs to do is agree to collaborate on a science-fiction novel with me. I understand his novels sell a lot more than mine!

[Robert Anton Wilson responded to Cliff: "No need to flip the penny at all—just prove that it 'is' 'normal' in 'all' respects, after first defining the terms set in dubious Korzybskian quotes."]

DAVID: Cliff, let's talk about God and the mind. What sort of association do you see between religion and mental illness?

CLIFFORD: Temporal lobe epilepsy [TLE] can produce profound religious experiences. Some researchers have gone so far as to suggest that the mystical religious experiences of many of the great prophets were induced by TLE.

This is not to demean religious experiences, because all experiences are mediated by our brain states. Perhaps TLE is a doorway to valid dimensions of reality. In my books *Strange Brains and Genius* and *The Paradox of God*, I discuss several nuns with TLE who "apprehended" God in TLE seizures and who described the experiences in glowing words. Even Ezekiel in the Old Testament had a TLE-like vision reminiscent of modern UFO reports.

More recently, at my weblog RealityCarnival.Com, I published an article going much further. . . . My controversial premise is that DMT in the pineal glands of biblical prophets gave God to humanity and let ordinary humans perceive parallel universes. As we discussed, the molecule DMT [N,N-dimethyltryptamine] is a psychoactive chemical that causes intense visions and can induce its users to quickly enter a completely different "environment" that some have likened to an alien or parallel universe. DMT is also naturally produced in small quantities in the pineal gland in the human brain. Some DMT experiences remind me of experiences of biblical prophets. Readers should visit RealityCarnival.Com for all the details and discussions.

I think that our brains are wired with a desire for religion and belief in God. If so, the reasons for our interest, and the rituals we use, are buried deep in the essence of our nature. Religion is at the edge of the known and the unknown, poised on the fractal boundaries of history, philosophy, psychology, biology, and many other scientific disciplines. Because of this, religion and God are important topics for contemplation and study. Even with the great scientific strides we will make in this century, we will nevertheless continue to swim in a sea of mystery. Humans need to make sense of the world and will surely continue to use logic and religion for that task. What patterns and connections will we see in the twenty-first century? Who and what will be our God?

DAVID: Speaking of religious experiences, what is your personal perspective on the concept of God, and do you see any teleology in evolution?

CLIFFORD: Sometimes readers of my Neoreality science-fiction series ask me why I write on God, strange realities, and religious subjects. As I said, I tend to be skeptical about the paranormal. However, I do feel that there are facets of the universe we can never understand, just as a monkey can never understand calculus, black holes, symbolic logic, and poetry. There are thoughts we can never think, visions we can only glimpse. It is at this filmy, veiled interface between human reality and a reality beyond that we may find the numinous, which some may liken to God.

I believe your use of the term "teleology" is related to the teleological argument for the existence of God that posits that order in the world cannot be accidental and that since there is design, there must be a designer. But what do you mean by God—the God of Miracles or the God of Order? Many scientist uses the word "God" to mean the God of Order, the God of mathematical and physical laws and underpinnings of the universe. Others may use the word

"God" to refer to the God of Miracles who intervenes in our affairs, turns water into wine, answers prayers, cures the dying, inflicts plagues on his enemies, performs various miracles, helps the Israelites destroy the Canaanites, and avenges the righteous people on Earth. I don't see how the existence of order (e.g., the structure of snowflake) or evolution forces us to believe in a God of Miracles.

When one looks at the amazingly complex "design" of the Mandelbrot set—the whirls, the bridges, the islands, and the infinite regress—we might be tempted to say there is a cosmic designer, but all we really have is the equation $z = z2 + c$, which is obviously not a God in any traditional sense.

On the other hand, some scientists feel we exist because of cosmic coincidences, or, more accurately, we exist because of seemingly "finely tuned" numerical constants that permit life. Those individuals who believe this anthropic principle suggest these numbers to be near miracles that might suggest an intelligent design to the universe. For example, we owe our very lives to the element carbon, which was first manufactured in stars before the Earth formed. The challenge in creating carbon is getting two helium nuclei in stars to stick together until they are struck by a third. It turns out that this is accomplished only because of internal resonances, or energy levels, of carbon and oxygen nuclei. If the carbon resonance level were only 4 percent lower, carbon atoms wouldn't form. Were the oxygen resonance level only half a percent higher, almost all the carbon would disappear as it combined with helium to form oxygen. This means that human existence depends on the fine-tuning of these two nuclear resonances.

Other amazing parameters abound. If all of the stars in the universe were heavier than three solar masses, they would live for only about 500 million years, and life would not have time to evolve beyond primitive bacteria. Stephen Hawking has estimated that if the rate of the universe's expansion one second after the Big Bang had been smaller by even one part in 100 thousand million million, the universe would have recollapsed. The universe must live for billions of years to permit time for intelligent life to evolve. On the other hand, the universe might have expanded so rapidly that protons and electrons never united to make hydrogen atoms.

All of these cosmic niceties have led the one-time agnostic physicist Paul Davies to write: "Through my scientific work I have come to believe more and more strongly that the physical universe is put together with an ingenuity so astonishing that I cannot accept it merely as a brute fact." Of course, these conclusions are controversial, and an infinite number of random (non-designed) universes could exist, ours being just one that permits carbon-based life. Some researchers have even speculated that child universes are constantly budding off from parent universes and that the child universe inherits a set of physical laws similar to the parent, a process reminiscent of evolution of biological characteristics of life on Earth.

DAVID: In your book *The Science of Aliens* you discuss the possibility that the alien abduction phenomena may also be the result of temporal lobe epilepsy, which you mentioned as being a possible explanation for some mystical experiences. What are your thoughts on how this relates to the strange contact experiences that people report with alien intelligences while they're under the influence of DMT, and do you tend to view these experiences as complex hallucinations or as "a doorway to valid dimensions of reality"?

CLIFFORD: This question is the key and is something I continually ponder. Refer back to my early discussions of DMT in this interview. As I said, I am very interested to learn why people using DMT often report seeing intricate palaces and temples, golden objects, and strange beings who sometimes seem to be fixing the tapestry of reality. The DMT reality seems to be utterly "real," and I hope we can gain information from this reality that will shed more light as to its validity or usefulness. I don't know what the DMT world means, but I consider it worthy of further research.

The DMT universe can overlap ours in various ways. For example, a DMT psychonaut, with his eyes open, may see a being perched on a tree in our world. This is a level 1 merging of realities, with the tree from our universe and the being from the DMTverse. Or the psychonaut can walk through a forest and around a lake and see a totally unrelated forest and lake in the DMTverse, with no correspondence to the real universe except for the fact that a forest and a lake exist. In this level 2 blending, it's as if the subconscious brain "sees" our traditional world but creates a DMT metaphor for it. A lake in one world is a lake in the world beyond. Level 3 blending can be particularly enchanting. The psychonaut may walk through an ordinary auditorium, seeing a completely different universe comprising a vast machine complex or palace of sparkling jewels. In this level 3 blending, the psychonaut is still able to spatially "navigate" both worlds simultaneously.

For example, the psychonaut may walk down an aisle, climb stairs, and avoid chairs in our world while traversing the DMT level 3 universe. The psychonaut doesn't "bump" into things. Researcher Benny Shannon has experimented with ayahuasca (a DMT-containing plant potion) and confronted various blendings of our universe and the DMT verse, and he himself has seen entire cities of gems and gold. He says, "It was as if a screen had been raised and another world made its appearance to me." Indeed, some psychonauts after seeing the celestial palaces have claimed these were the most beautiful images they had ever seen in their entire lives. I don't speculate that L. Frank Baum, the author of *The Wizard of Oz*, or the producers of the movie version have tried DMT, but the glistening emerald city and munchkins are images right out of a DMTverse.

In short, the molecule DMT can cause a transition from our world to another with no cessation of consciousness or quality of awareness. In this environment, the so-called self-transforming machine elves appear to inhabit this parallel realm. The DMT experience has the feel of reality in terms of detail and potential for exploration. The creatures encountered are often identified as being alienlike or elflike. If we could gain information from these creatures that we could not ordinarily obtain with our normal consciousness, wouldn't that be something special? Author Terence McKenna has used DMT and felt that "Right here and now, one quanta away, there is raging a universe of active intelligence that is transhuman, hyperdimensional, and extremely alien. . . . What is driving religious feeling today is a wish for contact with this other universe." The aliens seen while using DMT present themselves "with information that is not drawn from the personal history of the individual."

DAVID: What are your thoughts on the possibilities of extraterrestrial life, and what do you think an intergalactic zoo might look like?

CLIFFORD: I have no doubt that primitive life is common in the universe. Recent discoveries of life living miles under the Earth in utter darkness, or in ice, or even in boiling water, tell us: Whatever is possible in nature tends to become realized. My personal view is that almost everything happens in our universe that is not forbidden by the laws of physics and chemistry. Life on Earth can thrive in unimaginably harsh conditions, even in acid or within solid rock. On the ocean floor, bacteria thrive in scalding, mineral-laden hot springs. If microbes thrive in such miserable conditions on Earth, where else beyond Earth might similar life-forms exist?

The best way we can guess at how alien life might appear is to consider the evolution of animal shapes on Earth. The idea that alien evolution will lead to creatures that look like us is far-fetched—despite the fact that on *Star Trek*, Mr. Spock looks almost exactly like us even though he was born on planet Vulcan to a Vulcan father. Mr. Spock's mother was human, yet somehow his father from an entirely different planet was able to fertilize her—something less likely than you or I being able to mate with our close evolutionary cousins such as the octopuses and squids. Similarly, the aliens of Whitley Strieber's *Communion*, and also those drawn by people claiming to have been abducted by aliens, have faces vaguely resembling our own.

These creatures, like the aliens in Steven Spielberg's *Close Encounters of the Third Kind*, have large, smooth heads and huge black eyes. Again, they are also a little too human looking considering the quite different evolutionary pathways we'd expect on different worlds. Obviously, Hollywood production costs can be kept down if aliens are simply humans wearing sophisticated masks and makeup with dripping goo. Why is it that so many of the recent Hollywood extraterrestrials tend to be wet—the slimy goo variously suggesting amniotic fluid, mucous, evisceration, and dangerous body fluids? Perhaps all the alien drool reminds us of rabid animals and therefore is something to be feared.

In the DMT universe or temporal lobe epilepsy universe, there may be reasons why psychonauts see humanoid forms, but speaking from a purely evolutionary standpoint in our "real world," there are many reasons why human forms are unlikely. For one thing, the diverse rates and directions of evolution on Earth, with many types of creatures becoming extinct, show that there is no goal-directed route from single cells to an intelligent human. With only slightly different starting conditions on Earth, humans would not have evolved. In other words, evolution is so sensitive to small changes that if we were to rewind and play back the "tape" of evolution, and raise initially the Earth's overall temperature by just a degree, humankind would not exist. The enormous diversity of life today represents only a small fraction of what is possible. Moreover, if humans were wiped out today, humans would not arise again. This means that on another world, the same genetic systems and genes will not arise. This also suggests that finding another planet with humans, dinosaurs, or apes is more unlikely than finding an island in Lake Michigan where the inhabitants speak English through doglike snouts.

Given all this, I should point out that evolution on Earth tells us a lot about possible alien shapes. Although every detail must be different, there are patterns of general problems, and common solutions to those problems, that would apply to life on alien worlds. In the course of Earth's history, whenever life-forms have had a problem to solve, they have solved it in remarkably similar ways. For example, three very unrelated animals—a dolphin (a mammal), a salmon (a fish), and an ichthyosaur (an extinct reptile)—all have swum in coastal waters darting about in search of small fish to eat. These three creatures have very little to do with one another either biochemically, genetically, or evolutionarily, yet they all have a similar look. To a first approximation, they are nothing more than living, breathing torpedoes. Despite their differences they have evolved a streamlined body to help them quickly travel through the water. This is an example of convergent evolution, and we might expect aquatic aliens that feed on smaller, quick-moving aliens to also have streamlined bodies.

With convergent evolution, successful solutions arise independently in different animal lines separated in time and place. The reason for the similarity of solutions is clear: Animals encounter similar environmental problems and cope with them in a similar way because that solution is an efficient one. These universal solutions will be found on other planets with life.

DAVID: How do you think science, philosophy, art, and entertainment may have developed in an advanced extraterrestrial culture?

CLIFFORD: First let us ponder what aliens would consider as beautiful art. Would an alien race of intelligent robots prefer a combination of graffiti-like figures echoing the art of children and primitive societies, or would they prefer the cold regularity of wires in a photograph of a Pentium computer chip? If we were to give these aliens a musical CD, they should be able to conclude we have an understanding of patterns, symmetry, and mathematics. They may even admire our sense of beauty and appreciate the gift. What more about us would our art reveal to them? What would alien art reveal to us? Whatever their aesthetic differences, alien math and science might be similar to ours, because I believe that the same kinds of mathematical truths will be discovered by any intelligent aliens. But its not clear our art would be considered beautiful or profound to aliens. After all, we have a difficult time ourselves determining what good art is.

Because alien senses would not be the same as ours, it's very difficult to determine what their art or entertainment would be like. If you were to visit a world of creatures who primary sense was smell and who had little or no vision, their architecture might seem visually quite boring. Instead of paintings hanging on the walls of their home, they might use certain aromatic woods and other odor-producing compounds strategically positioned on their walls. Their counterparts of Picasso and Rembrandt wouldn't make paintings but would position exquisite concoctions of bold and subtle perfumes. Alien equivalents of *Playboy* magazine would be visually meaningless but awash in erotic aromas. Their culinary arts could be like our visual or auditory arts: Eating a meal with all its special flavors would be akin to listening to Beethoven's Fifth Symphony. If all the animals on their world had a primary sense of smell, there would be no colorful flowers, peacock's tails, or beautiful butterflies. Their world might look gray and drab. . . . But instead of visual beauty, an enchanting panoply of odors would lure insects to flowers, birds to their nests, and aliens to their lovers.

If we were able to extend our current senses in range and intensity, we could glimpse alien sense-domains. Think about bees. Bees can see into the ultraviolet, although they do not see as far as we do into the red range of the spectrum. When we look at a violet flower, we do not see the same thing that bees see. In fact, many flowers have beautiful patterns that only bees can see to guide them to the flower. These attractive and intricate patterns are totally hidden to human perception.

If we possessed sharper sight we would see things that are too small, too fast, too dim, or too transparent for us to see now. We can get an inkling of such perceptions using special cameras, computer-enhanced images, night-vision goggles, slow-motion photography, and panoramic lenses, but if we had grown up from birth with these visual skills, our species would be transformed into something quite unusual. Our art would change, our perception of human beauty would change, our ability to diagnose diseases would change, and even our religions would change. If only a handful of people had these abilities, would they be hailed as messiahs?

If technologically advanced aliens exist on other worlds, Earthlings have only recently become detectable to them with our introduction of radio and

TV in the latter part of the 1900s. Our TV shows are leaking into space as electromagnetic signals that can be detected at enormous distances by receiving devices not much larger than our own radiotelescopes. Whether we like it or not, Paris Hilton's sex video is heading to Alpha Centauri and *South Park* is shooting out to the constellation Orion. What impressions would these shows make on alien minds? It is a sobering thought that one of the early signs of terrestrial intelligence might come from the mouth of Bart Simpson.

Similarly, if we receive our first signal from the stars, could it be the equivalent of "The Three Stooges," with bug-eyed aliens smashing each other with green-goo pies? What if our first message from the stars was alien pornography that inadvertently leaked out into space? SETI funding would be even more difficult if the Reverend Jerry Falwell and other conservatives found that our first extraterrestrial message was of a hard-core *Playboy*—and our first images were of aliens plunging their elephantine proboscises into the paroxysmal esophagus of some nubile, alien marsupial.

As hard as it may be to stomach, our entertainment will be our earliest transmissions to the stars. If we ever receive inadvertent transmissions from the stars, it will be their entertainment. Imagine this. The entire Earth sits breathlessly for the first extraterrestrial images to appear on CNN. One of our preppy-and-perfect news anchors appears on our TVs for instant live coverage. And then, beamed to every home are the alien equivalents of Pamela Anderson in a revealing bathing suit, Beavis and Butthead mouthing inanities and expletives, and an MTV heavy-metal band consisting of screaming squids.

This is not such a crazy scenario. In fact, satellite studies show that the Super Bowl football action, which is broadcast from more transmitters than any other signal in the world, would be the most easily detected message from Earth. The first signal from an alien world could be the alien equivalent of a football game. Lesson 1: We had better not assess an entire culture solely on the basis of their entertainment. Lesson 2: You can learn a lot about a culture from their entertainment.

DAVID: Do you think that consciousness is created by the brain, or do you think that it can exist in life-forms without a nervous system, like a plant?

CLIFFORD: The question is difficult until you define the word "consciousness." If it is simply goal-seeking or avoidance behavior, many primitive animals and plants display this. Also, what do you mean by life-forms? Consider hive minds on Earth, which we can explain using a termite analogy. Even though an individual component of the hive mind is limited—as a termite has limited capacity—the entire collection of components display emergent behavior and produces intelligent solutions. Termites create huge, intricate mounds—taller than the Empire State Building when compared to their own height. These termites control the temperature of the mound by altering its tunnel structure. Thus, the component termites come together to create a warm-blooded super-organism. Is the hive conscious even if its components are not?

DAVID: What are your thoughts on artificial intelligence, and do you think a computer can ever become conscious?

CLIFFORD: Some say that computers can never have real thoughts or mental states of their own. The computers can merely simulate thought and intelligence. If such a machine passes the famous Turing test—a test to see if you can have a conversation with the machine and find it indistinguishable from a human—this only proves that it is good at simulating a thinking entity. Holders of this position also sometimes suggest that only organic things can be conscious. If you believe that only flesh and blood can support consciousness, then it would be very difficult to create conscious machines. However, there's no reason to exclude the possibility of nonorganic sentient beings. Some day we'll all have a Rubik's cube-sized computer that can carry on a conversation with us in a way that is indistinguishable from a human. I call these smart entities Turing-beings, or Turbings. If our thoughts and consciousness do not depend on the actual substances in our brains but rather on the structures, patterns, and relationships between parts, then Turbings could think. If you could make a copy of your brain with the same structure but using different materials, the copy would think it was you.

At a more liberal end of the spectrum are those researchers that say passing a Turing test suffices for being intelligent. According to this way of thought, a machine or being able to respond to questions in the sophisticated ways demanded by the Turing test has all the necessary properties to be labeled intelligent. If a rock could discuss quantum mechanics in a seemingly intelligent fashion with you, the rock would be intelligent. If the thing behaves intelligently, it *is* intelligent. When a human no longer behaves intelligently (e.g., through brain damage or death), then we say there is no longer any mind in the body, and the being has no intelligence.

We may like to digress and consider what it means for an intelligent machine, being, or Turbing to actually "know" something. There are many kinds of knowledge the being could have. This makes discussions of thinking things a challenge. For example, knowledge may be factual or propositional: A being may know that the Peloponnesian War was fought by two leading city-states in ancient Greece, Athens, and Sparta. Another category of knowledge is procedural, knowing how to accomplish a task such as playing chess, cooking a cake, making love, performing a Kung Fu block, shooting an arrow, or creating primitive life in a test tube. However, for us at least, reading about shooting an arrow is not the same as actually being able to shoot an arrow. This second type of procedural knowing implies actually being able to perform the act. (One might wonder what it actually means for a machine to have "knowledge" of sex and other physical acts.) Yet another kind of knowledge deals with direct experience. This is the kind of knowledge referred to when someone says, "I know love" or "I know fear."

Let's sum up. On one side of the discussion, humanlike interaction is quite important for any machine that we would wish to say has humanlike intelligence. A smart machine is less interesting if its intelligence lies trapped in an unresponsive program, sequestered in a kind of isolated limbo. As computer companies begin to make Turbings, the manufacturers will probably agree that intelligence is associated with what we call "knowledge" of various subjects, the ability to make abstractions, and the ability to convey such information to others. As we provide our computers with increasingly advanced sensory peripherals and larger databases, it is likely we will gradually come to think of these entities as intelligent.

Terence McKenna thought that "alien life" would first appear to us in the form of computer consciousness. He said in the May 2000 issue of *Wired*: "Part of the myth of the alien is that you have to have a landing site. Well, I can imagine a landing site that's a Web site. If you build a Web site and then say to the world, 'Put your strangest stuff here, your best animation, your craziest graphics, your most impressive AI software,' very quickly something would arise that would be autonomous enough to probably stand your hair on end. You won't be able to tell whether you've got code, machine intelligence, or the real thing."

According to Chworktap, the beautiful female protein robot in Kilgore Trout's *Venus on the Half-Shell*, "Anything that has a brain complex enough to use language in a witty or creative manner has to have self-consciousness and free-will." I don't know if I agree entirely with Chworktap, but I see no reason that consciousness would be limited to organic life-forms. Certainly within this century, some computers will respond in such a way that anyone interacting them will consider them to be conscious. The entities will exhibit emotions. Over time, we will merge these creatures. We will become one. We will download our thoughts and memories to these devices. Our organs may fail and turn to dust, but we will survive.

DAVID: When I interviewed Ray Kurzweil for this book, he told me that he thought that it would be around thirty years before we had computers that exceed human intelligence. How long do you think it will be before computers exceed human intelligence—if, indeed, you think that such a thing is possible—and how do you think the world will change if and when they do?

CLIFFORD: Computers, or computer/human hybrids, will surpass humans in every area, from art to creativity, to intelligence. I do not know when this will happen, but I think it very likely that it will happen in this century, in the same way that we will become immortal in this century because we will fully understand the biological basis of aging. Of course, computers already exceed human "intelligence" when it comes to winning chess or solving certain mathematical problems. I see no reason why this basic skill won't gradually metastasize into other areas like painting, music, and literature.

DAVID: What do you think happens to human consciousness after death?

CLIFFORD: If we believe that human consciousness is a product of the living brain, then consciousness evaporates when our brains die. When you fall asleep at night, consciousness seems to disappear, and then comes back upon awakening or when dreaming. If so, perhaps consciousness disappears when an individual dies as it does when a person enters nondreaming sleep. Some day we may prevent this death by uploading our minds to machines, so in that sense our consciousness will survive brain death. I have nonreligious friends who speculate that consciousness exists as some kind of fundamental property of space time, and I know of people who take DMT and who become certain that consciousness survives our bodily deaths, but of course all of this is speculation.

If we believe that consciousness is the result of patterns of neurons in the brain, our thoughts, emotions, and memories could be replicated in moving assemblies of Tinker Toys. The Tinker Toy mind would have to be very big to represent the complexity of our minds, but still it could be done, in the same way people have made sophisticated computers out of Tinker Toys. In principle, our minds could be hypostatized in the patterns of twigs, in the movements of leaves, or in the flocking of birds.

In any case, I believe that we all live happy lives, coded in the endless digits of pi. Recall that the digits of pi (in any base) not only go on forever but seem to behave statistically like a sequence of uniform random numbers. This means that somewhere inside the endless digits of pi is a very close representation for all of us—the atomic coordinates of all our atoms, our genetic code, all our thoughts, all our memories. Given this fact, all of us are alive, and hopefully happy, in pi. Pi makes us live forever. We all lead virtual lives in pi. We are immortal.

You can read a large group discussion of this topic, which I initiated at my Web site http://sprott.physics.wisc.edu/pickover/pimatrix.html. At this site, I state the controversial notion: "This means that romance is never dead. Somewhere you are running through fields of wheat, holding hands with someone you love, as the sun sets—all in the digits of pi."

My favorite novel dealing with near-death experiences is Connie Willis's *Passage*, which describes physicians studying and inducing near-death experiences. In my own novels, the characters often cope with death, uncertainty, and strange realities separated from ours by thin veils. For example, in *The Lobotomy Club*, scientists and amateurs perform brain surgery on themselves in order to see religious visions and a "truer" reality. The new reality turns into a nightmare filled with military conspiracies, insectile aliens, bioengineering, biblical imagery, and prodromic dreams.

DAVID: Have you ever had a psychedelic experience, and, if so, how has it influenced your writing and your perspective on life?

CLIFFORD: I have not had drug-induced psychedelic experiences, although many people who read my Neoreality books seem to think I have had some kind of hallucinations. In some sense, I have to put a damper on my creativity and visions. Some of my publishers even say I write too much and should slow down. Speaking about publishing, I find that selling fiction is much more difficult than selling my nonfiction. If the ability to find a publisher for nonfiction can be compared to walking across the street, finding a publisher for fiction is like walking from New York to California backward. Nevertheless, my mind, visions, and ideas continually fly. As Salvador Dalí said, "I am the drug!"

My Neoreality books deal with beautiful women and their surgically altered brains, fractal sex, Noah's Ark, hyperspace physics, hallucinating androids, prophetic ants, vitamin B12, cosmic wormholes, novel plastics, intelligent spiders, and quests for God and the structure of ultimate reality. Is that sufficiently psychedelic for you? My artwork is also quite psychedelic and featured at such places as Erowid.org, alongside art produced by people under the influence of psychedelic drugs.

DAVID: Do you think that the human species is in any danger of extinction? Do you think we'll survive the next hundred years?

CLIFFORD: The first question to consider is whether the human race could destroy itself even if it wanted to. The easiest Doomsday Machine to construct is the cobalt bomb cluster. Each cobalt bomb is an ordinary atomic bomb encased in a jacket of cobalt. When a cobalt bomb explodes, it spreads a huge amount of radiation. If enough of these bombs were exploded, life on Earth would perish. In another recipe for Doomsday, large hydrogen bombs are placed at strategic locations on Earth and exploded simultaneously. As a result, the Earth may wobble on its axis. If placed at major fault lines, the bombs could trigger a worldwide series of killer earthquakes.

It would also be possible to capture one of the larger asteroids and send it crashing to Earth by exploding nuclear bombs at specific locations on the surface of the asteroid. Biological Doomsday Machines include weapons utilizing bacteria, viruses, or various biological toxins. For example, a few pounds of poison produced by botulis bacteria is sufficient to kill all human life.

Many believe that the Earth is like an inmate waiting on death row. Even if we do not die by a comet or asteroid impact, we know the Earth's days are numbered. The Earth's rotation is slowing down. Far in the future, day lengths will be equivalent to fifty of our present days. The Moon will hang in the same place in the sky, and the lunar tides will stop.

In 5 billion years, the fuel in our Sun will be exhausted, and the Sun will begin to die and expand, becoming a red giant. At some point, our oceans will boil away. No one on Earth will be alive to see a red glow filling most of the sky. As Freeman Dyson once said, "No matter how deep we burrow into the Earth . . . we can only postpone by a few million years our miserable end."

Our good friends at the "Voluntary Human Extinction Movement" (www.vhemt.org) believe that we should be phasing out the human race by "voluntarily ceasing to breed" to allow the Earth's biosphere to return to good health. I don't see this movement making a major impact. Do you? Let's consider other possible agents that might decimate our population: prions (infectious proteins); nanotechnology gray goo (submicron-sized self-replicating robots programmed to make copies of themselves and which get out of control, forming a gray goo that envelops the Earth); and terrorists' production of a biological agent like Ebola (an infectious virus).

On the other hand, I'm a bit more optimistic in the short run. Some researchers have even suggested that humans are at less risk for extinction now than at any other time in history, and that risk decreases proportionately to advances made in technology. For example, aside from AIDS, it seems as if epidemics are less dangerous than in the days when the Europeans wiped out the South American Indians through disease and when Europe suffered from the Black Plague.

As I indicated, in this century, we will probably become immortal, due to our understanding of the biological basis of aging and our merging with computers. Long before the Sun envelops the Earth, we will have left it.

DAVID: What do you think of the possibility—which is a common theme in many science-fiction stories—that our own machines may one day rise up and destroy or dominate us?

CLIFFORD: I think it more likely that we will blend with machines. We will become them. Similarly, we may one day be able to download ourselves to software and dispense with our physical bodies.

DAVID: Assuming that we do survive, how do you envision the future evolution of the human race?

CLIFFORD: We'll become immortal. For the rich, genetic manipulation will cause us to become taller, more intelligent, more attractive, healthier, and stronger. For rich people, ugliness fades from the world. Our preoccupation with sexual pleasure will continue to increase in many segments of the population. One hundred years from now, humans will elect to have orgasms that last for hours, even days. With virtual reality, you'll be able to share the orgasm with whomever you want, from Paris Hilton to Queen Elizabeth.

Also, despite the opinion of people like George Bush, stem cell research will become more common and help us evolve and keep healthy. On one of my RealityCarnival.Com web pages, I wrote a letter to President Bush, asking him to keep an open mind and foster a liberal attitude with respect to a woman's option of having an abortion and with respect to embryonic stem cell research, which he has limited. The notion that an embryo or fertilized egg should be considered human is certainly open for debate. As reported in *Science* magazine, "zygotic personhood" (the idea that a fertilized egg is a person) is a recent concept.

For example, before 1869, the Catholic church believed that the embryo was not a person until it was forty days old. (Aristotle agreed with this forty-day threshold.) Thus, the church did not believe a human had a soul until day forty. If the early embyro was souless, perhaps early abortion was not murder. Pope Innocent III in 1211 determined that the time of ensoulment was anywhere from three to four months. If we truly believed that a zygote is a person, we would incarcerate women who use the pill because the pill may sometimes prevent the implantation of a fertilized egg. We do not jail such women or their physicians; hence, we do not actually believe a zygote is a person.

Because of various birth control methods, millions of unwanted children have not been produced and countless suffering has been abolished (including decreases in crime, child abuse, and ecological nightmares). If people can overcome the fallacy of zygotic personhood, we can then ease restrictions on human embryonic stem cell research, which has the potential to help people with Alzheimer's, Parkinson's, and diabetes. Although nonembryonic stem cells (such as multipotent adult progenitor cells) may eventually be suitable substitutes for embryonic cells, we should not restrict stem cell research now. Similarly, those who hope to ban cloning because it may entail the discarding of zygotes should rethink their position.

With women gaining more control over their reproductive fate, society has changed. Reliable birth control became as easy as taking a pill, which, along with education, is one of the greatest factors in helping women achieve equality with men and preventing overpopulation in less developed parts of the world. Although religious people may debate whether a fertilized egg (zygote) should be accorded the same rights as a child (and therefore destruction of the zygote should lead to imprisonment), no one debates that the pill and other methods of birth control have decreased the suffering of fully formed, multicellular humans. Very few people today believe in gametic personhood (the idea that sperm and eggs are people) or homuncular personhood (the eighteenth-century idea that the entire human organism—the homunculus—is contained in the spermatozoa); similarly, the notion of zygotic personhood may someday fade from the world scene. And this leads me to the more mind-boggling issues that we will face in the next century: the notion of cybernetic personhood.

In the coming years, we will be able to create sentient creatures in software running on computers. We will be able to simulate ourselves in software. This, of course, will affect laws, politics, and religion. The termination of sentient software may one day be much more egregious than termination of a zygote. Returning our attention to present technology, I hope that future U.S. presidents consider the appointment of individuals—both to the judiciary and to positions of policy making—who have not taken extreme positions in opposition to abortion or embryonic stem cell research.

Many colleagues believe that we'll enhance our senses using genetic engineering. Perhaps someday we will be able to have a whole range of new senses, like echolocation, infrared vision, and other senses we can barely imagine. Some say that increased racial mixing will continue to take place and that the last blonde will die in Finland in four hundred years. Because more than 50 percent of Jews in America are marrying people from other religions, the last practicing Jew will die in America in three hundred years. According to Alan Dershowitz, a Harvard study predicts that the American Jewish community is likely to number less than 1 million and conceivably as few as ten thousand by the time the United States celebrates its tricentennial in 2076. Jews may only consist of isolated pockets of ultra-Orthodox Hasidim.

Sometimes I mourn the fact that the ultimate fate of the universe involves great cold—or great heat if there's sufficient gravity to draw all matter together in a single point in a final Big Crunch. It is likely that *Homo sapiens* will become extinct. However, our civilization and our values may not be doomed. Our heirs, whatever or whoever they may be, may find practical ways for manipulating space time as they launch themselves throughout the galaxy. They will seek their salvation in the stars.

Future Cultures and Subcultures

An Interview with Bruce Sterling

Bruce Sterling is a science-fiction writer and social satirist who helped to create the cyberpunk genre and has had a large influence on computer culture in general. He has written more than ten bestselling science-fiction novels and three short story collections, but, more important, he helped to establish a cultural movement that has a deep and lasting effect on how people interact with technology. Sterling appeared on the cover of the very first issue of Wired *magazine—an indication of the essential role that he has played in the development of digital culture—and he continues to write a monthly column for the publication. Some of his books include* Involution Ocean, The Artificial Kid, Schismatrix, The Hacker Crackdown, *and* Tomorrow Now: Envisioning the Next 50 Years.

* * *

DAVID: How has your interest in science and technology influenced your fiction?

BRUCE: My father was an engineer, and there are a lot of oil and gas people in my family. An uncle of mine is an entomologist. So there was science and engineering in my family background. It was not some kind of alien thing. It was how we ate, really. I mean, that was our industrial base there. So I never felt alienated by it. Or surprised by it. It was just a normal thing for me. I'm still very interested in the oil and gas industry, although I rarely write about it. People like to call science fiction "science" fiction, but the more time I spend with it, the more I realize that it's not primarily concerned with science. You get your best effects out of areas that are better described as engineering or industrial design.

DAVID: How has satire played a role in your work, and why do you like to mix real facts with your fiction?

BRUCE: Well, people call that stuff satire, but I like to think of it in the terms that H. G. Wells did. He said that if you want to write about the future, you need to triple the phenomena that you're writing about—not because things always triple, but because if you double it, people think you're merely exaggerating. And if you quadruple it, nobody can tell what the hell you're talking about. So if you take some small phenomenon that looks like it's going to become a great commonplace someday, you start extrapolating it. You could blow it up to three times normal size, and point out that it may have a much stronger effect than it seems to be having at the moment—and that effect looks satirical.

It looks and smells like satire, but it doesn't necessarily have to be humorous. It may well be a rather accurate description of what's likely to happen. If you live in a growing town and the traffic triples, you will have big traffic jams. If you anticipate this in print, it may sound quite funny, but it's not very funny when you're actually in one. (*laughter*) It's not at all uncommon for traffic to triple in some places.

DAVID: You mentioned before that you have an interest in subcultures. What are your thoughts on how the counterculture of the '60s influenced what became the digital subcultures of the '80s, '90s, and today?

BRUCE: I'm interested in all forms of subculture, but I'm more interested in sociology than I am a committed believer of any kind of subcultural pitch. People that were very involved in a counterculture in the 1960s think they were inventing all that. The 1960s counterculture was just one of the larger ones, due to its generational cohort. But I've always been more interested in '70s, '80s, '90s counterculture than I was in that of the '60s. Actually, I'm more interested in the countercultures of tomorrow than I am in the subculture of any particular time and place. I've found that there are subcultural splits that go through every society. The question is not whether society is going to be segmented in subcultural ways, but exactly how those social divisions are going to manifest themselves.

. . .

DAVID: All previous forms of media—television, radio, newspapers, et cetera—have been monopolized by corporations. It seems that they can't monopolize the Internet. Do you think that this will make a difference sociologically?

BRUCE: I've got about fifteen different problems with that entire set of formulations there. (*laughter*)

If you mean that people who are using the Internet for noncommercial reasons are likely to dominate, yeah, I think there's a pretty good chance of that actually—because the Internet was not invented by corporations. It was basically invented by the military and science—basic science and computer scientists. A few DARPA grants here and there kind of got that whole thing steamrolling. And when the Internet was first invented—ARPAnet, Milnet, and so forth—there was never an idea that it was ever going to become a commercial operation.

So it's a very 1990s kind of rhetoric to say, well, everything is going to be privatized and commercialized by large companies—until you look at areas where this commercialization isn't happening, and those areas are frequently a lot worse: They are criminalized or militarized. After a while you may plead for your kindly corporate dominance—after you've seen the nature of paramilitary warlord regime.

The difficulty there is that, unless corporations have a stable democratic government to offer them a level playing field, they really behave in many ways that are menacing to their own self-interest. Microsoft has grabbed a lot of the operating system market, and they really are a monopoly. But the fact that Microsoft managed to choke off so much innovation through monopoly merely means that their industry as a whole is now being shipped off to India and China as rapidly as computers can be flung off the docks.

So that's turning out to be counterproductive behavior. The computer industry got all its cachet from being profoundly innovative, but if you have complete corporate dominance—from a plutocracy and a monopoly—then nobody's going to innovate, because that simply makes no sense. If you innovate when you have a quarter of the market, maybe you'll get half the market. But if you already have 95 percent of the market, there's no reason to do anything much, except post armed guards and clip stock coupons. So the fact that the U.S. Justice Department was too weak to break up Microsoft has had a shattering effect on the computer industry. A corporate monopoly is inherently unstable. It's just not going to work.

. . .

DAVID: Can you talk a little about the Dead Media Project?
BRUCE: Yeah, that was an effort of mine that bore fruit in a lot of peculiar ways. It was something that Richard Kadrey and I cooked up once over his kitchen table in San Francisco. It was during the height of the '90s tech boom. Kadrey and I were both quite close to that, and we were disgusted by the silly P.R. mess around new media—as if media were somehow inherently better, simply because they were new. It occurred to us that nobody was keeping track of all the forms of media that were no longer new, that were being exterminated.

So we decided we would use new media—the Internet being a newfangled thing at the time—to try and keep track of defunct media. We wanted to accumulate a list of the dead media, and see if we could figure out something about the nature of technological change in the media world, because that's something of profound interest to science-fiction writers of my generation. How are things changing? What are the driving forces? And so forth. So I worked on this for about four years, and I did assemble a pretty good list of dead forms of media. It's certainly the most extensive list I've ever seen. It's by no means complete, but it's the most complete I was able to do. And I even came up, finally, with a driving theory as to why media die.

DAVID: What was the theory?
BRUCE: I like to call it the Dairy Product Theory of Dead Media. The reason media die has nothing to do with their being media. That was the central problem with the Dead Media Project, because it's a category error. Media don't die because they carry messages from one person to another, in an effective way or a less effective way. They die for the same kind of reasons that dairy products die.

In other words, with dairy products, there's always a need for milk. Milk is one of the oldest consumables that the human race has ever created, packaged, and sold. But every epoch comes up with its own methods of delivering milk. The mistake would be to think that the milk was causing the changes—that it's because of milk that you no longer see, say, a horse-drawn wagon with big hammered-steel milk jugs in the back. That horse-drawn wagon, with the really big jugs of milk in the canisters, is gone now. But it's not because of anything to do with milk. It's because of new modes of transportation and storage.

The same is true for media. Media aren't evolving because of their innate "media-ness." They're evolving because of other reasons—electronic ones, mechanical ones, means of production, means of distribution, forms of wavelength regulation. In other words, there's very little that's media-like about media. They're not becoming more "media-ish." (*laughter*) The fact that they are media is not their driving force. The driving forces come from other aspects of technological development.

DAVID: When I interviewed Douglas Rushkoff a few weeks ago, he told me that he thought the media is alive—that it's actually a living entity of sorts, with an agenda to perpetuate itself.

BRUCE: Yeah, well, that's not too hard to imagine, given their behavior. There's Manuel DeLanda's book on the machinic phylum and so forth. But that's not a new notion, and it's not really going to get you very far as a serious mode of analysis, I don't think. It might be best described as a colorful metaphor. Believing that media is alive is like believing that the milk is alive in the can and the bottle. You know, sometimes milk really is alive. Yogurt has got living bacteria in it, but that doesn't mean that it's all some kind of amazing scheme by which little yogurt canisters are multiplying and spreading themselves around. There's no agenda there. It's just milk, okay?

DAVID: What do you think corporations in the future will be like, and do you think that the multinational corporations of the future will have as much political power as they do today?

BRUCE: That's a real difficulty there. People say "corporations" as if there's only one kind of them. There's the small regional ones, and there's the big multi-nats. Then there's NGOs [nongovernmental organizations], and there's the quangos [quasi-governmental organizations]. There's the defense companies that are really close to the government, and so forth and so on. Corporations are very ductile forms of organization. A profit-driven private sector doesn't necessarily have to look very much anything like today's corporations look.

If you look at current corporations, they no longer look very much like they did in, say, the 1980s. They tend to be very stockholder-dominated now. It's become easier for them to paste on new logos, spin off entire divisions, or engage in mergers and acquisitions. And fraud—that too. Through these other kinds of peculiar activities, you get these virtualized structures, and the offshore setups that are hanging on to some management corps in the developed world. They're no longer the classic, solid, white-collar megacorp notion—you know, the silk-hat Monopoly guy from the board game. I guess you might call them "rhizomatic."

But when I look at the trend there and try to figure this out, I think there's some kind of bleed-over between big corporations and nongovernmental organizations—because we really have a lot of problems that can only be dealt with successfully on a global scope. The nation-states are having a hard time getting their heads around that. But I think that, compared to governments, corporations are actually quite vulnerable. It's really kind of pitiful to see what happens to a McDonald's, or a Coca-Cola, or a Wal-Mart. Increasingly, they do get politically and socially polarized, and relentlessly attacked, and they're losing market share. Coca-Cola is not selling as well as it did. McDonald's is kind of dead in the water. Wal-Mart is a source of increasing political controversy.

It's tough to find anybody who will actually loyally work for a modern corporation. Stockholders day-trade them, and the CEOs rip them off. People come up with golden parachutes. Besides California rate payers, the primary victims of Enron—which was a malignant corporation by anyone's standards—are Enron employees. Those loyal employees got really burned by their own outfit there. So if you claim that corporations are dominating everything, and then ask: What are they going to be like? I don't know. That notion is subject to question. I mean, maybe, like Enron, they'll dominate politically and simultaneously implode. In which case they're just an inherently unstable way to try and run human affairs. And I suspect that's the case. The instability is in Schumpeterian "creative destruction," and it might even be construed as a virtue.

DAVID: Speaking of things being unstable, in your book *Tomorrow Now*, you talk about how a permanent state of disequilibrium can be a very creative space. Can you explain why you think this is so?

BRUCE: Well, it's not like we're getting a choice. (*laughter*) A human body is in a permanent state of disequilibrium. You're conceived. You grow. You're born. You age. You move through time, and you perish. And you never get to stop in the middle, just because you're happy right where you are, right? I mean, time flows through your being, and you don't get to opt out of that process. Human life is a permanent disequilibrium. And what you have to do is get up in the morning and keep putting one foot in front of another. (*laughter*) I think that's just a fact of life about the human condition, and the social condition, as well. In writing about permanent disequilibrium, what I was trying to do was get people used to the idea, so that they'd be willing to confront the truth there, and not feel some kind of existential horror about it. There needs to be some way for us to celebrate the truth without flinching, and deal with it as effectively as we can.

Whenever somebody comes up with some weird, static notion, like this poor Fukuyama guy who wrote his book about "the end of history" way back in 1992—well, history immediately continues, which makes him look rather foolish. It's very disillusioning to people when these grand, static formulations break down. You'd be a lot better off by realizing that history doesn't end—authors end, okay? History flows through people and renders us mortal. Francis Fukuyama would have been a lot better off writing a magisterial book called *The End of Myself*. That premise would have been a lot clearer. But unfortunately, he got kind of carried away with his methods of analysis there, and he didn't realize that the clock continues to tick, even though he really thinks he's got the grand scheme figured out. We're never going to get history figured out, although people always aspire to do that in some way.

Some particular zealots, having figured out our sublime and holy destinies, immediately want to go out and violently convince everybody else. That really causes a lot of unnecessary grief. What we really need is something more along the lines of a Soros "Open Society"—a society and a political arrangement, and an economic arrangement, an educative arrangement, and so forth, that just takes it for granted that our knowledge is inherently imperfect and we're going to keep making new mistakes. We're never going to get perfect, permanent answers. Not utopias. Not dystopias. Not the greatest, grandest ways to run things. Not so-called solutions to so-called problems. But decent, livable spaces in which we're able to make fresh mistakes. That's the best we should ask for, and that's the best we should be willing to ask for. And that is permanent disequilibrium.

DAVID: When I interviewed Ray Kurzweil for this book, he told me that he thought that it would be around thirty years before we had computers that exceed human intelligence. How long do you think it will be before computers exceed human intelligence, and how do you think the world will change when they do?

BRUCE: I think that whole idea is absurd. This is like asking when do you think a 747 will lay better eggs than an owl does? Computation has very little to do with what human brains do. We're abusing the term "intelligence" as a kind of smear-over, conflating term to try to unite cognition and computation. I don't believe those are even very closely allied things. I suspect that they're profoundly different phenomena.

DAVID: What do you think about the notion of artificial intelligence in general, and about the possibility of reverse engineering the human brain?

BRUCE: I think those are two different fields. I think you're very likely to see very powerful machines that are capable of very sophisticated forms of processing, but their activities are going to look less and less like "intelligence." I mean, there's just no good technical reason for these machines to behave in a way that resembles human cognition. That's like asking why won't this jet flap its wings? Well, a jet doesn't need to flap wings. There are no really big ornithopters. There's no good engineering reason to make an ornithopter. There are no birds that are as big as 747s because flexing wings can't support that much weight in the air. So you can call what a jet does "flying," and you can call what a bird does "flying," but, in point of fact, although they're bound by some similar laws of aerodynamics, they don't scale, one to another.

The things computers can do that are interesting have very little to do with Turing Tests, relating to people, talking, or understanding natural language. I'm very aware that there are a lot of people in the Kurzweil school who really want to scoop out their skull cavity and install a lot of silicon in there. And they believe this is really some kind of neat hack. But it's absurd. It's like sawing off your legs and grafting on roller skates. I think they're operating under a basic misapprehension. And I don't worry much about the issue—I think time is already telling, there. I never argue with hard AI [artificial intelligence] guys because they're more set in their ways than the Jesuits. It's theological, it's blue-sky handwaving, it's not practical. In the short term, there's very little that a Kurzweil-style AI machine could do that anybody would be willing to pay for or finance. And in the long term, we really will be reverse-engineering the human brain rather than trying to mimic it in silicon, and that's a whole different story.

DAVID: What do you think some of the most important technological advancements of the twenty-first century will be, and how do you think the world will change as a result?

BRUCE: Well, I'm kind of a Ubi-Comp groupie. I don't think the trend is about superintelligence. I think it's about distributed sensors. Like, for instance, I don't want a "smart" refrigerator. I don't want to converse with the Turing refrigerator. I don't want to have it sell me anything. But I would like it to be very efficient, and I would like it to know what's inside it. That would be handy. I'd like to be able to poll my refrigerator by cell phone from downtown: Is there milk? Yes. How much? So much. How old is it? It's smelling pretty funny. Thank you, refrigerator. Now, that should be like a set of text messages.

So I don't really need Jeeves the butler to be in my refrigerator. I don't need human interaction with mechanical devices. That's like putting a wooden horse's head on the front of an automobile. I think the most important technologies of the twenty-first century are going to be whatever technologies allow us to keep nine and half billion people on the planet, without drowning in our own spew—whatever allows us to feed and educate people, and keep the plagues at bay, while we're doubling our numbers and causing a really serious biosphere problem. Those are the big issues, the big opportunities.

DAVID: What do you think is the biggest threat to the human species?

BRUCE: Greenhouse effect.

DAVID: Are you optimistic about the future, and do you think that the human race is going to survive the next hundred years?

BRUCE: People always ask me that, but I think it's a bad question to ask. Are you optimistic about the future? Or are you pessimistic about the future? Nobody would ask that of somebody who was studying the eighteenth century instead of the twenty-first. Like, are you optimistic about the eighteenth century? Or pessimistic about it? I try not to allow a set of emotional attitudes to put blinkers on me. I mean, if I were optimistic about the eighteenth century, I could go and write a history of the eighteenth century that said "In the eighteenth century things were great!" And if I were a pessimist, I could say "The eighteenth century was a living hell!" But, in point of fact, the eighteenth century was both at once, depending on circumstances and point of view. And every other century has always been both at once. So I'm inclined to think that most future centuries will also be both at once, and that questions like "Are you an optimist?" or "Are you a pessimist?" are just an invitation to ignore a lot of the evidence.

DAVID: Do you think that the human species will survive the next hundred years, and if so, how do you envision the future evolution of the human race?

BRUCE: I don't think that every human being will be gone in the next hundred years. It would be difficult to exterminate a broadly spread species. It's like asking Do you think that every rat will be gone in the next hundred years? I mean, we're at least as inventive as they are. (*laughter*) It's possible that through some superb act of biological extermination we could wipe out every rat, but as long as there's breathable air and sunlight, there's bound to be a last few human beings left on, say, remote islands or whatever. Unless there's a catastrophe so huge that it kills off every large mammal, there's going to be some of us.

Now, I'm not saying there can't be catastrophes so huge that they kill off every large mammal. Like, if the Sun explodes, and fries the Earth, well, we're goners. But I'm pretty sure that a hundred years from now there will be some humans. They may not look or think much like us. I would expect there to be a pretty wide variety of them. The thing that worries me is that there might be just a few hundred thousand of them in a world that's so severely ruined that they're sliding into some kind of posthistory. Civilizations do crumble. Civilizations have been known to fall. Most of them have, always. And if you have one global civilization that's everywhere, all over the place, and it makes one really big mistake, you could have one very large barbarism in pretty short order. And, yeah, I find that prospect worrisome. But I don't really think in terms of complete apocalypse, because I just don't think that's very realistic.

DAVID: Have you ever had a psychedelic experience, and if so, how has it influenced your writing and your perspective on life?

BRUCE: I'm very interested in drugs, and I'm even more interested in neuro-chemistry. There has been a lot of skull sweat wasted in this line of work. My feeling about psychedelics is that it's a serious blunder in judgment to imagine that a psychedelic substance is actually "psychedelic" just because it makes you feel psychedelic. In other words, LSD is not a mystical substance. Basically, it's a poison. And if you take this poison, you'll have certain very remarkable mental effects. But it's wrong to think that you've been granted some spiritual source of mystical insight there. It's a toxin and you've been intoxicated.

I've noticed some wacky developments quite recently. There are some new genetic knockout mice who are immune to LSD. In other words, they simply don't have the neural pathway in the brain that responds to this particular narcotic. (*laughter*) So you could feed these lab rats LSD by the handful, and it doesn't even slow them down. (*laughter*) I find that hugely amusing.

DAVID: What kind of an effect do you think psychedelics have had on science fiction in general?

BRUCE: Well, there were guys like Philip K. Dick, who was a notorious pill head. I haven't really seen many writers destroyed by psychedelics. That's one of the least harmful drug problems a writer could have. The drugs that are really dangerous for writers are definitely alcohol and cigarettes. Alcohol just reaps writers by the hecatomb. Writers tend to be kind of melancholic, and when it's your business to talk a lot, or write a lot, alcohol tends to make you very loquacious. So it's easy to get a big substance dependency on alcohol in my line of work—and I've seen booze destroy a lot of my colleagues, or really hurt them. I never knew a writer who took a whole lot of LSD, or other psyche-delics, and became a genuine psychedelic casualty. I've seen plenty of musicians who were psychedelic casualties. With writers, that's a little rarer.

DAVID: What do you think happens to consciousness after death?

BRUCE: There isn't any. It's like going to sleep and not waking up.

DAVID: What is your perspective on the concept of God, and do you see any teleology in evolution?

BRUCE: No. I'm an atheist, and I think teleology is just a mistaken idea.

DAVID: Does it seem to you that anything is accelerating in the evolutionary or historical process?

BRUCE: Well, we're about to become the first species who ever got their mitts directly on their own germ plasm. That doesn't really have anything to do with evolution as we know it—that's just an ability to go and screw around with our own DNA. But we're doing that right now—those glow fish there. Those babies are the thin edge of the wedge. (*laughter*) I just wonder how many of those glowing DNA-altered fish sold this holiday season. I keep track of a lot of stuff like that, and that trend's definitely accelerating. I mean, when you see DNA technology hitting the toy market, that's a classic S-ramp curve about to blow there.

But it's a mistake to get all teleological and Lamarckian about it, and heap a lot of cosmological importance on it, as if to say Oh, now we're really accel-erating evolution. No, you're not, okay? It's like saying Oh, now we're running really fast because, look, I just bought this Cadillac. In a Cadillac, you could go a lot faster than any prehominid did, because you've got this artificial device here, but that doesn't mean you're out-evolving them. It merely means you've come up with this mechanical hack. So, yeah, there's all kinds of accelerations. It's just that you need to be very careful not to conflate different categories and read mystical overtones into them.

DAVID: Can you talk about the Viridian project, and what are your thoughts on the environmental crisis that we're facing on this planet?

BRUCE: I started doing this for much the same reason I wrote *Hacker Crackdown*, when the cops were showing up at the doors of friends of mine. Climate change is really starting to hit the fan. I'm from Texas, and I have fam-ily in the oil industry, so fossil fuels really paid for my education, home, shelter, and so forth. I'm somebody who's really profited a lot personally by the fossil fuel industry over the years, and now I see that this machine which fed me has lasted too long. It's lasted way too long, and it's getting more and more desperate, antidemocratic, and malignant. So technologies are not permanent installations. In the case of fossil fuel businesses, really, you're much better off with them in a state of disequilibrium than you are with them as permanent, corrupted institutions trying to reshape society in their own image.

So I got very interested in combating fossil fuel industries and combating the green house effect—not really through politics, although I think that's an interesting line of work. I wanted to talk about it from an industrial design perspective, because I just think my own energies are better invested that way. I'm very interested in industrial design, and I have a lot of friends who are designers. So there's a lot of design work to be done here, and a lot of design criticism to be done here. My feeling is, we really need a better understanding of what it is we're doing to ourselves and our society through continuing to rely on this fossil fuel for the industrial revolution—this two-hundred-year old, filth-spewing, smokestack technology. We really need to look at it very clearly and critically, and understand that, even if it looks cheap, we can't buy another planet if we wreck this one.

So I've been working on that since 1998 or so, and I've had a few setbacks, but I'm also happy to report some good news. Like, for instance, Austin, Texas, which is my home base, has recently declared itself to be the Clean Energy Capital of the World. I'm really excited—just thrilled, frankly—to be an industrial design critic, and science-fiction writer, living in the Clean Energy Capital of the World. That was a fulfilling thing for me to hear, and it was a political victory in a lot of ways. I feel like I'm living and working in just the area where I want to be living and working. So that's very satisfying.

. . .

DAVID: What gives you hope?

BRUCE: I like to quote Vaclav Havel on that topic. He says that "hope is not the conviction that things will turn out well, but the conviction that what you are doing makes sense, no matter how things turn out." I think that's just a more productive attitude. I think I am doing much the sort of things that I ought to be doing, and I think that my own activities make a certain amount of sense. I'd never claim that they make sense for everybody, but I feel they make sense for me, and I actively enjoy it when I'm able to do things that give me a sense of personal fulfillment. I like to increase the sensation of self-actualization—when you become more and more like yourself. To become more like myself—that doesn't really require a Pollyanna attitude on my part.

The thing that's good about self-actualization is that you're not aspiring to become perfect. You're not trying to become soulful, morally better, or angelically good. You're not subjecting yourself to some kind of idealistic framework from outside time and space. You become more willing to recognize yourself as a mammalian, physical, living entity, moving through time, having mass and occupying space. (*laughter*) I think since that's the truth, you should come to terms with that, and you should arrange your life in a way in which that knowledge makes some sense. So, I don't really have to drink a liter of hope to get out of bed in the morning. What I need to get out of bed in the morning is something to compel my interest—and there's a lot of that stuff around right now.

Bio-Media Theory

An Interview with Douglas Rushkoff

Douglas Rushkoff is a media theorist and social commentator. His books, articles, newspaper columns, talks, and NPR commentaries thoughtfully explore the psychological and sociological consequences of technology, mass media, advertising, and youth culture. He is one of the most widely read media critics in America and is considered one of the world's experts on youth culture and advertising. Some of his books include Cyberia, Media Virus, Playing the Future, *and* Coercion. *Rushkoff was the correspondent for PBS's award-winning* Frontline *documentary on teenage culture,* The Merchants of Cool. *His weekly commentaries air on CBS's* Sunday Morning, *National Public Radio's* All Things Considered, *and appear on the back page of* Time *magazine. He lectures regularly at conferences and universities around the world and has served as an adjunct professor of communication at New York University. He also served as an advisor to the United Nations Commission on World*

Culture and on the advisory boards of the Media Ecology Association and the Center for Cognitive Liberty and Ethics.

*   *   *

DAVID: What do you think adults can learn from youth culture?

DOUGLAS: Why, they can learn about the future. Everybody tries to forecast the future using all sorts of strange methodologies about what's going to happen. So much effort has been expended exploring the question Where's the human race going? When all that you have to do is look at a kid. A kid is basically the next model of human being. So, if you want to know where evolution is taking us—whether it's physical evolution or cultural evolution—you look at kids, because they are quite literally the future.

The other thing we can learn from kids is the trending of our cognitive and neural habits. You can see most readily the different ways that kids draw connections between things than we do—the different ways of processing information—if you can hold back from being judgmental about it, for just a moment, to look at what it is that's going on for them and inside them. I mean, yeah, there are many tendencies that are very upsetting—a shortened attention span, less memory, less reading, and less consideration, okay, okay, okay. But if you look beyond those surface observations and focus instead on children's cognitive functioning and pattern recognition, it becomes a lot more interesting.

You can start to see the differences between the way kids process information and the way we do as being almost as profound as the differences between the way literate culture looked at things from the way oral culture did before it. There are some extraordinary shifts taking place. Certain things were lost when we learned to write things down. Memory, for one. But other things were gained.

. . .

DAVID: Could you define what you mean by a media virus? How is the concept related to Richard Dawkins's concept of memes, and how can media viruses be used to help prevent what Noam Chomsky calls "the manufacture of consent"?

DOUGLAS: Yeah, well, in the hopeful vision I guess it could prevent that. A media virus is really just an idea that's wrapped in a shell of media. If a real virus, a biological virus, is DNA's code wrapped in protein, a media virus is ideological or conceptual code—what Richard Dawkins calls memes—wrapped in a media shell. And the point of a viral shell is to allow it to pass unrecognized through the body, or from body to body. So it's got to really have a way of transmitting, a reason for it to move from person to person.

So a media virus, say the Rodney King tape, is first and foremost a media story, not about Rodney King, but about the tape itself. The reason why that homemade, camcorder video of a black guy getting beaten by white cops spread around the world overnight was not really so much because a black guy was getting by white cops. That happened all the time. The reason that it spread around the country was because the real story was someone caught this on camcorder. So this was a story about media. The shell of the Rodney King media virus is the tape itself. It's not the carrier, that it's on videotape. But rather, it's the story of media being used in a new way.

Media wants to grow. Media is a living thing. So media passes stories about media more than it passes anything else. But once that virus is spread, it releases its code, and that decides whether or not it's going to replicate and survive. And the code of this virus really did challenge our cultural code. Just as a biological virus, the genes inside it, the DNA inside it, literally interperlates itself into our own genetic code. It turns our cells into virus factories. The media virus uses its ideological code, its memes, to interperlate itself into our cultural code. So if we have cultural weaknesses, if there are gaps, conflicts, or contradictions in our cultural code, then the meme will find a place to nest, and the virus will end up replicating.

So, whether it's Madonna talking about sex, or Howard Dean exploiting Friendster or meetup.com, media viruses are launched when people use a medium in a new way. Then, once they have your attention, if the viruses can release ideas, code, or concepts, even, that challenge the weaknesses of the culture at any given moment, then they'll succeed and they'll move on. Unfortunately, the main group that took up the notion of media viruses were marketers, and it quickly became what they're calling "viral marketing." It's all based on *Media Virus*. So, on the one hand, I launched a terrific virus. But, on the other hand, it mutated into something that I didn't expect.

I did see media viruses as way to break down the predictability of the media space, and to challenge a lot of the authorities that people like Chomsky are talking about, by creating a bottom-up media, a way for ideas to spread, and a new channel for activists to get their ideas spread faster and better than anyone else. And sometimes it works. There are thousands of terrific blogs out there, and uppity Web sites, from Smoking Gun to Matt Drudge, and there are all sorts of great stories about ideas that have trickled up. But the powers that be tend to imitate the properties of media viruses, the same way that Miller or Budweiser can create a fake microbrewery to make people think that they're drinking a local beer. Or Starbucks creates fake local coffee houses, that don't have the Starbucks name on them, just to look like their own competition.

DAVID: What are some of the other ways that major corporations have used media viruses?

DOUGLAS: One campaign, which was based on Media Virus, that I was told about by the creative people responsible for it was a Calvin Klein campaign, where, apparently, they had all these photos of underage kids in their underwear, and it was reminiscent somehow of child porn. All the Christian groups and child protection groups complained, and Calvin Klein took it off the billboards, or out of magazines. But it had been their intent the whole time to do a campaign that they would be forced to take down, because they knew they would get far more secondary media attention than they could ever pay for. So for two or three days every newscaster is carrying the Calvin Klein story. So they get name out there. And they get their name out there as a dangerous company that's doing cool, weird, sexy, rule-breaking stuff, which then, I suppose, makes their underwear seem sexy and naughty, and cool for people to use.

So that would be a more commercial use of a media virus. I guess the thing that bothers me most about it is not just that it was for commercial culture, or corporate culture, but that it was kind of disingenuous to begin with. It wasn't really an advertising campaign. It was an advertising campaign created to get taken off the air. In other words, because it was so thought out in a certain way, it just doesn't feel genuine to me.

DAVID: What do you mean when you refer to corporations as being an empty set of operating commands, or as dead things, with nobody really in charge?

DOUGLAS: When I'm talking about corporations being mindless usually what I'm trying to do is empower the people that are working for them. It's funny, a lot of times I'll be invited to speak at a conference, or even at a corporation, to all the workers and people there, and people in the counterculture get all upset. They think, Oh, it's this horrible sellout thing I'm doing to take money to talk to their employees. But what I'm trying to demonstrate to the employees, what I'm trying to explain to them, is that the corporation doesn't really exist. The corporation is paperwork. It's a list of rules, through which people are supposed to interact, or priorities that they're supposed to follow, but there's nobody home.

I mean, the worker is listening to the executive, who's listening to the CEO, who's listening to the shareholder, who's just Joe Public finally. It's the same person walking into the store. So it's very easy to say, Oh, corporations are to blame, these horrible entities, but corporations are not conscious. Corporations are groups of people acting in concert, following a set of rules. And what people forget is that those rules can be changed. We're not here to be at the mercy of a piece of paper. A corporation is like a computer program. What I'm saying, most simply, is that this means the people who think that they are the victims of the corporations they are working for—or that they have shares of, or that are in their communities—have access to the codes through which those corporations exist.

DAVID: How does this type of corporate structure allow for underground artists, psychedelic tricksters, and political activists to "sneak" their unconventional ideas into the public domain?

DOUGLAS: There's a lot of different ways that activists, and wonderful strange people, can get involved in changing the reality in which they live. Sometimes I think the most valuable thing is just to do things that change people's conception of stuff. In other words, rather than actually taking down a corporation, just demonstrating to everyone in a community that they don't have to buy their stuff at Wal-Mart. I mean, that, in and of itself, is kind of an eye-opener. Or that there are maybe laws protecting them. Or just that they have a say in what goes on. That they can choose how they think. That they don't have to work seven days a week. That they might have enough stuff. That there are ways to have fun without buying products. That they can get laid without having those jeans. Those are the things. That's the area that's most interesting to me.

As far as weird people being able to get their messages disseminated by media companies, yeah, that happens, too. I mean, because some of them are so big, one right hand doesn't know what the left hand is doing—so that Warner Music ends up publishing *Cop Killer*. Or Paramount-Viacom ends up creating *Beavis and Butthead*, which ends up really killing the rock video as a revenue stream and as a marketing tool. Because now you've got *Beavis and Butthead*, the creation of a wonderful crazy animator down in Texas, Mike Judge, where they're deconstructing MTV on television. And fourteen-year-olds are watching that, realizing, Oh, that's how rock videos are put together. And that's the way they're supposed to work on my head. So people wonder why they don't show rock videos on MTV anymore, and that's really the reason. It's because those two little animated creatures deconstructed it, and were there someone in charge, they probably wouldn't have let that happen.

DAVID: Who are the different audiences that you address in your books, and why do you think it's important to break down the concept of "us" and "them"?

DOUGLAS: When I wrote *Coercion*, which was my sixth or seventh book, I wrote that because I realized my other books were too advanced in some ways. Books like *Cyberia*, *Media Virus*, and *Playing the Future* are celebrating interactivity and our ability to become the authors in our own media space—the people who hack through the systems one way or another, spread their messages, and build their own reality. That was exciting to me. And there were thousands, or maybe hundreds of thousands, of people out there who were excited about this opportunity. But what I realized was that the majority of people in America not only didn't know that opportunity existed, but didn't even know why they should. Or that they were not conscious people looking to make a change in the world, but were, pretty much, unconscious people, at the mercy of the media messaging they were receiving.

I realized not everyone had gone through all the stages that my friends and I had gone through, that most people were still in the thrall of the mainstream media and the marketing universe. So what I needed to do was take a few steps back and say, Okay, everybody, you know there's this media space that we all live in, and certain people tend to dominate the messages that you get. And many of the places where you walk are owned by corporations who have a very vested interest in you buying things, and that you are constantly under some level of assault, of manipulation, by all these various forces.

While you can't walk around paranoid, constantly deconstructing everything coming at you, or you won't have a very fun existence, you should at least be able to live on a more level playing field. When you go into a retail or a corporate environment you have to understand that there are a lot of tools being used—from architecture to language and tone of voice, to lighting, to the very paths and surfaces you walk on, that are designed to either intimidate you or lead you to make certain choices and have certain behaviors.

DAVID: What do you mean when you say that your not counterculture, you're "pro-culture"?

DOUGLAS: What I'm trying to do in most of my work is break open the rhetoric that has allowed us to stagnate. There are certain patterns of language that reinforce notions about ourselves, and our relationship to the world, that may be more destructive than we realize. And that by keeping our language alive, by understanding what we're saying when we say it, we become a lot more aware of our conditioning. So if we who care about the future, we who care about the environment, if we accept that we are the counterculture, what have we accepted? We have accepted that we are literally against culture. So now we've cast ourselves as kind of the bad guys, the underdogs, the ones who are fighting against something. Well, what if we decided no, we are not the counterculture minority fighting against this great overculture. No, we are real people. We are culture. George Bush is the counterculture. *I* am the culture.

What is a culture? A culture is like yogurt. A culture is a living thing. This is not just a pun, or a metaphor. The culture is the life. It's the fertilization. It's the thing that actually propels us into a future. It's great. It's fecund, moist, real, growing, and diverse. It's in constant communication with itself and with other ones. It's wet, sexy, and real. That is what culture is. That's the petri dish. That's the yogurt. That's the moss on the side of the tree. That's the culture. Counterculture, to me, would mean, dry and sterile, unloving and unsexy. The counterculture are the people who want to kill culture. They're the people who want to prevent fertility and diversity, the exchange of ideas, fluids, psyches, and everything else.

So, by looking at words, and being willing to reclaim certain language, we can end up shifting our perspective on things tremendously. If you walk outside thinking of yourself as part of culture, then you start saying Well, what are the obstacles to culture? And you realize marketing is an obstacle to culture—because what do marketers do? Marketers try to make people feel unsexy and uncreative, so that they're dependent on a product to bestow some kind of sexiness or creativity upon them. Wow, so that's interesting. So what is Nike? What is Jordache? What are Levi's? Is that culture, or is that counterculture? Oh, now I'm arguing they're counter, they're against culture. So what's proculture? Is pro-culture the thrift store? Is pro-culture the Dead show? Is pro-culture sex with your girlfriend or wife? That's where culture lives. Pro-culture is nursery school. That's culture.

DAVID: How have Noam Chomsky and Marshall McLuhan influenced your perspective about the media?

DOUGLAS: I guess Chomsky influenced me in the sense that he certainly seemed to have a very clear vision on the interplay between money, power, media, messaging, and consciousness—and how tightly controlled this public relations-run spectator democracy is, and how that works. But I generally accept his work as a challenge to prove him wrong, to accept it as a gauntlet. In other words, here's how things are, or here's how things could be. Or here's one way of understanding this. So what I think is: Well, what am going to do about that? How am I going to arrest that? How am I going to help people recontextualize that? Where are the unseen triggers? Where are the unknown access points to power that Chomsky doesn't see?—but I, as I younger and more optimistic soul, can find and then share with others. So that's really the way he has impacted me most. It's like, okay, it's a really bad trip—but what I can I do to flip it?

McLuhan influenced me in that he helped me see that I come from a tradition. The tradition is not really one of media theory as much as a trickster tradition. There are some people around who, in their work, either tickle, cajole, or trick people into seeing things in new ways. The object of the game, for me, is to exist in this kind of liminal space between the way things are and the infinity of the way things could be, and help people open their minds to other possibilities. To help people across this chasm of uncertainty, so that they can live in a space of possibility.

Most people are afraid of possibility because they can't deal with a shifting reality, and they can't accept their own responsibility for the way things are. Most people cannot cope with a reality that works like a lucid dream, even though they happen to be living in one. So they would rather shut down, and they would rather agree to the consensus reality where they are victimized and unhappy, than accept a more plastic, open-source conception of reality where anything and everything is possible.

DAVID: How has your experience with psychedelics influenced your writing and your perspective on life?

DOUGLAS: I think it's very hard for anyone who has had psychedelic experiences to ever know how many of the insights that they might credit to psychedelia might have happened anyway. In other words, sometimes I think, Okay, it's all the acid. That you have one acid trip and, basically, you never come down from it—just the rest of life kind of comes up to it. (*laughter*) That there's a full categorical shift in the way you understand the world, that your perspective is forever changed, and that's it.

But I talk to a lot of people who've never had psychedelic experiences—at least chemical or plant-induced ones, or who have never even smoked pot—and they still seem just as aware of the fact that we're all living in reality tunnels, and that we chose different tunnels. And they can have moments of a broader perspective, where they see the way all these things are arbitrarily chosen, and that we've been living in a certain picture frame, and how you can pull out of that frame and see all these other possibilities. So the only thing I know for sure is that psychedelics provide a very tangible and experiential metaphor for the interchangeable contextual frames that we use to understand the world we live in.

For me, certainly, psychedelics were a valuable medicine—for a kid who, at nineteen, was really trapped in doing premed and becoming a doctor. I was going to do all this stuff I didn't really want to do. I actually made the decision to go be a theater person before I'd had any kind of drug experience, but it definitely helped. Afterward it helped me see the validity of that decision, and it helped me understand that all this recontextualizing I had been doing, all of the frames within frames. All of the theater that I was so interested in was not for the play, but for the proscenium arch itself, and for the ritual that was going on in the room. All of that had a shamanic history, and it was a bit more universally applicable than I had realized. It wasn't just something that happened in a theater; it's something that happens in the world at every moment. We are contextualizing and recontextualizing things based on assumptions.

DAVID: What do you think happens to consciousness after death?

DOUGLAS: I really have no idea. I would guess it goes on for a few minutes. You get to heaven, and you have those great life-after-life experiences, and then . . . (*laughter*) nothing! (*laughter*) I would think the only way for a person to have anything approaching consciousness after death—real death, when the body actually stops metabolizing, or there's just no metabolic processes and the brain is really dead dead—would be, while that person is alive, to learn to identify so profoundly with something other than his or her own ego so that when the self dies, the identification goes on. But most of us really believe in the illusion of individuality. We believe who we are is us.

So, in a sense, it blows the question out of the water, finally, because you say, Well, what happens to consciousness after death? Well, what happens to your consciousness after someone else's death? Not a hell of a lot. I mean, you might feel bad that they died, but their consciousness is gone, except for the part of it that's now in everybody else.

It certainly shouldn't be anybody's goal to extend consciousness after death, because that's still just a person trying to project their ego. But I would think a fringe benefit of developing true compassion for other people is that if you do identify with other people, other things, and other systems—things that are beyond the four walls of your own limited personal consciousness. Then the death of you or me is inconsequential. But I think that for 99.9999 percent of people the chances are that they just die.

DAVID: So you think death may be different for some people than other people?

DOUGLAS: Possibly. I would think that the only way out would be to get out while you're here. I don't think you can get out after you're dead.

DAVID: What is your perspective on the concept of God? Do you see any kind of teleology in evolution, and how has Judaism affected your views on spirituality?

DOUGLAS: I think we are no better than fungus on a rock hurling through cold and meaningless space, and that we were not put here with purpose by a supreme being. But I do believe that God is something that can evolve. I think of God as an emergent phenomenon, rather than a preexisting condition. So I think we can make God. I think we can conceive God. I think we can start to behave in godly ways. But I think God is something we build together. God is something we make. God is the result of love and ethical action, higher states of consciousness and coordinated action—things like that.

Not for many people, but for me, this teleology is absolutely consistent with the intention of Judaism—which was to get people to stop worrying about God, particularly idolatry, and start worrying about one another. What the Jews keep doing is smashing idols. They took idols off the Ark and left empty spaces there—literally empty spaces. And the empty spaces were protected, sometimes protected by cherubs—like on the top of the Ark of the Covenant. These are all empty places. That's why I wrote this book called *Nothing Sacred*. The idea is that this "nothing" is sacred, because only when you have an empty space can you create a dynamic or a voltage between people, and that's what makes God happen—this communing or community between people. These resonant living fields of interaction between loving human beings is what makes God possible. But I don't believe in God as a separate thing. I guess I'm a bit like Teilhard de Chardin with this idea of evolution groping toward complexity, rather than us being set in motion by a supreme being who wants us to return to him.

DAVID: How do you integrate your psychedelic experiences with your interest in Judaism? I think for a lot of people it's hard to understand how organized religion could be compatible with a psychedelic experience.

DOUGLAS: Organized religion isn't really compatible with any experience. I don't even see it as compatible with Judaism. Organized religion is not something I'm interested in, and it may not be compatible with a psychedelic experience or with the genuine expansion and development of consciousness. I don't look at Judaism as a religion. I look at Judaism as the process by which we get over religion. Most religions were born that way. Most religions were born as fresh breezes, as ways to lift people from the self-protective crouch of religion—whether it was Taoism lifting people out of Confucius, Judaism lifting people out of child-sacrifice to the god Molech, or Christianity trying to lift people out of the restricting rule sets of Jewish law into a more all-encompassing spontaneous experience of love. Each one of these new religions starts as a way to break the attachment to religion, to just live a good life, and they end up eventually turning into religions themselves. So it's that moment of liberation that you want to preserve, and that you want to keep reliving every time you get attached to something.

That's why the Jewish mythology is still very effective for me, because it's all about breaking out of slavery, the leaving Egypt, which in Hebrew is Mitzrayim. It's leaving the narrow place, the idolatrist place, by smashing the idols—which is what the plagues really are, the desecration of the Egyptian gods that we used to worship—and moving into a society that cherishes life. That's why they say "l 'chaim! l 'chaim," or "to life," and this is the central Jewish belief. That was an illegal sentiment in ancient Egypt, because that was a culture that worshiped death. You asked me what I thought happens after you die. Well, in Judaism it doesn't really matter what happens after you die, because you're here. What matters is what you do here, and if something happens after you die, you'll worry about it then. The reason to do great things here and now is not because you want to be rewarded after you die. The reason to great things here and now is because that is actually the most fun and meaningful way to live.

DAVID: Do you think that the human species is going to survive the next hundred years?

DOUGLAS: Yeah, a hundred years isn't so long. It really isn't. A hundred years is really just like three generations. Yeah, they'll still be people here. In a thousand years? Who knows? I don't think it's a matter of whether or not there's any people around. I think it's a matter of whether the civilizations that we built will be around. I think it's a matter of whether we can sustain a level of consciousness and complexity. I think they'll be people for a long time, even if they go back and live in tribes, and live off the old warehouses of Coke or whatever until they learn to make food again. I think there will be people for a long time, even after the environment gets bad. I mean, humans are fucking up the environment for sure, but Nature fucks up the environment even more sometimes, at least as far as people are concerned.

If Nature threw one good ice age or one good drought on us, we might be finished. We've been so lucky over the last few thousand years to have had this very temperate mild environment in which to live. That's why all us little mammals have been able to run around and do all this. Nature could whack us way harder than fluorocarbons are going to whack us. And, in that sense, it's almost important that we have a certain amount of AmGem, and Genentech, and other bizarre genetic science going on—where people are figuring out how to grow wheat on rocks, or soy on the ocean, because we just may have to. And we have to, not just because we are fucking things up so badly, but because Nature really can turn on a dime, and the environment can change profoundly in a half century. We've seen it happen before. The Sahara desert was fertile at one time. The deserts of Iraq were the most fertile part of the world that we even knew about. So things shift. Things move around.

DAVID: How do you envision the future evolution of the human race?

DOUGLAS: I don't know. I hope people become more conscious and aware of each other. If there's any real plot to be followed, then I'd hope for the human race to become a more coordinated being. Right now people don't want to coordinate because they think it would mean the loss of individuality. But what they don't realize is that the only way they're ever going to find their individuality is by coordinating. So it's not a matter of becoming the superorganism, as defined by the prefascist philosophers, or Hegel or those guys.

It's not a superorganism. But there is an organizational level that we're capable of. Rather than a collective unconscious, there's a way to have a collective consciousness. I think the only reason why people don't have it is because they are afraid of it. They're afraid of the loss of privacy. They're afraid of losing what they think of as their self. But what people are going to have to slowly learn—and it may take thousands of years to do this—is that the self separated from human community doesn't even exist.

The self only exists in relationship to other people—just like a Web site only exists in its links to other places, or from other places really. So eventually people will see their way through what looks like a paradox to them now, and instead see it as the crucial dynamic through which people can evolve into something greater than the little, isolated, lonely, puny intelligences they are today.

. . .

DAVID: What gives you hope?

DOUGLAS: Interactions with happy people. As long as I can have a meaningful interaction with another person and experience the creation of joy from what wasn't there before, I have hope—because it means that humans are still capable of manufacturing love and joy where there wasn't any before. Not finding light, but doing light. As long people can do that, then I still have some faith in the relatively infinite capability of people to re-create reality on their own terms.

Quantum Sociology and Neuropolitics

An Interview with Robert Anton Wilson

Robert Anton Wilson is a writer and philosopher with a huge cult following. He is the author of over thirty-five popular fiction and nonfiction books dealing with such themes as quantum mechanics, the future evolution of the human species, weird unexplained phenomena, conspiracy theories, synchronicity, the occult, altered states of consciousness, and the nature of belief systems. His books explore the relationship between the brain and consciousness and the link between science and mysticism, with wit, wisdom, and personal insights. Comedian George Carlin said, "I have learned more from Robert Anton Wilson than I have from any other source." Dr. Wilson earned his doctorate in psychology from Paideia University and was the associate editor of Playboy *magazine. He is perhaps best known for coauthoring the science-fiction trilogy* Illuminatus! *Some of his popular nonfiction books include* Cosmic Trigger, Prometheus Rising, Quantum Psychology, Everything Is Under Control, *and* TSOG: The Thing

That Ate the Constitution, *a satirical commentary about the loss of constitutional rights in America.*

* * *

DAVID: What is "maybe logic"?

BOB: A label that got stuck on my ideas by filmmaker Lance Bauscher. I guess it fits. I certainly recognize the central importance in my thinking—or in my stumbling and fumbling efforts to think—of non-Aristotelian systems. That includes von Neumann's three-valued logic [true, false, maybe], Rapoport's four-valued logic [true, false, indeterminate, meaningless], Korzybski's multi-valued logic [degrees of probability], and also Mahayana Buddhist paradoxical logic [It "is" A, it "is" not A, it "is" both A and not A, it "is" neither A nor not A].

But, as an extraordinarily stupid fellow, I can't use such systems until I reduce them to terms a simple mind like mine can handle, so I just preach that we'd all think and act more sanely if we had to use "maybe" a lot more often. Can you imagine a world with Jerry Falwell hollering "Maybe Jesus 'was' the son of God and maybe he hates Gay people as much as I do"—or every tower in Islam resounding with "There 'is' no God except maybe Allah and maybe Muhammad 'is' his prophet"?

. . .

DAVID: You once appeared in a photo on the front page of the *New York Times* receiving medical marijuana in front of City Hall in Santa Cruz. How has marijuana helped you to deal with the symptoms of post-polio syndrome, and what are your thoughts about the political debate over medical marijuana?

BOB: First of all, I've had post-polio syndrome (PPS) ever since I recovered from the polio. Most of my life, from age five to sixty, the symptoms remained minor—annoying foot spasms at times, leg pains when standing in long lines. After sixty, the pains got worse, not just on the long lines at airports, but even on comparatively short lines in banks or markets. At sixty-eight, the pains got more frequent and more intense, even when I didn't have to stand on lines. Then I started falling down at unexpected times, and the pain became even more excruciating.

This happens sooner or later to most polio survivors and often hits some in their forties, so I feel lucky to have had sixty good years. Current theory attributes PPS to muscle damage during the polio; I evidently walked around with only half of my muscles for over six decades. My doctor recommended megadoses of vitamins and nutrients, to repair the damaged muscles as far as possible, and marijuana to stop the pain. I get the marijuana free from WAMM, a group of neighbors and friends with other medical problems that pot seems to help—muscular sclerosis, AIDS, cancer, and a few others.

It has worked wonders for me. Not only does it kill pain, but the high also increases general good humor and optimism. I sincerely believe that optimism—or "faith healing" or "Christian Science" or "mind over molecules" or "spontaneous remission" or whatever you call this—works better with pot than without it.

The political debate? To my admittedly simple mind that fines down to: Do I trust my doctor, and my own brain and my senses, or do I trust a Tsar three thousand miles away who can only know better than us if he has direct guidance from God? Well, I don't believe in mystical Tsarism; I prefer constitutional democracy. The Tsar does not seem any more infallible to me than the Pope, and I refuse to let him sentence me to a life of continuous agonizing pain. The Tsar's goon squad keeps trying to shut WAMM down, and if they succeed, I'll just buy my weed from back-alley dealers.

Meanwhile, I've worked at learning to walk for the third time, and at seventy-two can report considerable progress . . . .which the pessimists will call wishful thinking, I suppose. At least, I've gotten to a point where I only spend part of each day in a wheelchair. At the worst, three years ago, I spent the whole day there.

. . .

DAVID: Where do you think the human race should be focusing its scientific efforts right now?

BOB: Biotechnology. I've said and written for thirty years that the health and longevity researchers seem on the outskirts of major breakthroughs. These breakthroughs now seem less than ten years away, maybe only five. Of course, Bush has banned the most promising areas of research, but he can only enforce that Tsarist infophobia in the U.S. The research will continue in the civilized, or nonTsarist, nations.

DAVID: What is your perspective on telepathy, psychic phenomena, and synchronicity?

BOB: That whole area seems enormously intriguing but badly in need of heavy doses of maybe logic. I find most of the debate weary, flat, stale, and unprofitable, because both sides seem overly dogmatic. If they took every "is" out of every sentence and replaced it with a "maybe," they might begin to make sense. Of course, the dogmatic deniers seem much sillier to me than the believers, because the believers at least use probability theory with some skill. They also do scientific investigations which the deniers shun "as the devil fears holy water." Have you ever heard of any scientific investigations by the Commitee for Scientific Investigation of Claims of the Paranormal? I haven't. They rely entirely on abstract monkish logic, innuendo, invective, smear, and out-right libel.

DAVID: What are your thoughts regarding the possibility that people can communicate with extraterrestrial or extradimensional intelligences while in certain altered states of consciousness?

BOB: I estimate a 99 percent probability that we can, in such states, communicate with intelligences seemingly not our own. I've done it. I still remain unsure, how-ever, if the Higher Intelligences contacted dwell in outer space, in other dimen-sions, or in circuits of my own brain not identifiable as "me" or "my ego." I'd love to live in an open democratic society where research on this became legal and widely published. Creating such an open society remains a major goal of the Guns and Dope Party. We favor total freedom for orgonomic medicine, LSD research, cloning, and every other alternative that the Tsarists have made illegal.

DAVID: How has your use of psychedelics influenced your writings and your view of the world?

BOB: Well, I've moved from atheism to agnosticism, with somewhat pantheis-tic leanings. I just don't want to sound too pretentious about it. I don't claim to know anything about any gods or goddesses, but I suspect a good deal. I suspect that some form of "divinity" probably exists, but it seems to me immanent and decentralized, not transcendent and authoritarian. More like Internet than like a monarchy. Aleister Crowley said "Every man and every woman is a star." We in the Guns and Dope Party have changed that to "Every man and every woman is a Tsar." That not only signifies scientific and political freedom, but something in the neigborhood of Vedic identification of the true self with divinity, or at least the Quaker "inner light."

DAVID: How has marijuana helped you with your creative writing process?

BOB: I have always had strong tendencies toward compulsive rewriting, polish-ing, refining etcetera, and marijuana has intensified that. In fact, these days I seldom stop fine-tuning my prose until editors remind me about deadlines. As Paul Valery said, "A work of art is never completed, only abandoned," and I regard even my nonfiction as a kind of art.

DAVID: Are you still as optimistic about the future now as you were when you wrote *Cosmic Trigger*?

BOB: More so, but only because I don't think politics has as much importance as most people imagine. The real changes occur first in pure science, then in technology, then in social forms; the politicians then run around in front of the parade and pretend they're leading it—like Al Gore claiming he invented Internet. If you only look at Dubya and Osama, the world looks like a Dark Age madhouse, but look at biotech and computer science, and space colonies and a much more hopeful scenario dawns. Politics always represents organized info-phobia, science represents infophilia, and over a span of generations, infophilia always wins out.

DAVID: What is infophobia and infophilia?

BOB: I coined the term "infophobia" to synthesize Dr. Timothy Leary's work on neuropsychology and Claude Shannon's mathematical theory of information. Basically infophobia represents an attitude of fear toward certain types of signals. Some people are afraid of TV. Some are afraid of Internet. Some are afraid of learning foreign languages, etcetera.

Infophilia represents the opposite extreme—the desire to learn many symbol systems, and use them for fun and profit. Primarily, I feel that anything that accelerates the flow of information helps solve all of our problems; anything that jams the signals, distorts them, warps them, or just tells flat lies, increases all of our problems. I consider this a scientific foundation for the first amendment to the Constitution, and for civil liberties in general. Or, as Paul Krassner summarized it, "Fuck Censorship!"

DAVID: Do you think that the human species is going to survive the next 100 years, or do you think we're going to drive ourselves into extinction?

BOB: Maybe we'll destroy ourselves and maybe we'll achieve what Bucky Fuller called total success in Universe. I see no social profit, and no personal psychological profit [except to masochists], in assuming preordained failure and general disaster. I assume the unknown future remains unknown, so why not try for the best we can imagine?

DAVID: What do you think is the biggest threat to the human species?

BOB: Stupidity, especially in the form of those "faith-based organizations" so beloved by Tsarists. All my hope centers around research-based organizations.

DAVID: Assuming that we do survive, how do you envision the future of the human race?

BOB: Mix Dr. Timothy Leary's SMIILE scenario—Space Migration + Intelligence Increase + Life Extension—with Trotsky's Perpetual Revolution, and/or Jeffersons's "revolution every ten years," and serve piping hot. With relish.

DAVID: What do you think happens to consciousness after death?

BOB: I haven't died yet, so I can't speak with any assurance about that. My guesses remain guesses. I grant equal respect to the opinions of all men, women, and ostriches, but no matter how sure any of them sound, I still suspect them of guessing, just like me. I wish they would use that liberating word "maybe" more often in their speculations.

If I must flounder around in metaphysics, "the great Serbonian bog where armies whole have sunk," I know of only five possibilities: (1) heaven, (2) hell, (3) reincarnation, (4) "union with God" or some other entity a lot like "God," and (5) oblivion. Only (1) heaven seems frightening to me; an eternity of "bliss" with nobody around but Christians—such messmates as Pat Robertson, Jerry Falwell, and others of that ilk—really sounds awful. There's even a sinister rumor that the streets "are guarded" (brrrrrr!) by the United States Marines.

Fortunately, according to the leading proponents of this model, I can't get sent there because I don't believe in Christ. Oh, goody.

Of course (2) hell sounds almost as bad, but it has its good points. Everybody I admire from all history will get sent there, so the conversation should prove lively and stimulating. Besides, I find it impossble to believe that "God" (i.e., the assumed "Mind" behind the universe) suffers from the kind of sadistic psychosis necessary to delight in eternal torture, and if "He" (or She or It) does have that kind of nasty streak, well, as a part-time Buddhist, I'll just have to forgive "Him" (or Her or It). I've started practicing for this even-tuality by forgiving all the people who've made this planet a good simulation of hell.

(3) The reincarnation model seems cheerier and somewhat less goofy than these morbid notions, so it doesn't bother me. I even wish I could believe in it.

(4) "Union with God" seems a great idea to me, if I understand it, like an acid trip that never ends. Now, that's what I'd prefer, if I have any choice in the matter.

Finally, there's (5) the oblivion model. I've never understood why so many people, like Woody Allen, find oblivion totally dreadful. If you're oblivious, that implies no experience and, of course, no experiencer either. How can you fear or even resent what you will never experience? It seems to me that only an advanced case of narcissism, or a mangled confusion of the map with the territory, can explain the bum rap that oblivion gets from most people. We all go there every night, between dreams, and it doesn't hurt at all.

DAVID: What is your perspective on God, and do you see any teleology in evolution?

BOB: Well, since the only kind of divinity that makes sense to me seems decentralized, I assume it must possess what cybernetic theory calls "redun-dance of potential control"—maximum feedback all around. In organisms, groups (flocks, herds), machines and groups of machines, that implies change and evolution, which in a feedback system means learning, and that seems like a kind of teleology.

By the way, Norbert Weiner pointed that out way back in 1948 in his book *Cybernetics: Control and Communication in the Animal and the Machine*, and the whole Internet revolution dates from that, but I guess most biologists felt daunted by his mathematics. They still seem to think we would have all remained amoebas except for "copying errors." I'll believe that when I believe that if we all threw our junk in the same field for 4 billion years it would accidentally organize itself into a jet airliner.

. . .

DAVID: What gives you hope?

BOB: The research of psychlogist John Barefoot, which indicates that optimists live roughly 20 percent longer than pessimists. Why should I make myself miserable with gloomy thoughts, cut my life by one-fifth, and miss out on the biotech revolution, just to become fashionable with the New York intelligentsia?

Napalm, Silly Putty, and Human Nature

An Interview with George Carlin

George Carlin is a writer, stand-up comedian, actor, and proponent of free speech. His irreverent, controversial, and thought-provoking stand-up routines have gotten him arrested, earned him four Grammy Awards, and tested the limits of free speech in America. Carlin has had numerous successful albums, four of which went gold. His first album, FM & AM, *won a Grammy Award for Best Comedy Album in addition to its gold status. His album* Class Clown *featured the recorded debut of the "Seven Words You Can Never Say on Television" routine—which resulted in a legal battle that went all the way to the Supreme Court. Carlin has written and performed in thirteen HBO specials, starred as a cab driver in the Fox television sitcom* The George Carlin Show, *and has appeared in many films, such as* Dogma, Prince of Tides, *and* Jersey Girl. *He received a Hollywood Walk of Fame star at the corner of Vine and Selma streets. Some of his albums include* A Place for My Stuff, Playin' with Your Head,

Parental Advisory: Explicit Lyrics, *and* Complaints and Grievances. *He is also the author of several books, including* Sometimes a Little Brain Damage Can Help, Brain Droppings, Napalm & Silly Putty, *and* When Will Jesus Bring the Porkchops?

* * *

DAVID: Can you talk a little bit about your creative process?

GEORGE: Here's how my creative system works. I'm going to talk about my own case, although I sometimes think it applies to all of people who create, and it probably does. But I can best speak about my own situation, what happens over the years, if you're curious, you read, and try to absorb and soak up information. I quit school when I was sixteen, yet I had a good mind, so I had the need to educate myself, and fill myself with just plain facts and information. I found it interesting to learn secondhand all about Shakespeare, and then some of the classics. Not that I know much about them, but I know the references when I see them.

When you quit school at an early age, I think you have a lifelong need to show the world—and maybe yourself—that you're really smart after all. So there was this drive to interpret the world. Most art is an interpretation of the world around the "artist," whether it's in paint or in music. I'm not trying to sound grand here with this overuse of the word artist, but I think there's no other good word for it. So I'll use it, and risk sounding somewhat self-important. It's an interpretation of the world around you. It's the world through your filter. You re-create the world and say, Here's the world as it comes through me.

Now I'm sixty-six, and over the years I noticed that what occurs as you age is an accumulation of information, data, knowledge, and what I'm going to call the matrix of the mind. There's just a rich, textured, field of information and impressions that have been all networked by the brain. The neurons are always working, creating new neural networks, and working out connections between things. You don't even have to work on that. So a person who's in his sixties has a much richer interpretation of life as he sees it today than he did when he was twenty, because at twenty he had less in his matrix. It just wasn't there experientially.

So that's what happened to me over the years. I developed and matured as an individual/creative person, and my writing matured as well. First of all, my technique improved. For one thing, I got better at the actual writing. And secondly, the comparisons, the information that comes in now is compared against this richer field in my brain. So it has more life to it. There's more discovery and reality in it for me than there was when it was a little more simplistic.

Now, in terms of actually functioning day to day, here's what I do. If you buy that brain hemisphere theory—and there's some question about it now—then

I'm right-brained, because I have this free-flowing, creative side. But I'm also extremely left-brained. I'm very organized. I have what you would call obsessive-compulsive tendencies. Now, I don't have a problem with it. A shrink once taught me to use this to my benefit, not to my detriment. Because it can hurt a person's life. It can interfere with life. But it can greatly benefit you if it's channeled correctly.

So what I've always done is try to channel my compulsive need to have order in my physical world and in my work. The more organized my files are—they're now computer files, although they used to be hard pieces of paper—the more I have to draw from. Because you don't remember—certainly not consciously—everything you ever heard. So you write things down. I write notes down all the time—anything I think of that has promise for me. Anything that I think fits into my world of what I want to comment on, or know about, I write it down. If I'm in a car, I'll use a little hand recorder.

Then, regularly—every couple of weeks—I harvest these accumulated notes. Every two weeks or so I put them in the proper places in their files—whether it's under "animals," "colors," "clothing," "male/female," "race," "politics," "driving," or "cats and dogs." These things go in their proper files, and as you put them in, you see the rest of the file, and it makes an impression on you—even if you're not consciously trying for it. It goes through the system once again. It goes through the neural system, and so these things just become richer and richer.

Then files have a way of maturing on their own, to where I really love it. I look at the thing, and I say, This is good. I got to tell people this. Boy, wait'll they hear this. That's the impulse behind the showoff—wait'll they hear this. So I get that feeling, and I know I'm ready, or sometimes not, because I don't have enough time in my shows. I have an hour and twenty minutes that I do. I do an HBO show every two years, and that's an hour's worth. So if you start out with an hour's worth of stuff, by the time you get finished with it in a couple of years, it's an hour and a half, and you don't get to do it all.

So there's this great surplus. And I just write all the time, in some form or another—whether it's writing notes, harvesting the notes, or taking things from the files and actually doing the writing. That is what I do, and then I channel it on to the stage. The stage goes into HBO and CDs, and now I have this book outlet. I've done two books that have done very well, and I'm writing a third one now. It's called *When Will Jesus Bring the Porkchops?* and it's another collection, but this the best one. I guess, unintentionally, I saved a lot of the best stuff from the first two books. I mean, I'm proud of those first two books, but I know I saved a lot of real gold, and now I'm going to get to use it in this book. So that's the process.

DAVID: How has a sense of justice motivated you?

GEORGE: Comedy is grievances. It's a recitation of grievances—whether they're inconsequential, superficial—like "my wife shops too much," or "kids today," all those old-fashioned themes—or, if it's deeper, and somewhat more thoughtful, about social imbalance and inequities, and the folly of human behavior. It's usually a complaint. So I think inherent in some of that complaint is a sense of wanting more balance, more fairness, and I guess that can translate to justice.

I'm sure there are examples in certain comedy we can find that would be specific to justice itself, in the broader sense of justice. Then there's a lot, which is less defined, but leans in that direction—of things that look to redress imbalances and inequities. It's all about dissatisfaction. My comedy is about being very dissatisfied with my fellow humans and with the people in this country. Basically I think the human species is a failed species.

I mean, we had a great opportunity, with great gifts. We had this wonderful intellect that raised us up, that gave us the ability to objectify and say, I am here. It is out there. It hasn't been used for the wrong purposes, but the emphasis has gone in the wrong direction. We were given two great things that distinguished us from other animals, or made us special—and that was the ability to cooperate, but then we also had the natural lower-brain need to compete. So competition and cooperation together are what made this species leap, leap, leap forward. But now, I think, competition far outweighs the ability to cooperate.

There's no real enlightened self-interest. There's no foresight. There's no planning. I mean, there's a modicum of it you see. They'll talk about this or that five years down time, but no one is sitting around making concrete plans for things that will happen. They wait for them to happen. They wait for emergencies. They wait for near emergencies. Then it's patchwork, and then there's no money for it. Then some other group has a complaint. It's just that the competing interests prevent a real, honest beneficent development of the species. I'm talking now partly about the culture, apart from the species, as I mention some of those things.

There are two things in our culture, I think, that lead us astray. I think we turned everything over—mankind in general, not just our culture—to the high priests and the traders. Everything was turned over to those who wanted to control us through mysterious beliefs. And we had an impulse to connect to the universe. They knew that. The clergy, in general, were very, very devious and clever. They knew people had a need to connect to the "One" of some sort. They know there's this longing to rejoin nature, because we now feel outside of nature. We objectify. We say, Man against nature. Well, that's absurd, because man is obviously a part of nature.

So when we distinguish ourselves, we set up this battle. And they knew we have underneath that a longing to correct that, to reunite. So they twisted and distorted that into these narrow, superstitious belief systems, where you have this invisible man in the sky who's judging you, going to put you in fiery place.

They manipulated people—some of whom were simply weaker, and some of whom were just easy to manipulate. The traders, the businesspeople, the commercial, the merchant class, they turned everything into acquisition and ownership—and, to oversimplify, "having the latest thing."

People have material needs, but you don't need a deodorant for every different day of the week. You don't need 400 varieties of mustard. There are over 400 different varieties of mustard that some place in Menlo Park, I believe, has at some supermarket there. I counted 151 different choices in the cat food section alone, forgetting dogs. At the car wash I counted over one hundred twenty separate ways of changing the smell in your car, whether it was beads, or a little sachet thing, or oils, or sprays, or charms that you hang from the mirror. One hundred twenty of them, if you counted all the scents and all these delivery systems. This is what I call too many choices. There are too many choices in America.

These are the trivial things that we're given. We're given many choices to distract us from the fact that our real choices have been diminished in number. Two political parties. Maybe three or four large banks now. Credit card companies, just a couple, a handful. Newspapers, reduced. Ownership of media, reduced, down to five or six big companies now. Big stock brokerage firms, reduced in number. All of these important things we have less choice. Then we're distracted with these frivolous choices: 21 flavors of ice cream, 35 flavors of popcorn. You see specialty shops with 35 flavors of popcorn, like chocolate-walnut popcorn. These are absurd distractions from what we are doing to ourselves, because we engage in this. It's not really all imposed. So that's my feeling.

. . .

DAVID: Why do you think people create taboos, and why do you think it's important to break taboos—and find humor in many of the things that a lot of people wouldn't dare joke about?

GEORGE: I'm not well read enough, but I've heard passing references to the effect that there are taboos in all societies, and in primitive societies. It sounds like it's related to the superstitious impulse behind certain religious things—like there's a need to have things that are out of reach, beyond, or, in this case, unmentionable. I think it's important to break taboos for the same reason it's important to break laws and rules—because either you're a slave to them, or you're taking matters into your hands.

No one has to come see my shows who doesn't like me talking about white Christians. They are free not buy a ticket. They're free to leave at any time. So I'm not imposing anything on anyone. Therefore I feel free to cross the line. I've found out most of these things about my own comedy in looking back—either a year, two years, five years, or ten years—and finding out what it is I do. I don't set out with these things in mind that are now ways I have of analyzing, but I look for where the line is drawn on any subject. I look for where the line is drawn by these taboos, and I deliberately cross that line. I try to do it with wit and humor, and good rational and logical underpinning.

I like good ideas. I don't want just do something for its own sake to bother people, but if I can bother them with a logical argument about something they have agreed to in society simplistically—like children are sacred, the cult of the child, this cult of professional parenthood, and of course religion, and respect for policemen and the law, and all of these untouchable areas. I like attacking those beliefs, but with good sound thinking, and an unusual approach. If I can find a new direction into an old subject, that's what you're up there for.

Now, all of these socially critical aspects of the work are secondary to the main thing you're up there for—that's to entertain. And that means two things to me. Not just getting laughs, which I love. I love big jokes, and I try to have good big fat home-run jokes. All of them. All the time. Fast. Lots of them. But when you're not joking, you can also still engage their imaginations with thought and dazzle them verbally—by showing jazz riffs and verbal flights and passages that have an entertainment value of their own, that people aren't even fully aware of. So the job is entertaining and engaging imagination. Laughter is part of it. Thought is part of it—not making people think. I never set out to do that. Sometimes interviewers will ask me, Do you like to make people think with your shows? I say, no, I like them to know I'm thinking. Then I like to show them that. And they take and do what they want. But, generally, I try to make it entertaining.

Primitive societies, or social groupings, had shamans, and some of them even more recent in time. Shamans were tricksters. There was a tradition of the trickster, and the trickster was a clown, a humorous fellow. His task was to trick the gods, to humor the gods into laughing, so that there was access to the divine—because laughter is a moment when we are completely ourselves. It's that disarming moment, or disarmed moment, when something strikes us, and we laugh without even knowing it, trying it, or being able to prevent it. It just happens. No one is more himself than the moment when he's laughing at a joke. It's at those moments that people's defenses go down, and that's when you can slip in a good idea. So if the good joke carries a good idea, the entrance is open at that moment. I learned that one time and saw how it definitely applied. And I've always been kind of charmed by that notion.

DAVID: You've said that America's only public metaphor for problem-solving is declaring war. What is your perspective on the American government's War on Drugs and War on Terrorism?

GEORGE: I've done some writing about the whole metaphor of war. I mean, they have a War on Trash, a War on Cancer. Some of them are absurd. I've kept track of them. I have about thirty of them, and I wish I could think of some of the more trivial ones. But let's keep it with America for now. America is a kind of friendly aggressor. We've been very aggressive at taking over the world with our culture in order to impose our business structure on the world, for free market capitalism. Apparently, it's one of the better systems, by the way, for getting more things to the most people. I can't deny that. Some of these distortions have their own oddly beneficial aspects to them, and I don't know enough about things to pull that apart properly.

But let me just say that the white Europeans have always exploited the dark, the black, the brown, tan people. The northern hemisphere has always plundered the southern hemisphere. And there are interesting, or sound, historical reasons why this happened. But it doesn't gainsay the fact that I think there's a highly developed ability, for want of a better word, to dominate others and use them for our profit. We want to impose democracy where we can, and we want to impose market capitalism, because, basically, I think we want to sell refrigerators.

I think we look at a place like Bosnia and we say, you know something, if these people all had fucking laptops, and cell phones, and microwaves, we could sell a lot of merchandise. I think that's in there somewhere, this need to conquer and overcome other people in order to have them become part of the marketplace. I really don't think there's a lot of ideology to it. I really don't think it has anything to do with "spreading democracy" and giving people "free choice," because there are no free choices. The whole system is rigged. The whole system is rigged against the Little Man. There is an ownership class in America. I call them the People Who Own Everything.

And people say, Oh, your conspiracy thing. Listen, don't be making fun of the word "conspiracy." It has meaning. Powerful people have convergent interests. They don't always need a meeting to decide on something. They inhabit the same gentlemen's clubs or golf clubs. They sit on the same boards of directors. They're on the same board of trustees at the university. They all have this common ownership background of the American enterprise, and they are very few in number. They control everything, and they do whatever they want. They have a system called the two-party system that keeps the people at bay. They give them microwaves. They give them fannypacks. They give them sneakers with lights in the heels. They give them Dustbusters, and whoopee cushions, to keep them distracted, and keep them just calm enough that they're not going to try something.

Now, of course, the ownership class has all these fucking guns, and weapons, and helmets, and radios, and radars, and night vision and everything— so there's never any hope anymore of a real revolution. They got that covered. But for a long time they just kept it all down by giving the people just what they needed, and then running things themselves. They give them this illusion of choice between liberals and conservatives. But you'll notice that anyone who's an extreme liberal or an extreme conservative is marginalized. They're not on mainstream television. That's why Fox has tried, I guess, so hard to push a very hard right-wing conservative line and make it commonplace in America to be hearing those things. Right-wing radio does that.

But essentially, the real freaks, on either side, are not heard from. They are marginalized. The Ralph Naders of the world, for instance. They give them a modicum of time to make it appear like he has a slight voice. But he's ridiculed. They marginalize you by calling you a kook. Or it used to be a communist, or fanatic, or whatever the word is they use when you cross the line, and you really are radical. And radical just means root; it comes from the word "root." So it's root thinking. If you're a radical thinker, they have no place for you.

So they control this center, and they keep the people relatively quiet. Even a Clinton—I mean, you say, well, what about Clinton? He was very oriented toward people's needs and everything. Yeah, but he was backed by the Bilderbergers. I mean, they have bend in them. The ownership class has a flexibility. People say, Well, I say people have no voice. And they say, What about the antiwar movement and Vietnam? Yeah, how long did it take? And it didn't happen until the ownership class decided it was no longer in their interest. Same thing with the civil rights movement. They decided this is no longer in our interest to maintain this system. Let's bend a little. And they bend a little.

DAVID: What is your perspective on our vanishing constitutional rights in America?

GEORGE: First of all, people are dreaming if they think they have rights. They've never had rights. There's no such thing. They say God-given rights. If you ask them, Where do these rights come from? They say, Well, they came from God. They're God-given rights. And I say, Well, let me tell you this. The American Bill of Rights has ten stipulations. The British has thirteen. The Dutch, the Germans, the Belgians—all of them have different numbers of rights in their constitutional guarantees, different numbers of rights. Why would God give different numbers, of different rights, to different people, in different places? Amusement? Oversight? What's going on?

So clearly these things have nothing to do with a God, if there even is one. These are privileges, which are temporarily granted to the people to keep them placated so that the market economies, and market constitutional systems— the parliamentary or president, whatever kind of democratic institutions they are, parliamentary or otherwise—so that they can function. And the people are happy. There's a balance. And that's the way things are handled, but rights can be taken away. So they're not really rights, if they can be taken away by human beings. The Japanese Americans who went to the camps in 1941 had rights, but suddenly someone says, Well, not that one they don't have. Lincoln suspended habeas corpus.

It's capricious and arbitrary, and people are wrong when they think they have rights. I say, If you think you has rights, you is wrong. I've written a thing on this; it's going to be in the next book. In fact, it might even be in the next HBO show. It's what I call the "Patriotic Suite." I have this seven-part thing, that's all about red, white, and blue, swearing on the Bible, taking off your hat, saluting the flag, and all this stuff. And one of them is about rights. There has been a long progression of erosion of Americans' stated rights—or the way they're interpreted in the Bill of Rights in the Constitution—long time cutting away, cutting away, cutting away.

Now, it has taken a huge leap with the Patriot Act. The Ashcrofts, the disciplinarian, authoritarian, strict, Calvinist, Christian mind-set is in a position of power now, and they're just shredding that Bill of Rights. Not that it wasn't under attack before they came along, but they've really jumped on the bandwagon with this 9/11. I would not be surprised if 9/11, if that whole thing—and this will get all the anticonspiracy people interested—were not staged by the Bush-Carlyle Group empire. The Bush empire, the dynasty, that whole, entire secret society sort of ownership. I don't know. I'm clearly in over my head here, because it's a thing that I think about sometimes, but it would make a lot of sense for them. Here's the *New York Times*. On the front page today, "United States Uses Terror Law"—that would be the Patriot Act—"to Pursue Crimes from Drugs to Swindling." So they're branching out now.

You asked about the War on Drugs. Obviously, drugs represent a form of freedom and personal choice. So here's one thing where you have no freedom of choice. You're told you can do this, but you can't do that. You can't drink after 2:00 A.M. in this state. But you can drive across the border, and you can drink until 4:00 A.M. in that state. There are all these forms of control. People think they have freedom of choice in this country. Here's your fucking choice— paper or plastic? That's your choice. Will this be charge or cash? That's your choice. Visa or MasterCard? Coke or Diet Coke? Smoking or nonsmoking? Window or aisle? Those are your fucking choices America. You have no choices. They're imposed.

DAVID: Some of your humor stems from a playful deconstruction of language. Why do you think it's important to reflect on our use of language, and how do you think our use of language affects our view of reality?

GEORGE: Well, we think in language. We think in words. Language is the landscape of thought. It's how thought is realized and, obviously, how we communicate ideas. It's how we individuate ourselves, how we are human individuals that are separate from others. And there's some virtue to it, in separation, earlier I was saying. We're completely at odds with nature, and that's true. But it is important to understand your identity, and your place in the scheme of things, and in the universe even. So that all comes from having language available for thought and expression.

The language attraction in me came from the family. It's very heredity. My mother's father, Dennis Bearey, was a New York City policeman at the turn of the last turn of the century, the 1900s coming in. He was self-educated. He had quit school, come to America, young, and taught himself. During his adult years, he wrote out most of the works of Shakespeare longhand, copying them from a book, because of the joy the language gave him.

So that's a pretty dramatic expression of appreciation for language. He was Irish, and the Irish have that gift of, perhaps, you know a little bit disproportionately to some other cultures—although there are great writers everywhere. But the Irish really have the gift of gab. The ratio of poets, playwrights, and authors to mechanics is much different in Ireland. So he had that. He gave that to my mother. She got it hereditarily, and it was reinforced at home, because at dinnertime they would discuss—not all the time, I guess—but they would often discuss language, and Shakespeare's use of it.

My mother was very careful with me to point out good writing. She would call me into her room. I'd bring her her newspaper, and she was tired after work. She'd be reading, and she'd say, "George, come here. Look at this. Look at this word. Look how this sentence *cuts*"—she was dramatic the way she spoke—"this sentence just *cuts* right through." So I had the genetic marker for it, and then she encouraged it by pointing out the joy in savoring the graceful and incisive use of language.

So, to me, language is just my instrument. I have the computer open here. I was working on the book, and I just have the greatest joyful feeling when I'm altering a sentence. When I'm fixing a paragraph, it's just like some kind of union with something. I don't understand it. I know there's a joy. I have a woman in my life, Sally Wade, and we have a joyful wonderful life together. And that's a separate form of joy, being with Sally, enjoying each other. But being at that computer, with the words, is just . . . I don't know, somehow, it goes to my foundation.

Yeah. Boy, when they came up with being able to highlight a whole paragraph and move it somewhere else—holy shit, did they change the world! I mean, you say, wait a minute, this goes at the end. I can't imagine how people did that with yellow tablets, or dipping a pen or a quill. And these great things that came out of what must have been such a long laborious process. Having to do something over, or delete something, and put an insert, and all; you know, it must have been a mess. I did it, and I don't remember how messy it was. But, boy, my writing changed qualitatively, not just quantitatively, with my use of the word processor. I noticed that the thinking and the writing, as they are combined, became more complex and more interesting. And I'll use that word "textured" again. It just really changed the quality of what it was, not just how fast I could do it, or how much I do. So I'm glad you know. Obviously you know that.

DAVID: You said before that you're not trying to get people to think in your comedy routines. However, I still wonder if you aren't sometimes trying to educate people. Is this ever part of your intention?

GEORGE: Well, let me cop to one thing that I'm aware of. Someone once said, If you scratch a cynic, you'll find a disappointed idealist. That really rang a bell with me—because I recognized that, within me, there is this flame of wishing it were better, wishing people had better lives, that there was more of an authentic sharing and harmony with nature. So these complaints, this thing that sometimes reads as anger to people, is largely a discontent, a dissatisfaction, sometimes a disappointment in what we have allowed, passively or actively, to happen to us, as a species and as a culture.

I know that I would have been a good teacher. Had I gone on and had a continuing formal education, I would have made a good teacher. I would have made a good trial lawyer, because I like persuasion. I like the art of forensics, of using language and thought to shape . . . I guess we're talking about to shape other people's thinking. Sure. I mean, it has such a potentially pretentious ring to it, to me, that I shrink from it. But words are words, and descriptions are descriptions. You have seen something that is true.

Someone recently—a woman at a dentist's office—gave me, not quite a thesis, but a paper that her son wrote at Berkeley, comparing certain aspects of Kierkegaard to some things I said about religion and politics. And boy, I mean, I was a little flattered to be thrown into philosophical company like that, but the things he pointed out hit me, again, right on the button—because they were about the need to tell people that it's up to them. It's not up God. It's your responsibility.

Whether it's citizenship, or whether it's morality, things don't come from God. Things come from you, and things that you want to change in the world have to start inside yourself. You can't just acquiesce. You can't be at the mall, with a fannypack on, scratching your nuts, buying sneakers with lights in them. You have to be thinking. You have to be resisting. You have to be talking.

So these things are pointed out to me sometimes in passing, or directly, and, frankly, I'm impressed by them, and, naturally, I'll use the word "flattered" here again. I think flattery is usually artificial, so I don't like the word "flattery." It usually suggests insincerity to me. But complimented, I mean, just really complimented by it. Because, to take myself seriously here for a moment, an artist, a creative person, I often don't know the things that I'm doing. Not all artists are the same, but this is true in my case, and I'm sure it's true in some other cases as well. They don't know some of the underlying things that are happening. They just do it, because there's a certain satisfaction, a certain joy. It fills some need.

And yet another person can come along and point out things that they don't see. I've seen this with people who wrote certain things about Lenny

Bruce, that I'm sure Lenny didn't sit around and think of. But they would interpret him, and they would say, Do you see what he's doing here? Do you see what this is? Do you see how this fits with that? So, to a person who's looking carefully, it's true that there are probably some things about my work that reveal idealism and whatever the other qualities are that are more high flown, less concrete and earthy. Things that are more substantial.

. . .

DAVID: How has marijuana and your use of psychedelics affected your comedy career and your perspective on life?

GEORGE: What they did was affect my consciousness, obviously, and that affects everything about you. So, naturally, in this line of work it's extremely important, extremely influential. Your consciousness influences the work.

I was an early pot smoker. I was smoking pot when I was thirteen in 1950. It was an unheard of act in an Irish American neighborhood. People didn't know anything about it, and considered it to be on a level with heroin. I mean, it was just . . . (*George speaks in a scratchy, old-geezer voice*) marijuana—you smoke one of those things, and yeah, boy, you're gone for life. So, we were kind of a daring little group of us. We were on a new generational cusp.

We lived in West Harlem, white Harlem we called it, between Columbia University and all of the institutional establishments. Let me tell you what was in my neighborhood. Right across the street from my house was the entrance to Teacher's College, Columbia University. Barnard was there. Columbia University was there. St. John the Divine, the largest cathedral in America. Riverside Church, a twenty-three story gothic tower, was at the end of my block, with the biggest carillon in the world. Union Theological Seminary, the largest multidenominational Protestant seminary.

Literally around the corner from me, without crossing the street, was the Jewish Theological Seminary. Again, largest of its kind. Diagonally across the corner was Julliard School of Music, when it was still uptown. We played and fooled around at Grant's Tomb. So we had this incredibly high-powered institutional neighborhood, full of learning and striving. Harry Emison Fasdigger was the pastor over at Riverside Church, and I know that it had an effect on me. But I choose to hang around the other direction. I went down the hill to Harlem, toward the Latin, and black, and working-class Irish—because that's were the fun was! There were good smells coming out of the windows. The music was great. And my peers were there.

So we were on the beginning of the generation. The kids who were a little older than us, my bigger brother's guys—they were still street fighters and drinkers, and wore the big shoes. We had gravitated from the big shoes, and the peg pants, into conservative three-button charcoal suits, like the black dudes wore. We got into rhythm and blues. We got into pot smoking. We were a change. And that's why that piece of material in one of my albums—*Occupation Fool*—is called "Grass Swept the Neighborhood," because it changed us.

I think that marijuana is a consciousness-altering drug which has a cumulative effect. I also think it is a self-limiting drug, if a person is paying attention. It is a drug that suggests its own disuse, eventually. Some people maintain a certain consumption, at a good level, and they're not just half asleep all the time, and can't think. They save it for night time, or the weekend, or whatever, and that's different.

But generally marijuana, and LSD, and they're both, I think, essentially hallucinogenics. I'm not 100 percent sure of that. I wouldn't be on record with that, but they're certainly not in the narcotic classes, stimulants, or any of those things. They are separate. LSD—originally as unaltered by man—along with peyote, pot, and those forms of hallucinogens are all completely natural. They come from nature, and the only things that are done with them is they're passed from one person to another. It's these other drugs—where we get in the laboratory, or the garage, and we start altering their molecular structure—that are the deadly ones. The really deadly things have come from man's altering of nature, of the parts he can manipulate.

Pot is an herb. It's very natural. It obviously has some healing qualities and some palliative qualities. I think it changed my thinking. It fostered offbeat thinking, the kind of alternative thinking that was already an internal part of me—this disbelief in the received wisdom, and in the authority, as it was passed along. I think it fostered that. Then it changed my comedy. I was a straight, mainstream, suit-and-tie comic for ten years, from 1960 to 1969 or '70. I had a two-tiered life going on, and I didn't even know it.

One of them was this lawbreaking, school-quitting, pot-smoking person, with no respect for authority. The other one was a mainstream dream. I wanted to be in the movies. I wanted to be Danny Kaye. Well, you can't be Danny Kaye if you're going to be this other thing. So I lived two lives. My professional life was this straight path of pleasing the public. It wasn't until the late '60s that things changed, and this was because of the alternative culture—the people I could really identify with, what's called the counterculture. This began to manifest itself through the youth culture, with its disrespect for authority, free love—and "let's get high," and "here's how I feel," and "here's what's going on in my mind and my heart." All those things had been suppressed in America— some voluntarily, some not—prior to that. The '50s are notorious for that. But jazz and the beatniks were the exception. The bohemian world. But they were just starting.

Anyway, I was attracted to this other thing in the late '60s, because all my friends were musicians who had gone through the changes already. I was a big pot smoker. But slowly I used a little peyote, a little mescaline, and these tendencies in me to be myself, and not play a fake role as a people-pleasing, mainstream comedian, came to the fore. I became more myself. The comedy became more personal, therefore more political, and therefore more successful. I think you can never be successful unless you are yourself, at least certainly not successful in the good, rich sense of the word. So, suddenly, I also became materially successful. People started buying albums. I had four gold albums in a row. So the LSD, directly—in conjunction with its role in the counterculture, and my taking of it, those two things—definitely changed my life, because my creativity shifted into a very high gear.

DAVID: What do you think happens to consciousness after death, and what is your perspective on God?

GEORGE: I don't know. It's obviously one of the most fascinating things that we don't know. I profess no belief in God, which by definition is true, especially if we take the accepted definition of God. But to be an atheist is to also have a belief, and have a system, and I don't know that I like that either. And yet I shrink from the word "agnostic," because it seems like a handy weigh station to park at. I don't know. And I'm satisfied not knowing, because it allows me to be filled with speculation, and imagination, about all the possibilities.

I find it interesting to read about, or listen, to people who have highly developed beliefs in an afterlife—forgetting now Christians, God, and religion—and second chances, reincarnation, other planes of existence, other dimensions. Now, we get into the physical realm of the *universes*—which is interesting because *universe* means "one," and here we are talking about multi-universes.

DAVID: I actually asked Stephen Hawking—the renown physicist—about that once. He often writes and lectures about multiple universes and baby universes. I asked him how there could be more than one universe, when, by definition, the word "universe" means everything that exists. He told me that "a universe is a set of related events." Apparently, you can have many self-contained "sets of related events" that have no influence upon one another, and each one is considered its own universe.

GEORGE: Well, it's just fascinating, and you get lost in the possibilities. There's no way to hang your hat on any of these things. There's just no way to say, Ah, this a good one. I'll go with this. Because they're all titillating, and they're tempting. And they're all entertaining to the way I've developed my mind. I find it highly entertaining to consider wormholes, and alternate parallel universes, and all the things that Robert Anton Wilson sometimes writes about.

It's just endlessly entertaining and fascinating. So I'm quite content in being in this position. I think there's a certain arrogance of spirit that says, Here's the way it goes. Here's what happens. Or to narrow it down to two things or so, maybe it's okay. I don't know. But for me, I can't live that way. I have to keep all the doors open, just for the fun of it.

I don't care what happens to me after I die, but I know this. I know that if there's some sort of moral reckoning, I know I'll come out clean. I know I've never done a mean thing intentionally to anyone. I know I've only tried to make people feel better, and be more at ease. I don't mean professionally. I mean in personal relationships. I try to put people at ease, make them feel good. And I know that if there's some sort of reckoning by something, that says, Well, let's look at your record here, I'm clean. So I'm happy with that.

DAVID: Do you think that the human species is going to survive the next hundred years, and if so, how do you envision the future evolution of the human race?

GEORGE: I would guess that some cataclysm, man-made or nature-made, might happen. Obviously not real original thinking here, but I'll try and give a personal shape in a moment. Some sort of cataclysm will alter this thing. There are too many people. Let's say that the American Dream—and they call it a dream because you have to be asleep to believe it—is spread everywhere, and everyone in India, and everyone in China, has a car. Actually China—everyone has a car, or two cars, and big cars.

Okay, now, I'm a little bored by environmentalists. I'm a little bored with the whole almost-Christian fervor of these people. I do like vandalism, by the way. I like the big spikes in the trees. I like vandalizing the SUVs. That's fun. But the idealistic sitting around—all that shit—it kind of bores me. I understand the importance of it, but it bores me. But I also understand the fact the Earth is an organism and that life is completely interdependent, everything upon everything. And if you alter one thing, in some minute fashion, you alter everything. And sometimes it's not so minute. And there comes a tipping point. And if everyone has a car, and everyone is spewing out shit, think of the consequences. And even if they try to fix that, and then they go to the next thing, they'll fuck it up. We will always overstep. We will always use our brains to our self-disadvantage, ultimately.

And they'll be a tipping point. It'll either be environmental, or one of these lovely germs will get loose. Let's face it, if everybody, if all these countries in the world—and there's a lot of them now—are playing around with all of these different lovely microbes. We don't even need to list them, because we all know what they are. Ebola, Jesus. Plague. Smallpox. All these things for which there is no cure or prevention, at least not now. I'm sure the people in charge have gotten their shot. But, sooner or later, someone drops a vial. Sooner or later, somebody takes something home. Sooner or later, a window is left open in a building. Something in the perfection of the system slips, and there'll be, perhaps, that kind of a disaster. It could be locally contained. They might be able to put a ring around it, and say, Well, this part of the world is unlivable for the next thousand years.

But hey, we're all going to eat, and we all get fucking hats, and we're all in good shape. So things will go on. But then there might be something wide enough, whether its nuclear, or any of these lovely chemical things we have. Or nature, like just plain old volcanoes coming of age again, or some other huge geologic disturbance. Nature usually works very slowly. But suddenly, the slow process becomes a very rapid change. Volcanoes, and magma, and all that stuff build very slowly. But when they reach a threshold, they look—vvwoooom— and it's happening instantly. A mountain range has come up.

But anyway, what I'm trying to say is, what might happen to the human species is that it becomes greatly reduced in numbers, greatly reduced in its ability to use technology to any benefit. I mean, people may sit around, and still have their laptops, but if there's no Internet, or if there's no electricity, then you can't charge whatever the fuck it is.

I'm just saying, the systems will be compromised enough, and the numbers reduced, so that a—not a fresh start, because it won't be that—but a regearing. Maybe they'll be a hundred thousand people left. Maybe they'll be 10 million. Maybe they'll be scattered. Maybe they'll all be in one corner of the world. Maybe they'll have a little technology. Maybe nobody will have anything. So, I mean, it's just, again, one of those wonderful things to speculate on. I have no idea. But I hope it's dramatic and funny. Please God, let it be violent, and let it be funny. That's all I ask.

Realist and Surrealist

An Interview with Paul Krassner

Paul Krassner is a rare blend of satirist, stand-up comedian, prankster, and political activist. He is perhaps best known for publishing the satirical political magazine The Realist, *which was the first adult satire magazine. Krassner wrote for* Mad *magazine in the 1950s, and he cofounded the radical left-wing Youth International Party (Yippies). When ABC newscaster Harry Reasoner wrote in his memoirs, "Krassner not only attacks establishment values; he attacks decency in general," Krassner named his one-person show "Attacking Decency in General," receiving awards from the L.A. Weekly and DramaLogue. Krassner's comedy albums include* We Have Ways of Making You Laugh *and* Brain Damage Control. *He is also the author and coauthor of numerous books, including* The Winner of the Slow Bicycle Race *and* Confessions of a Raving Unconfined Nut.

* * *

DAVID: Why do you think it's important to blur the line between psychological dualities like reality and fantasy, or tragedy and absurdity?

PAUL: I think that each of those dualities are two sides of the same coin. There's an old saying that comedy is tragedy plus time. And if there is a line between them, that line is blurring—because time is accelerating in terms of the rate of information rising from the underground. For example, graffiti like "Watch out for the secret war in Peru" took maybe ten, fifteen, even twenty years to rise to mainstream awareness. But now, because of technology, and the fierce competition, it takes a much shorter time. So print reporters check the Internet, and news and information comes out much faster than before—so that the line has been blurred because of that.

Not only is there less time now between the tragedy and comedy, but I've seen it happen simultaneously. An example would be when the Branch Davidian headquarters were on fire in Waco. Jay Leno did a joke on *The Tonight Show*, where he said that there were two kinds of Branch Davidians—regular and crispy. And the fire was still going on at that time. That's why when 9/11 happened, everybody was saying, Is it too soon to be funny? "How much time will it take?" Larry King asked. "A month? Six months?" It was as if there were timetable.

I performed around three weeks after 9/11 in San Francisco. It was going to be a rally for a couple of referendums on environmental issues for the election. Ralph Nader was supposed to do this, but then he was morphed into an antiwar leader when he spoke. And of course there was a connection between energy sources and the impending attack on Afghanistan. But that was an audience which really had already been self-selected. So I could do controversial material and have it accepted easier with that particular audience.

DAVID: How have some of your satirical writings turned out to be prophetic?

PAUL: Oh, many things have come true. I did a piece for *The Nation*, I think, maybe eight-ten years ago, on growth in fear stocks, like, for example, the security industry and security guards would be much bigger. And, of course, that's come true. It's happened quite often. I remember when Don Johnson was on *Miami Vice*, and he had this five-day growth of beard, as a kind of trademark. So I had predicted that special razors would be manufactured that could do that, and they were. So it's the same information that was seen differently by myself and an entrepreneur—who thought, Ah, yeah that's not a bad idea. It was the same idea, of course, but they perceived it as a way to make money, and I perceived it as a way to make a comment on a possible cultural trend.

. . .

DAVID: How has your experience with psychedelics influenced your satirical writings, your comedy, and your perspective on life?

PAUL: On some levels, it's impossible to know. On other levels, there are concepts that I probably wouldn't have gotten without them—like saying that what really gets you high is the glue that's on the rolling paper, not the pot inside the joint. I don't think I would have come up with that concept, among many others, if I hadn't been high. I wouldn't have a lot of the stuff I've done on stage, which is just talking about experiences like taking acid at the Chicago Conspiracy Trial. Obviously I couldn't write about those things, or talk about them, if I hadn't done them. It would never have occurred to me to have those kind of stories.

But also, it's the process. I mean, sometimes it's impossible to know. If an idea comes to me, and I'm stoned, how do I know whether I would have gotten that same idea if I were not stoned? Or vice versa even? So I just surrender to the process. But I know that being stoned seems to help me make connections and to extrapolate on notions. There's a lot of comics who get ideas when they're stoned, and will then put those ideas into the material when they write something. Whereas, say, George Carlin has said that he will work on, work on, work on something, and then smoke some pot to help him fine-tune it. Then there are people who will perform when they're stoned. So there's all different levels of the relationship.

DAVID: Robert Anton Wilson told me that when he edits his writing, he often alternates between being stoned and straight.

PAUL: Oh, right. Yeah, because sometimes, let's face it, you get an idea when you're stoned, and you look at it when you're not stoned, and you realize that it may not be such a great insight after all—like about the importance of flushing the toilet as an exercise in responsibility, for example.

DAVID: What was it like to accompany Groucho Marx on his first acid trip?

PAUL: It was enlightening and enjoyable—just in the sense of seeing him as himself, not as his character. This happened at the home of an actress who lived in Beverly Hills, who was not there at the time, and she had a large collection of classical records and Broadway musicals. One of them was *Fanny*, and there was a song on the album called "Welcome Home." And the song went, " 'Welcome home,' says the chair. 'Welcome home,' says the clock." All these various pieces of furniture in the house say "welcome home" in the song. And Groucho was sort of following the lyrics of that, with his exaggerated Groucho walk, saying "welcome home to the chair," and just acting out the lyrics—as though he actually was being greeted by the clock, the chair, and the rest of the furniture.

We talked about his favorite contestant on *You Bet Your Life*. He said it was an elderly gentleman with white hair who was very chipper in mood. When Groucho asked him what he did to retain his sunny disposition, the contestant said, "Every morning I get up and I make a choice to be happy that day. I know that I have the choice of whether or not to be happy." Then at one point

Groucho went to urinate, and when he came out he started talking about how the human body is a miracle. He said, "You know, everybody is waiting for miracles to happen, but the whole human body is a goddamn miracle."

We spoke about humor. At one point Groucho said that "everybody has their own Laurel and Hardy. A miniature Laurel and Hardy, one on each shoulder. Your little Oliver Hardy bawls you out—he says, 'Well, this is a fine mess you've gotten us into.' And your little Stan Laurel gets all weepy—'Oh, Ollie, I couldn't help it. I'm sorry, I did the best I could. . . .' "

We had been talking about *The Realist* slogan—"irreverence is our sacred cow"—and he said that reverence and irreverence weren't separate things. He said that you could be irreverent about the things that you felt a reverence for, because reverence and irreverence were the same thing. There's a quote saying, essentially, that you can make fun of the things that you love without loving them any the less. And that's how I interpreted Groucho saying that irreverence and reverence were the same thing.

DAVID: What do you think happens to consciousness after death?

PAUL: Oh, I think it dies with your physical body. That's my belief, and it's a pretty basic belief. It's like a Philip Wiley story, where an angel falls down from the sky, in front of this air force major, and he has to change his philosophy. So if I believed that that my consciousness survived after my physical body died, I would have to change my philosophy.

DAVID: What is your perspective on the concept of God?

PAUL: One of the few things I remember from my entire higher education was a sociology professor saying that if horses had a deity, it would look like a horse. Your question is one that I deal with all the time because there is so much use of the word "God," and I always wonder what people visualize when they pray, because God is such an inconceivable concept to me. I think that's why they have figures like Jesus, because then, at least, they can visualize something that they can relate to.

So I think that whatever concept of God that people have will work for them. I had a Donald Duck with eight arms—which was called either "Donald Sutra" or "Shiva Duck"—and this was my visual mantra. In other words, I feel that if the universe is infinite, then the number of paths to connect with the universe is also infinite. So the concept of God is inconceivable for me. An all-powerful, conscious being is inconceivable—and congratulations to those who can conceive of that. I'll stick with evolution, and even that's pretty hard to conceive of.

DAVID: Do you see evolution as being a completely blind-chance process, or do you ever entertain the idea that there could be some type of intelligence or design built into the evolutionary process?

PAUL: I think of it as cosmic accident and coincidence of various forces. And for the same reason—because it's impossible for me to conceive of an intelligence that could make such a design. I finally came to the conclusion that God is evolution. That concept first came to me when we were on that little vacation in Florida. We went to the Sea Aquarium on acid, and I was having this non-verbal relationship with a dolphin. I remember I asked the dolphin, "Why are you always smirking?" And the dolphin said (and I willingly concede that this was a projection on my part), "If God is evolution, then how do you know he's finished?"

Then I even made a joke to myself—which was that the dolphin was a actually a sexist pig, or he would not have given me the male pronoun for God. So I told this to dolphin expert John Lilly when I took a workshop with him, and Lilly just changed one word, like he was correcting a term paper or something. He said, "No. If God is evolution, then how do you know you're finished?" And that was an epiphany, because that was the moment that I remember thinking, Oh yeah, okay, it's my responsibility now to evolve—and I appreciated the concept of conscious evolution.

DAVID: Does it seem to you that something is accelerating in the evolutionary or historical process? What do you think it is that's accelerating?

PAUL: Yeah, inevitability. The sad thing is that there's so much human suffering because of America's national karma. But when they say, Well, why do they hate us? It comes out that it's not because they resent our freedom, or McDonald's, so much as that they saw on their own TVs, Palestinians who had been bombed by Israelis—and they're holding fragments of the bomb, in effect saying, "made in USA." So that's what I mean by inevitability.

But it seems to be accelerating, and it is getting weirder and weirder—because of the kind paranoia that makes people accept invasions upon their freedoms and, in some cases, even welcome it. So I just see all kinds of scenarios, and they're not all as optimistic as I would like them to be. This is why you have to make a separation between what you see is happening and how you live your own life. Harry Chapin—the late singer and songwriter—and I were once talking about hope, and he said to me, "If you don't act like there's hope, there is no hope." So even if it's a placebo—placebos work!

DAVID: Are you optimistic about the future? Do you think that the human species will survive the next hundred years?

PAUL: Your guess is as good as mine. When I think about this question my thoughts immediately go to my daughter, in terms of her reality, and also as a symbol of the future. But then I think, even if I didn't have a daughter, there are the children of the world, and whatever the human race is, it's amazing. I mean, we went from living in caves to talking on telephones without wires that take photos—it's just bizarre.

So I've become as much in awe of technology as I am in awe of nature. And I don't know. There are people like Ted Turner who say they give humanity a fifty-fifty chance of surviving. I see all the things—about the hole in the ozone, global warming, and all. I get a lot more e-mail than I can handle physically, but even just scanning, you can see what's happening with the water around the world and child slavery still going on in Haiti. But, at the same time, I see a kind of mass awakening now, the way it happened in the '60s. So that gives me hope, even in the face of all of that pessimism.

DAVID: How do you envision the future of the human race?

PAUL: At one end of the spectrum is total control, a fascist state. Just because the year 1984 is over doesn't mean the concept is. The other end of the spectrum is a bursting of freedom. But I don't know how you get from one to the other.

I used to live in La Selva Beach, by Monterey, in central California. I lived right on a cliff, overlooking the ocean, and I would just see everything in metaphors of waves. I would think that there are people who are on the crest of a wave. But you can't have a crest without a wave that follows it. So I began to apply that metaphor to many things, like say feminism. At a time when they're still performing involuntary clitorectomies on the other side of the globe, here it's just a matter of getting equal pay, among other causes. So I think of the people on the front lines of feminism as being on the crest of that wave, and another wave will follow sooner or later. That's the vision, and that wave metaphor applies to everything. Feminism is just one example.

But my epiphany occurred when I was researching conspiracies from political assassinations to the Manson murders and went nuts from information overload. I came out of it with the understanding that I couldn't save the world, that I had to start with myself—which is what John Lilly implied. So I just had to get some elbow room, work my way out, and realize that I wasn't the only one. If I was the only one, then there would be no hope. But there are people all around doing that, although it doesn't make the news. So people could begin to get despairing over just seeing the—I hate to sound like George Bush—but just seeing the bad things that make the news.

So I don't know. I try to think, Well, what will be different about our future generations? Will they have computer chips in their foreheads? And if they did, what would those computer chips do? Would they be like, instead of taking pills, you just press an area to change your mood? I think that, because everybody has their own vision, what results is an amalgam of all those visions—competing with each other, complementing each other. So that's why I love the unknown—even if I'm afraid of it.

Raising the IQ of the Global Brain

An Interview with Peter Russell

Peter Russell is a bestselling author, filmmaker, and management consultant. He is considered one of the leading thinkers on the nature and evolution of consciousness. Russell is probably best known for his pioneering book The Global Brain, *which builds on James Lovelock's Gaia hypothesis, by exploring the notion that the human species might be playing the role of a giant evolving brain in our planetary biosphere. Some of Russell's other popular books include* Waking Up in Time, The Consciousness Revolution, *and* From Science to God. *Common themes in his books include the integration of science and mysticism, avoiding ecological catastrophe, the relationship between personal transformation and global change, and the future evolution of the human species. Russell earned an honors degree in theoretical physics and experimental psychology—as well as a master's degree in computer science—at the University of Cambridge, England, where he studied under Stephen Hawking. Russell has also*

created award-winning films based on The Global Brain *and* The White Hole in Time, *and is a fellow of the Institute of Noetic Sciences.*

* * *

DAVID: What inspired your interest in the evolution of consciousness?

PETER: I think that was always there in the background. Many people ask me if I had a transformational moment, and I didn't really. As a teenager I was fascinated by the mind. I read stories about yogis, started exploring hypnosis, and I built equipment that modified brain wave patterns. Although I was studying mathematics and physics then, and getting more and more fixed in that direction, I was always interested in the mind. So I knew there was something there, and my interest gradually evolved.

At the time I wasn't interested in spirituality at all. I rejected religion when I was about thirteen. I thought it was a load of mumbo-jumbo that didn't make sense at all and didn't agree with the scientific worldview. Although I wasn't interested in the spiritual aspects of consciousness, I was interested in the untapped potentials of the mind. I think that's what eventually led me to explore meditation when I was in my early twenties. That's when I started getting really interested.

DAVID: What sort of paradigm shift do you think is necessary for Western science to begin to get a grasp on consciousness?

PETER: I think the essence of the paradigm shift is to let go of the idea that the material world—the world of space, time, and matter—is the fundamental reality. In some sense that's already happening in modern physics. We're realizing that space, time, and matter don't really exist in an absolute way. That came out Einstein's revolution. But, at the moment, we still think that consciousness emerges from the material world—and that, I think, is the fundamental problem with the current paradigm. Consciousness is so fundamentally different from material things.

We assume matter is unconscious, and then somehow this magical thing happens—when you put matter together in the form of a complex human brain consciousness somehow emerges out of it. The huge problem there for the current paradigm is how does matter, which we assume to be unconscious, ever lead to something so different as subjective experience? So I think the essence of the paradigm shift is challenging that assumption. That's the assumption that science won't let go of, and challenging that assumption means saying maybe consciousness does not come out of the material world. It does not emerge from matter. Rather, consciousness is fundamental to the cosmos.

What I find fascinating is that when we make that shift, it doesn't change anything at all in modern science. Physics, chemistry, biology, mathematics—they all stay exactly the same. But it adds a whole new understanding of human experience and spirituality. That's common in paradigm shifts: The old model is still valid, but as a special case. So the materialist worldview still has its place, but it's a special case of considering only physical reality.

DAVID: Why do you think evolution appears to be accelerating, and what do you think it is exactly that's accelerating?

PETER: What is accelerating is the rate at which new developments come into existence. People talk about time accelerating, but time doesn't accelerate. Time can't accelerate, because what do you measure the acceleration against? You got to have some standard of time. What is actually accelerating is the rate of change. I think the reason for this is because there's more potential for change as the universe gets more complex. When the universe was very simple, and bacteria were just reproducing by division, change was very slow. When sexual reproduction evolved change got much faster, because it was a more complex system. When multicellular organisms evolved, like mammals or ourselves, it got even faster. Each new level makes it easier for the next level.

With human beings, we've moved on to a whole new arena of evolution, and one which can move even faster. We're no longer bound by genetic biological evolution. You could even argue that we've stopped evolving physically. We've taken off the pressures of natural selection. We give everybody equal chances at mating, and we look after our sick. So we've taken off the pressures for biological evolution. Where we're evolving is in our understanding, our knowledge, our values—in our consciousness—and that is going much faster. We're seeing changes in human culture which are happening in decades, rather than thousands or millions of years.

DAVID: Our biosphere is currently facing one of the largest mass extinctions in its history. What do you think can be done to help turn this situation around?

PETER: The reason for this mass species extinction is that a species on Earth is destroying the atmosphere, polluting the seas, ripping out the rain forests, and in other ways disturbing the ecology. In the past it seems that it was probably asteroid or comet impact, or maybe huge volcanic eruptions, that really affected the species. When you had these mass species extinctions they were due to natural causes, which will happen from time to time. What's happening now is something which is the result of human activity.

I think nature is remarkably resilient and adaptive, and if we just got out of the way, I think nature would adapt and recover over thousands of years. The longer we go on with our current mode of civilization, we are just creating more and more problems. We're just making things worse and worse and worse, which means it's going to be harder and harder for the environment to adapt, and we're just creating a deeper and deeper crises. I think in the long term it will recover. But, in some way, we just need to end this crazy way in which we treat the planet.

DAVID: You've used two interesting metaphors to describe the role that you think the human species is playing on this planet. You've said that we're like neurons in an emerging global brain, and that we're also like an out-of-control cancerous growth on the planetary body. Can you talk a little about these two metaphors, and also about how your concept of the global brain relates to the Gaia hypothesis?

PETER: Yes. The idea of the Global Brain started for me a long time ago, when James Lovelock came out with the Gaia hypothesis. The idea was that you can consider the whole biosystem of the Earth as a single integrated system—much as if it were a living organism in its own right. You can then start drawing parallels between systems in the overall biosystem and an organism, and the functions they perform. So, for example, the atmosphere is a bit like the circulatory system, carrying nutrients around the planet. The rain forests resemble the lungs exchanging carbon dioxide for oxygen. As I began to draw parallels, I was forced to ask: What is humanity doing here? Life's existed on this planet perfectly well for three and a half billion years. Human beings are a very recent occurrence; they've appeared in just the last .01 percent of the planet's history. The biosphere survived perfectly well without us. What function do we perform, if any?

Then I realized what it is that human beings do that no other species does—the processing of information. We are information processors par excellence. That's come about primarily because we have developed the most sophisticated language and communication system on the planet. That suggested to me that we're like the nerve cells of the planet. Then I started looking at how the brain develops in the growing fetus. There's this massive population explosion of nerve cells around the second or third month. The number of brain cells grows exceedingly fast, and then, just before birth, it slows down and stops. The brain is, in a sense, fully grown. Then what happens is the nerve cells begin connecting up. The development of the mind, the intelligence, the creativity, and all of that, is not because the brain grows more cells. It's because the cells start interconnecting.

It struck me that humanity's going through a parallel thing. Human beings have suddenly appeared on the Earth, and now we've gone through this massive population explosion—which is now beginning to tail off, thankfully. The current estimates are it'll probably stabilize somewhere around twice the current size, or maybe less, if we don't destroy ourselves in the process. And we're now going through this phase of beginning to connect up. It started off with things like the telephone, then radio and television, fiber optics and satellites, and now the Internet, and who knows where it's going to lead. But we are beginning to connect in the same way as the cells in a brain connect.

But, at the same time, we can't ignore the fact that we are also acting in a crazy way. If we continue doing what we're doing, we're not going to be here much longer. The human species may still be here, but there's not going to be this wonderful high-tech culture with everybody communicating with everybody else. We've already damaged the environment and upset the weather patterns. We may be reduced back to hunter-gatherers or something. We're in a very dangerous situation indeed.

So I wondered, What is it also about human beings, that as well as making us so intelligent, also leads us to behave in ways which are insane? It is really insane. To realize you're destroying the planet, your support system, and then to continue with policies that promote yet more destruction is insane.

So I started thinking, Where does this insanity come from? What's it about? It became obvious that we are stuck in a rather self-centered mode of consciousness, in which our individual needs take priority over the needs of the collective. Then I realized that's what happens in cancer. Cancer cells are "rogue cells," cells that somehow lose their connection to the whole organism. They're very selfish cells. And I think, by and large, humanity has become a very selfish species. Cancer cells are also stupid. Ironically, if a cancer becomes malignant, and it's successful in its growth, it destroys its host organism—and hence itself—just as humanity seems to be doing. In addition, cancers can grow very fast when they become malignant, which, again, is what is happening with humanity.

I once saw a picture of a cancer growing in the human body, and then seeing a picture of a city sprawling out into the surroundings and thought, My God, it's the same type of system. When you look at the way the cancer is eating into the body, it's just like the way the city eats into the environment. Then I looked deeper and realized that what happens with a cancer—why the cells turn rogue and become selfish cells—is a result of the genetic programming being disturbed in some way. Whether it's due to a virus, pollution, radiation, for some reason or other the genetic code gets disturbed, and the cell loses its connection with the whole.

In the contemporary world, our psyche has become similarly disturbed. We've got faulty programs running us. We're often driven by old survival programs. They may have been valuable when we were in the jungle, and our physical survival was at stake. We needed them then. But today most of us have most of our physical survival issues pretty well handled most of the time. But we still have these old programs running our thinking. And these programs tell us that if we're not at peace, if we're not happy, we need to do something about it. There's something wrong with the world around us, and we need to change it, or control it in some way. That is the cancerous programming that is running humanity, driving us crazy, and causing us to destroy our environment. So, ultimately, I see very close parallels, not only between the performance of cancer and the behavior of human beings on this planet, but also in the deeper root causes of what's behind them both.

DAVID: Do you think that the human species will survive the next hundred years, or do you think we're in danger of extinction?

PETER: I really don't know. It's a wide-open question. We may create so much disruption on the planet that it will be impossible for a higher life-form such as human beings to exist. If we destroy the ozone layer, which is still a possibility, we destroy life on land. That's the bottom line. Life has only existed on land for the last 10 percent of Earth's history, and it only existed on land because the ozone layer had formed, protecting the land from the ultraviolet light of the sun. Before that life had to be in the sea, because water filters out the ultraviolet light. If we destroy the ozone layer, it's not just that we're going to have to wear factor 70 sun cream the whole time and wide rim hats. We may protect ourselves, but we'll lose all of our food. The crops, the trees, the bees, and the rest of life will die. If we destroy the ozone layer, the surface of the planet, the whole land of the Earth will become desert—probably for hundreds of millions of years. That is still a possibility, although, thankfully, it looks like we got a handle on that. It's probably the one environmental issue that we have handled. We've cut back enough on CFCs [chlorofluorocarbons] that it looks like the ozone layer may hold. But who knows? That scenario could still happen. We could destroy life on land, in which case we won't be here.

What's also clear is that it looks like we've messed up the world's weather system. The evidence for this is now coming in month by month. The biggest concern at the moment is shifts in ocean current and what's that going to do to weather systems on a huge level—what that's going to mean for agriculture, and the conflicts between people that it's going to produce. Who knows how that's going to play out?

My suspicion is that humanity will continue. But I don't think Western civilization will continue—and to be quite honest, why should it? If you gave every species on Earth one vote, how many species would actually vote for the continuation of humanity? Maybe a few cockroaches and brown rats, and other species that are dependent on us. But if you look at what Western civilization does to the environment, I don't think it has any justification to demand it continue to exist. When most people talk about saving the world, if you question them deeply, what they're really saying is they want to save this particular culture so that they can continue to exist.

DAVID: Assuming that humanity can get its act together in time, and we do survive, how do you envision the future evolution of the human species?

PETER: I think it's something that's already happening now, and that the future evolution of our species is in terms of our consciousness and our values. If you look back through history, there have been these lights of consciousness—we call them saints, yogis, the enlightened ones—who stepped out of this egocentric, materialistic take-what-I-can-for-myself mode of consciousness. There have been people who have moved through that into a whole other way, a way that is full of compassion, understanding, and love, that is not self-centered, that is not concerned with taking from the environment or with individual gain or profit. I think that is the direction in which we are headed.

At the moment, I think we are halfway through our inner evolution. We have woken up to our individuality, to our individual consciousness. Yet because we haven't woken up to what really lies behind that, we got in this pattern of trying to defend our little egocentric mode of consciousness, not realizing that it's just a passing phase. The sooner we move through this stage, the better. We'll be disturbing the environment less, and able to cope better with whatever problems may be coming.

I feel that that's the inevitable direction of the evolution of consciousness. Everything moves toward that end. Everything evolves toward greater freedom. That's true in the material plane, and consciousness has to move in the same direction. We have to move out of this very trapped mode of consciousness, into the sort of freedom and liberation which the great saints, yogis, and mystics have discovered. I think that is our true destiny, our true heritage.

DAVID: What do you think happens to consciousness after death?

PETER: I have no idea. I've studied the near-death experience a bit, and it fascinates me. It would seem that one way of understanding it is that the individual consciousness is dissolving back into the infinite consciousness. The consciousness that I experience has this individual limitation because it is functioning in the world through my body, through my nervous system, through my eyes and ears. That's where our sense of being a unique individual comes from.

When we begin to die, and let go of our attachment to the body, consciousness lets go of that identity which it gained from its worldly functioning and reconnects with a greater infinite identity. Those who've had near-death experiences often report there seems to be this dissolving of the senses and a moving into light. Everything becomes light. There's this sense of deep peace and infinite love. Then they come a threshold, beyond which there is no return. But we don't know what happens beyond there because the people who come back haven't gone beyond it.

When I think of my consciousness, when I think of "me-ness," it seems to be something that is created during this life through this interaction with the world, but doesn't exist as an independent thing. I think that a lot of our concern about death comes from wanting to know what is going to happen to this "me" consciousness. Is "me" going to survive? I believe that this thing we call "me" is not going to survive. It's a temporary working model that consciousness uses, but in the end it's going to dissolve. A lot of our fear of death is that we fear this loss of "me-ness," this loss of a sense of a separate unique identity. It's interesting that people who've been through the near-death experiences, and experienced this dissolving of the ego, and realized that everything is okay when that happens, generally lose their fear of death. They feel incredible liberation in life.

DAVID: What is your concept of God, and what type of relationship do you see between consciousness and what you would define as God?

PETER: For me the two are almost synonymous. But first, I should explain what I mean by consciousness. When I'm using the word "consciousness," I mean it in the sense of that fundamental essence of ourselves. The one thing we cannot deny is we are experiencing beings, and in that sense we are conscious. We can be conscious of anything. I may be conscious of my thoughts, my dreams, the outside world, my fears, whatever. It's all happening in consciousness. Consciousness is the space in which the phenomena of the mind take shape.

If you look to the mystics, people who have really traveled deep into the mind, and explored the innermost essence of the mind, they claim to arrive at a state of pure consciousness—consciousness before it takes on a particular form, whether that form is a thought, an experience, a perception. They report that pure consciousness has divine qualities. There is an incredible sense of ease, peace, and release. There's a sense of deep love, compassion, understanding, and forgiveness. As I said earlier, it also has qualities of light. And it's timeless, eternal. Now, these are all qualities which we traditionally ascribe to God. God is love. God is light. God is eternal. The peace of God that passes all understanding. The forgiveness of God. So there's very close parallels there between the experience of pure consciousness and the qualities ascribed to God.

What I think has happened over time is that some people have had an experience of pure consciousness. It's the natural state of consciousness. Once we let go of all our doing and inner egocentric machinations, we discover this pure consciousness. Those who've have had this experience have found it so transforming they have wanted to talk about it, share it with others. If you live in a culture that believes in some higher deity or God that has these qualities of infinite love, compassion, peace, then it's very easy to imagine that you have had a direct contact with God.

My feeling is that these qualities are intrinsic to consciousness. The divine isn't something that's out there; it is our own essential nature. It is the essential nature of everything in the cosmos. When we experience it, there is this incredible, almost overwhelming sense of freedom. Monotheistic cultures have identified this as the divine, and called it God. But for me, God isn't a supreme being out there, looking over us, judging us, keeping an eye on us, intervening in the world if we petition him, she, or it correctly. God is our own essence, our own true nature. When you see the divine in this way, so much of spirituality makes new sense.

It also answers the question of "How do I relate to God?" because that's really about "How do I relate to my own innermost essence?" That does not mean relating to something separate from me. It's just opening up to my own source, my own deepest nature. So I don't have to go anywhere to look for the divine, apart from just stilling my own mind and being with my true self. It is who I am in my deepest sense.

DAVID: Peter, do you see any teleology in evolution? Do you think that evolution is a blind chance process, or do you think there's any evidence of intelligent design?

PETER: That's a hard one. I mean, the answer is hard to phrase correctly. I don't think it's teleology in the sense that there is predetermined purpose or goal. But I do think there is a direction to evolution. There's an overall trend toward the emergence of greater complexity and greater organization and, with that, greater intelligence and self-awareness. As the universe unfolds, and grows into higher and higher levels of complexity, it moves toward greater and greater levels of awakening. What we now understand from chaos theory, and system theory, suggests that the evolution of complexity is a natural thing. It doesn't require any sort of intelligent design to create more and more complex systems. With that comes increasing consciousness and awareness. I think that process is inevitable. So it terms of teleology, I don't think evolution was destined to produce human beings like ourselves. That's what has happened on this planet. On other planets similar processes are also happening in terms of pushing toward greater complexity and greater awareness. But I have no idea whether they're going to end up looking like the human form or not.

DAVID: Have you ever had a psychedelic experience, and if so, how has it influenced your perspective on science and spirituality?

PETER: Yes, although I don't think it influenced my perspective on science greatly. I see science as a valid way of exploring the nature of the material world and arriving at consensus truth about this world. The problem with science is that it assumes this material reality is the only reality. I was aware of these limitations to science before I had a psychedelic experience. Having that sort of experience just confirmed my understanding that science was a partial perspective on the cosmos—valid within its own frame of reference, but only partial.

What changed was my appreciation of the spiritual. I realized there was validity to a lot of what the great spiritual teachers, saints, and mystics had spoken about. And I realized there were other ways of construing reality, other ways of creating one's own experience. But the most important part of the psychedelic experience was that, at times, I could let go completely of the ego mode and be with an experience without the illusion of the ego—of me here experiencing something. I could touch into that sense of oneness that the mystics have spoken about.

It was many years ago, back in the '60s when I did this. And, for me, it was a factor in my saying that I need to look at Eastern mysticism much more deeply. Because I think, like many people back then who tried these substances, it led to a different appreciation of reality, a whole opening up to a new way of seeing things and a new understanding of spirituality. However, the next day you're back with memories, or maybe some shift in experience, but over time it fades.

I realized that yogis, monks, and others in the East had been exploring the mind, in natural ways, for thousands of years, and come up with a wealth of wisdom about how to tap into these deeper states of consciousness. They learned how to dissolve this sense of ego through natural means, such as meditation and other such practices. So you could say that the psychedelic experience spurred me to find ways of raising consciousness that didn't involve psychedelics. And that's really been my mission in life—to draw upon what these inner seekers and explorers have found, and to try to integrate this into my own life, and pass it on to others, because that is the most important need in the world today.

DAVID: Do you see psychedelic plants as playing a role in the Global Brain, as being part of a natural system to raise consciousness? Terence McKenna and Timothy Leary spoke about the idea that a symbiotic relationship between the human species and psychedelic plants might be wired into us by higher design.

PETER: Again, there's the danger of teleology here. I think they have played that role, but that is slightly different from saying they are there in order to play it. If you think back to our early hunter-gatherer ancestors, they would have come across fruits, nuts, plants, and mushrooms. Sampling them, they would have learned what was poisonous, what killed them, what made them sick, what nourished them, and what made them healthy. And they would have learned that certain plants produce a different state of consciousness. Maybe there was some sense of liberation, perhaps a simple spiritual experience, or maybe a very profound spiritual experience. Those experiences that they found valuable would have been sought out, and perhaps made into a ceremonial event. So I think it's very likely that psychoactive plants played an important part in the development of probably just about every culture on the planet.

Indeed, we don't have to think back fifty thousand years to imagine how our ancestors may have lived. We only have to go to the Amazonian rain forest, or areas of Africa, to observe indigenous peoples to get an idea of how we might have lived. And when we do, we find that they do use these plants in ceremonial events. They have discovered things in their particular region of the world that seem to do this, and they revere them very much. So I feel these plants have played a role, but I wouldn't go so far as Terence to say they are there in order to do that. I just think that is what has happened.

DAVID: How do you think science and spirituality can be reconciled?

PETER: First of all, by realizing that spirituality is not talking about the same world as science. I think this is where the apparent conflict over reconciliation comes from. Science believes that religion and spirituality are talking about the material world. So when they find religious texts talking about the birth of the cosmos, God creating the world in seven days, Adam and Eve, or whatever, they just say that's clearly wrong. And if you believe that the religious texts are actually talking about the physical cosmos, then it is clearly wrong.

But I think that spirituality needs to recognize that as well. A lot of the debate is because religions feel threatened by science. But they're mistakenly taking spiritual statements to be referring to the physical world. But if you recognize that the spiritual traditions come out of a deep personal understanding of the nature of the human psyche, how the mind gets trapped, and how to liberate it from the ego mode, you can see they have great value. Religions have often taught this is in terms of allegory, which has given us the mistaken understanding or belief that they are describing the physical cosmos. I don't think they are at all. Science is describing the physical world, the material cosmos. Spirituality is describing the inner landscape, and how to work with that by using inner technologies. Once you see that they apply to two different complementary realms, there is no conflict. They don't need to be reconciled. They only need to be reconciled if you think they're describing the same world. When you see them as describing two fundamentally different aspects of the cosmos—the external physical and the internal psychic—then they can coexist quite happily, and learn from each other.

DAVID: What gives you hope?

PETER: People. Individuals who can overcome great difficulty in their own lives. Individuals who can shine with light and love in adverse circumstances. Individuals who can be at peace with what they have. I think this is the hope for the world—the awakening of individuals. Just seeing this in friends, who really do get into working with themselves, and freeing themselves from whatever it is that's holding them back—whether it's old childhood stuff or something else—and begin to change the way they relate to their family situation, and through that become somebody different in their little bit of the world. That gives me hope. More and more people transforming gives me hope.

The second thing that gives me hope is the youth today. When I say youth, I mean teenagers and people in their early twenties. I see so much wisdom there. I'm not saying they all have it, but even 10 percent would be significant. But some of them have an understanding, a compassion, and a wisdom that didn't exist when I was that age. Back in the '60s, many of us thought we were pretty hip and wise. And we probably were by the standards of the time. But I think if you could take some of these kids today, and put them in a time machine, and take them back to the '60s, people there would not know what to make of them. The awareness they have is something we were all groping toward back then. What we're seeing now is people two generations further on. We've had shifts in attitude toward pregnancy, childbirth, and raising children. We've had media shifts, shifts in education, shifts in awareness of the environment and the crisis we're in. All of that has helped to raise consciousness.

Ultimately, this is the way paradigm shifts happen—from one generation to another. In fact, it was Max Planck who pointed out that a new scientific truth does not triumph by convincing its opponents and making them see the light, but rather because its opponents eventually die, and a new generation grows up with a new way of thinking. It's amazing to look at some of these younger people, at the light and wisdom that they have. And some of them are now beginning to have their own children in their early twenties. What will their kids be like in another twenty years?

This light moving from one generation to another gives me hope. It is a collective evolution. If I look at myself, and where I am in terms of my own awareness and awakening, I've come some way in the last forty years. But the upcoming generations are in the same place as me. It's not that they are forty years behind me in terms of their evolution. We're all in the same place. We are all evolving together. It isn't that I've been on this planet forty years longer than them, therefore I'm forty years smarter than them. It's that our culture as a whole is forty years older, our culture as a whole is forty years smarter. So that gives me hope—just seeing the light in the young generation, because it means we're all moving forward.

Quantum Spirituality

An Interview with Deepak Chopra

Deepak Chopra, M.D., is a physician, inspirational speaker, and a prolific writer. Dr. Chopra combines conventional Western medical approaches with traditional Ayurvedic medicine from India and is one of the leading figures in mind/body medicine. His work has had a significant influence on many Western physicians, and he helped to bring the notion of holistic medicine to many people's attention. Dr. Chopra has written over thirty books (both fiction and nonfiction) on the topics of alternative medicine, self-improvement, and spirituality—including Timeless Body, Ageless Mind, How to Know God, *and* Quantum Healing. *Dr. Chopra lectures around the world and has made presentations to such organizations as the United Nations, the World Health Organization in Geneva, and London's Royal Society of Medicine. He attended medical school at the All India*

Institute of Medical Sciences, where he was trained as an endocrinologist. Dr. Chopra is the founder of the Chopra Center for Well Being in Carlsbad, California.

*   *   *

DAVID: How has your understanding of quantum physics and Hinduism influenced your perspective on the nature of consciousness?

DEEPAK: I'll give you my perspective on Vedanta. I think Hinduism is a corruption of Vedanta, and I'm not very keen on the Hindu rituals. But Vedantic understanding of consciousness, as the ground of existence, has really influenced my understanding of how the universe works. I am convinced by everything I know scientifically that consciousness is not an epiphenomenon—that it's the other way around. Matter is the epiphenomenon. Consciousness conceives, governs, constructs, and ultimately becomes the physical reality.

I believe that consciousness is the ground of being, and it differentiates into both observer and observed. Today from the perspective of quantum physics we also know that matter is energy and information. But energy and information are a potential, unless there's an observer to collapse the potential into a space-time event. So I think quantum physics, in many ways, validates the original insights of Vedanta.

DAVID: What are your thoughts on telepathy and psychic phenomena, and why do you think so many scientists have such difficulty accepting the possibility that these phenomena actually exist?

DEEPAK: I think scientists who do not understand nonlocality will have difficulty in understanding, or accepting, these phenomena, because the phenomena can't be explained by conventional science, or even by information technology. The only way these phenomena can be understood is the actualization, simultaneously, in information and nervous systems, that are separated from each other in space-time, from a common nonlocal domain.

As we understand more about the physics of nonlocality—which is really an elaboration of the Einstein-Padolski-Rosen equation and Bell's Theorem—we will have a better way to explain these phenomena. So-called telepathy, precognition, remembrance of other lifetimes, and prophecy are all examples of simultaneous actualization of information in different nervous systems from a single underlying nondual, nonlocal consciousness.

DAVID: One of the themes of your spiritual books is that we create our own realities through the choices that we make in life. However, it seems that much of what happens in life is beyond our personal control. I'm wondering if you think that our personal choices explain everything that happens to us. If we are 100 percent responsible for the creation of our own realities, how do you explain the atrocities and abuse that small children sometimes face in this world?

DEEPAK: I think you're asking a question that has been asked forever—and that is, is there free will, or is it a deterministic universe? In the enlightened mind, it's a completely free world and universe. In the conditioned mind, it's a determined world. We cannot squeeze the soul into the volume of a single body, or even the span of a lifetime. So the atrocities and abuse that happens are an interdependent co-rising of a turbulence in the collective ground of consciousness. And it can be very easily understood, if you put it in that context. If you think of a person as an individual, then, of course, there is a great difficulty in explaining these phenomena. From the Vedantic perspective, the person is an illusion. There is no such thing as a person. A person is in the interwoveness of interbeingness and does not have a separate identity. So whatever happens is a result of an interdependent co-arising of space-time events from the virtual or nonlocal domain.

DAVID: What is your perspective on God, and do you see any teleology in evolution?

DEEPAK: God is the source of all the information, energy, space-time, and matter that structure the universe. God is the generator and organizer. God is that which creates, organizes, and differentiates itself—himself, or herself—as the physical universe. If by teleology in evolution you mean purpose-driven evolution that results in a creative universe, I don't see any way of avoiding it. It has to be a fundamental aspect of evolution.

DAVID: What do you think happens to consciousness after the death of the body?

DEEPAK: Nothing happens to consciousness after the death of the body. When two people are speaking on the phone, and the lines are cut off, nothing happens to them. If the room I'm sitting in is destroyed, nothing happens to the space I'm in. Consciousness just loses a vehicle to express itself. If I destroy my radio set the broadcast is still happening, but it's not being actualized in the physical form, because the instrument is missing. So I think that when the instrument gets destroyed, consciousness ceases to express itself in the realm of space-time and causality, until it finds another vehicle to express itself. And, after a sufficient period of incubation, it does do that, by taking a quantum leap of creativity.

DAVID: You know, Deepak, even though I sense that there's wisdom in what you're saying, I have to admit that I always have this scientific skeptic inside me that questions all spiritual and mystical assertions, when they are expressed as facts. I'm curious as to how you can be so sure about things that have mystified human beings since the beginning of time—such as the nature of God, the existence of a soul, and what happens to consciousness after death. What gives you such a sense of certainty about your spiritual ideas?

DEEPAK: The only thing that can give you any degree of certainty is direct experience, and I come from there. Science is just one of the ways to express the truth, and it's really not an adequate way. Science is not an adequate way to express the truth; it's just a way to express our conceptional map of what we think the truth is. The conceptional map of science keeps changing. So I think science is extremely inadequate as a way of understanding reality. Reality is the observer, the process of observation, and that which is observed. Science addresses only that which is observed, completely excluding both the process of observation and, more fundamentally, the observer. So actually, even though I express my ideas in a scientific vocabulary, because that seems to be the fashion of the day, I really don't think science is adequate to address these deeper questions.

DAVID: But still, I don't understand how you can be so certain. I mean, you say that your experience gives you a sense of certainty—but we can certainly be fooled by our experiences.

DEEPAK: I'm more certain that I exist than of anything else. Then, in the certainty of existence, is the certainty of consciousness. The fact that I exist is the only thing I can be certain about. Everything else is really a perceptual artifact. I spend three hours in meditation every day, and I've been obsessed with these ideas ever since I was a child. To tell you the truth, I don't think I'm certain about anything else. I think the only thing I'm certain about is the nature of God and the existence of the soul.

I'm not certain about what I see or perceive, because I really know, from the depth of my being, that if you can think about something—if you can conceptualize it, if you can visualize it, and if you can experience it through your senses—then it's not real. It depends on something that you can't conceptualize, that you cannot visualize, that you cannot experience through your senses, and yet is much more real than anything that you can conceptualize. So conceptualization, visualization, perception, understanding, intuition, creativity, meaning, purpose, and decision making all depend on consciousness.

So, to me, consciousness or God is not difficult to explain; it's impossible to avoid. Everything else is very difficult to explain. How do you explain perception? Your brain only recognizes pH, body temperature, biochemical changes, and electromagnetic impulses. That doesn't tell me how you experience a red rose in your consciousness, how you feel beauty or, for that matter, how you experience sexual orgasm. Nothing that we explain in science really explains anything.

DAVID: At times, in certain states of awareness, I've thought to myself, Consciousness isn't the hard thing to explain, it's unconsciousness—that's the real mystery.

DEEPAK: Yes, that's true.

DAVID: In your book *How to Know God* you map out the stages of spiritual evolution as you've come to understand them. In reading the book, I was surprised that you didn't give any credibility to the psychedelic experience as being a genuine source for religious or spiritual insight. You mention it briefly and then seemed to swiftly dismiss it. I was surprised that you didn't give any credence to the work of people like Aldous Huxley, Alan Watts, Huston Smith, Ram Dass, and many other important religious scholars who believe that psychedelic drugs like LSD, or shamanic plants brews like ayahausca, can sometimes trigger powerful religious experiences. Have you ever had a psychedelic experience yourself, and why did you so quickly dismiss the idea that psychedelics can sometimes trigger true religious experiences?

DEEPAK: First of all, I grew up in a tradition that is so grounded in the understanding of consciousness that psychedelic experiences are considered hardly important—although in India, in rituals, we do occasionally use things like bhang, which is a form of marijuana, and mushrooms as well. I personally have used everything, including LSD, but that was when I was a medical student, more out of curiosity than anything else. And I do believe that these experiences can sometimes open a window to the transcendent and to the nonlocal domain of existence.

I had a wonderful experience when I used them—but I was seventeen, and that was a long time ago. I didn't feel the need to rely on drugs, and, as a physician, I've met many people who have suffered from psychosis, and other kinds of problems, as a result of relying on drugs, or psychedelic chemicals, to have an experience. As far as the work of Aldous Huxley, Alan Watts, Huston Smith, and Ram Dass goes, I think that they're very important religious scholars, and I believe what they're saying is very authentic. And I do think that they had great insights to give them a glimpse of this deeper reality. It just happens that I came from a tradition where this was almost taken for granted.

DAVID: Do you think that the human species is going to survive the next hundred years, or do you think we're going to drive ourselves into extinction?

DEEPAK: I think it's a fifty-fifty chance, and either way is really what the universe must intend. The universe could be saying *Homo sapiens*, or the human species, was an interesting experiment, and didn't work. After all, like our scientists, nature, God, or the Universal Being does try experiments. Dinosaurs were an experiment. There are many other experiments. From God's point of view, the human species could be a very interesting experiment—to give a creature free will, a nervous system that, at least, seeks enlightenment, and has self-consciousness. However, human beings have also very successfully destroyed the ecology, and we do stupid and silly things, like kill each other in the name of God.

So human extinction would not necessarily be a bad idea from the universe's point of view, to move on to something more interesting. But, on the other hand, I think humans also have the opportunity to move into a new phase of their own evolution, take a quantum leap of creativity, and actually fully develop the supernormal *sidhis* that the greatest spiritual traditions have talked about. And, in so doing, humans would also realize their inter-beingness, their oneness, and become much more compassionate and loving. If that happens, that would also be a really wonderful thing. I think we're at a crossroads at the moment, and it will be very interesting to see what happens. But either way, it will be very interesting.

DAVID: What do you think is the biggest threat to the human species?

DEEPAK: I think the biggest threat to the human species is ignorance, lack of awareness, and not knowing the true nature of one's own potential. This results in a very limited sense of identity, and leads to greed, to self-absorption, to a rapacious consumption-oriented society, and also to violence. I would say it is the limited identity that people have as a result of ignorance.

DAVID: Assuming that we do survive, how do you envision the future of the human race?

DEEPAK: If we do survive, I think human beings will develop new forms of cognition and perception, as well as new abilities—such as the ability to heal and the ability for nonlocal communication. We'll, once again, restore the ecological balance of nature and achieve the ability to transcend tribal tendencies, create a new civilization, and seed the galaxies with new life.

DAVID: How do you envision advanced extraterrestrial life in the universe?

DEEPAK: I think if the human species survives, we will certainly have the means, the technology, and the ability to seed not only our galaxy, but other galaxies, with life-forms. You could easily e-mail genetic codes to other planets in different galactic systems and, through robotic technology and remote control, reassemble life on other planets. And I'm only talking about technology. As we understand the nonlocal nature of the universe, quantum creativity, and discontinuity, then it might be possible for consciousness to travel to different dimensions and then reassemble the physical form in these different dimensions. So the possibilities are endless.

. . .

DAVID: What gives you hope?

DEEPAK: I believe, as I was taught by my spiritual masters, that hope is another sign of despair. So I never hoped. I'm always trying to maintain a sense of being where I'm independent of both hope and despair.

Here, Now, and
Tomorrow

An Interview with Ram Dass

Ram Dass is one of the most respected spiritual teachers in the world. His books and lectures are responsible for exposing many westerners to Eastern philosophy, and he has been an inspiration to many people. He is the author of twelve books about topics such as personal transformation and compassionate social action—including the classic book on Hindu philosophy, Be Here Now. *Ram Dass, who was born with the name Richard Alpert, earned his Ph.D. in psychology from Stanford University. In collaboration with Timothy Leary and others, Dr. Alpert researched the psychological effects of psychedelic drugs at Harvard University. This research lead to a storm of controversy and eventually to their dismissal from the Harvard faculty. Dr. Alpert traveled to India, where he met the spiritual teacher Neem Karoli Baba, who gave him the name Ram Dass, which means "Servant of God." Ram Dass created the Hanuman Foundation, which developed the Prison Ashram Project, designed to help inmates grow spiritually during*

incarceration, and the Living-Dying Project, which provides support for conscious dying. Ram Dass also cofounded the Seva Foundation, an international service organization dedicated to relieving suffering in the world, which works in public health and social justice issues and has made major progress in combating blindness in India and Nepal.

*　*　*

DAVID: What originally inspired your interest in the evolution of human consciousness?

RAM DASS: I'm inclined to immediately respond "mushrooms," which I took in March of 1961, but that was just the beginning feed-in to a series of nets. Once my consciousness started to go all over the place, I had to start thinking it through in order to understand what was happening to me. It wasn't until after I'd been around Tim Leary, Aldous Huxley, and Alan Watts that I started to reflect about issues like the evolution of consciousness.

DAVID: What drew you to study psychology?

RAM DASS: I'm embarrassed to admit what drew me to psychology. I didn't want to go to medical school. I was getting good grades in psychology. I was charismatic and people in the psychology department liked me. It was as low a level as that. My whole academic career was totally out of Jewish anxiety and issues surrounding achievement and adequacy. It was totally sociopolitical. It had nothing to do with intellectual content at all. I taught Freudian theory. Human motivation was my specialty, so I thought a lot about all that stuff. That served me in very good stead because it's an exquisitely articulated subsystem. If you stay in that subsystem, it's very finite and not very nourishing. But when you have a meta-system, and then there's the subsystem within it, then it's beautiful. It's like a jewel, just like with chemistry or physics. But when I was in it, it was real. When I was a Freudian, all I saw were psychosexual stages of development. And as a behaviorist, all I saw were people as empty boxes.

DAVID: How has your experience with psychedelics effected your view of life?

RAM DASS: It had no effect on me whatsoever and nobody should use it! (*laughter*) The predicament about history is that you keep rewriting the history. I'm not sure, as I look back, whether what appeared to be critical events are really as critical as I thought they were, because a lot of people took psychedelics and didn't have the reaction I had. That had something to do with everything that went before that moment. In a way I just see it as another event, but I can say that taking psychedelics and meeting my guru were the two most profound experiences in my life. Psychedelics helped me to escape—albeit momentarily—from the prison of my mind. It overrode the habit patterns of thought and I was able to taste innocence again. Looking at sensations freshly without the conceptual overlay was very profound.

DAVID: How did you then make the transition from Dr. Richard Alpert to Ram Dass?

RAM DASS: Initially it was all very confusing. I was teaching a course in human motivation. I took my first psilocybin on Friday night, and by Monday morning I was lecturing on stuff which was basically lies as far as I was concerned. (*laughter*) So, that was weird because my whole game started to disintegrate at that point. I still stayed as Mr. Psychedelic Junior in relation to Tim, and publicly my gig was turning on rich people and dealing and giving lectures on the psychedelic experience. By 1966 I looked around and saw that everybody who was using psychedelics really wasn't going anywhere. I was around the best of them, but even if they had the Eastern models, they couldn't wear them—the suit didn't fit. I realized that we just didn't know enough. We had the maps but we couldn't read them.

Then I went to India in the hope that I could meet somebody there who could read the maps. I met Neem Karoli Baba and he gave me the name Ram Dass, and that put it in a bigger context than the drugs. The experience wasn't any greater than the drug experience, but the social context of it was entirely changed. Neem Karoli took acid and said that these substances were known about for thousands of years in the Kulu Valley but that nobody knew how to use them anymore. I asked, "Should I take it again?" He said, "It will allow you to come in and have the darshan of Christ. You can only stay two hours. It would be better to become Christ than visit it, but your medicine won't do that." I thought that was pretty insightful. LSD showed you an analog of the thing itself, but something in the way we were using it couldn't bring us to the thing itself.

DAVID: Can you tell me about your relationship with Neem Karoli Baba?

RAM DASS: He is the most important separate consciousness in my life, even though he died in 1973. He's more real than anybody else I deal with. It's like having an imaginary playmate that is so hip and so wise and so cool and so empty and so doesn't give a fuck and so loving and so compassionate—so any way you can go. It's such fun. He is the closest I've ever come to finding unconditional love. He didn't even want to stay alive. Most people you meet might say, "I'm an unconditional lover," but you go to kill them and they go, "Nooo!" (*laughter*) But it's not him, he's just the form of it. Once Maharaji was warning this girl off this dubious guy she had met. She said, "He's only my friend" and Maharaji said, "Your only friend is God." I really heard that. Your only friend is the reflection of the mystery in each form. And that's what you want to be friends with—not with the story line.

DAVID: Have you ever had an experience that you would call an extraterrestrial contact?

RAM DASS: No. I assume there are lots of beings on every plane all around the place, but I myself have not had experiences of that kind. By extraterrestrial, do you mean beings on the physical plane, like other beings in the solar system?

DAVID: Not necessarily. A lot of people have used the term "extraterrestrial" in the context of a psychedelic experience, where they've encountered entities that seemed to have evolved either on another planet or in another dimension.

RAM DASS: I've met many beings on other planes but I don't call them extraterrestrial. Maharaji is not on this plane anymore—but he's here. He's present as a separate entity, and the form I see him in is the form my mind projects into him. I've also written prefaces for three volumes of the books on Emmanuel. Emmanuel speaks through a woman called Pat Roderghast, and he is an absolutely delightful spook. I know Pat very well and I know Emmanuel quite well now. I asked him what to tell people about dying and he said, "Tell them it's absolutely safe." What a superb one-liner. He also said, "Death is like taking off a tight shoe." He's just like this friendly, wise uncle. In the preface I say, I don't know whether this is vertical schizophrenia or whether it's a separate entity, and I don't really care. I'm experiencing it as a separate entity and my criteria is whether I can use the material, not whether it's real or not.

DAVID: What is your concept of God?

RAM DASS: I think it's a word like a finger pointing to the moon. I don't think that what it points to is describable. It is pointing to that which is beyond form that manifests through form. A God defined is a God confined. I can give you thousands of little poetic descriptions. It's all, everything and nothing. It's all the things that the Heart Sutra talks about. It's God at play with itself. God is the One, but the fact is that the concept of the One comes from two, and when you're in the One, there's no One. It's zero, which equals one at that point.

DAVID: What do you think happens to consciousness after death?

RAM DASS: I think it jumps into a body of some kind, on some plane of existence, and it goes on doing that until it is with God. From a Hindu point of view, consciousness keeps going through reincarnations, which are learning experiences for the soul. I think what happens after you die is a function of the level of evolution of the individual. I think that if you have finished your work and you're just awareness that happens to be in a body, when the body ends it's like selling your Ford—it's no big deal.

I suspect that some beings go unconscious. They go into what Christians call purgatory. They go to sleep during that process before they project into the next form. Others I think go through and are aware they are going through it, but are still caught. All the bardos in the *Tibetan Book of the Dead* are about how to avoid getting caught. Those beings are awake enough for them to be collaborators in the appreciation of the gestalt in which their incarnations are flowing. They sort of see where they're coming from and where they're going. They are all part of the design of things.

So, when you say Did you choose to incarnate?—at the level at which you are free, you did choose. At the level at which you are not, you didn't.

Then there are beings who are so free that when they go through death, they may still have separateness. They may have taken the Bodhisatva vow, which says, "I agree to not give up separateness until everybody is free," and they're left with that thought. They don't have anything else. Then the next incarnation will be out of the intention to save all beings and not out of personal karma. That one bit of personal karma is what keeps it moving. To me, since nothing happened anyway, it's all an illusion—reincarnation and everything—but within the relative reality in which that's real, I think it's quite real.

DAVID: How has your stroke changed your body physically and mentally?

RAM DASS: It damaged my brain in such a way that I'm unable to move my right arm and leg. The whole right side of my body is pretty much numb at the skin, but there is plenty of pain. The stroke has also affected my ability to speak. I have difficulty expressing concepts. The dressing room for concepts—where I dress them in words—has been harmed by the stroke. I have the concepts but no words to play with.

DAVID: What have you learned from your stroke?

RAM DASS: One of the things my guru said is that when he suffers, it brings him closer to God. I have found this too. The stroke is benevolent because the suffering is bringing me closer to God. It's the guru's grace, and his blessing is the stroke. Before the stroke I enjoyed playing golf, driving my MG sports car, playing my cello. Now I can't do any of those things. I can't do, do, do all the time.

The way I approach what happened is that with the stroke I began a new incarnation. In the last incarnation I was a golfer, a sports car driver, a musician. Now I have given all that up. The psychological suffering only comes when I compare incarnations—if I say, Oh, I used to be able to play the cello. So I say my guru has stroked me to bring me closer to a spiritual domain. I've learned that silence is good. I knew that before but I've learned it thoroughly now. I've learned about helping. In my life before, I was a "helper," and serving was power. Now I am helpless. Instead of my book *How Can I Help?* now I can have a book called *How Can You Help Me?* From the point in the morning when I wake up, I need help: Going to the bathroom, eating, going anywhere, I need to ask for help from those around me. That's powerlessness. But I've learned that even that role can be played with compassion, so that my helpers and I can serve each other.

DAVID: How has your stroke affected your spiritual outlook?

RAM DASS: It's gotten me deeper into karma yoga. This is my karma, and it is also my yoga. I think that it's taught me more about how suffering is a stepping-stone toward a spiritual goal. My stroke has also affected people. I was a spiritual friend for many, many people—through my books, tapes, or lectures. I was an identification figure for them, and the stroke shook them. They couldn't figure out why a person with such spiritual *naches* could suffer a stroke.

It undermined the feeling that only good comes to those who are good. I wanted to open the hearts of people, and my stroke did this and much more than my books, tapes, or anything else.

. . .

DAVID: Have you had any psychedelic experiences since your stroke?
RAM DASS: Sure.
DAVID: Have they been any different from the experiences you had prior to the stroke?
RAM DASS: No, they were not particularly different. But I think that psychedelic experiences helped me gain perspective. They helped me escape from the perspective of minds around me—the healers who are focused on the body. I needed to use a psychedelic to focus on the spirit.
DAVID: What else has your stroke taught you about consciousness?
RAM DASS: I think that it's increased my humanness. It's a strange thing to say, but when I started out my spiritual journey I was a psychologist, and I was busy being an ego. Then I got into my spiritual nature. I was a soul, and pushed away my ego and body. Now I'm not pushing away these things. I'm making friends with my body. The stroke taught me to honor those planes of consciousness which include the physical. Since my stroke, some of my friends say they've found me human, and that I was never human before. They mean I'm inhabiting my ego. Now they can find me as an individual, whereas before they could only find me as a soul.

. . .

DAVID: Do you think that the human species is going to survive the next hundred years, or do you think we're in danger of extinction?
RAM DASS: Yes, I think that we're in danger. We're in danger of being poisoned by our minds. Thought processes cause wars. But we will survive.
DAVID: How do you envision the future evolution of the human species?
RAM DASS: As one consciousness spread out into many multiple forms. Most of us who have done psychedelics, yoga, and so on have touched this plane of consciousness. With one consciousness the social games would be different, because we wouldn't be playing the games of country and so on. When there is only one consciousness, the concept of "us and them" sort of disappears. It stays in place, but its effect on you becomes less and less.

Medical Freedom and Cannabis Consciousness

An Interview with Valerie Corral

Valerie Leveroni Corral is the cofounder and director of the Wo/Men's Alliance for Medical Marijuana (WAMM), the most highly praised medical marijuana collective in California. Corral was the first person in California to challenge the marijuana laws in court, based on the necessity defense, and win. She also helped lead the 1996 battle to pass Proposition 215, the state's medical marijuana law. An article in the New York Times *referred to Corral as "the Florence Nightingale and Johnny Appleseed of medical marijuana rolled into one." Corral has testified before California State legislative committees of the Senate and the Assembly. She has received proclamations and resolutions from Santa Cruz City and Santa Cruz County and was Santa Cruz County Women's Commission Woman of the Year. Corral has served as a guest speaker to numerous other city councils, county supervisors, classrooms, health services agencies, and universities. She has presented her scientific observations to the British*

Parliament House of Lords and served as a Canadian federal case expert witness in the case Her Majesty the Queen v. Terry Parker 1998.

*   *   *

DAVID: How did you become interested in altered states of consciousness?

VALERIE: I was raised Catholic. I was convinced that I was being watched, interminably observed. God, Santa Claus, the watcher was always there to see if I was bad or good. Still, from an early age I simply knew I had goodness in my heart. I knew it, and I harbored no guilt about that—a realization that was certain to lead me from the church. But not before I had my first altered state experience.

I was nearly fourteen, just pubescent. I was with my family. It was Christmas Eve mass, midnight mass, in Reno, Nevada. There were Gregorian chants. There was incense and the cadence of Latin. I was intoxicated by that rhythm; it was hypnotic. It was an emotional time for our family. My brother was preparing to leave for Vietnam. (That's another story, one that still haunts me.) But the spell of that moment carried me until I floated into a dream. Then I looked around and I started to get nervous, like I shouldn't be having this weird episode in church, and I thought that I might get in trouble or something. My dad noticed and nodded me outside. I stumbled over a clutter of feet, out of the pew, fumbling toward the door. It closed behind me, and I was free. I laid down in the snow and then—whoosh!—I was soaring. I just laid there. I was free and I felt utterly divine, or something like I imagined divine to be. After that catechism seemed like an assault, an attempt to minimize my thoughts, to make me feel smaller, afraid. The church and the government are alike in that way.

DAVID: How did you first learn about the medicinal benefits of marijuana?

VALERIE: Oh, that was my husband Mike's insatiable curiosity. He, of course, wanted the best for me, for me to be well, and he was overwhelmed. After my car accident in 1973, which left me epileptic, he had been my sole caregiver. He was there for me around the clock, serving and rescuing me from one disaster after another. The difficulty that my illness presented in his life, in our lives, called for some kind of change. He was my devoted caregiver and none of this, not my life nor wellness, would be possible without his courage, service, and love. He saved my life and offered me hope where there was none. I was so sick.

This particular illness damaged so many things—psychically as well as physically. Just as illness can enrich the spirit and enhance our lives as we come to understand it, it is also true that it can undo us, damage our soul and pain the heart. It can do this to our loved ones too. I was like that—selfish in my suffering. It can get to be "all about me," and that can be ugly, so I had to practice some other way of being. I found that marijuana really helped me practice making that mental shift necessary to discover the healing path. That doesn't mean I believe in a panacea. I don't really—not anything you can take anyway. But I do believe we are creatures of habit, so I try to have some influence over mine.

Sometimes I would have up to five grand mal seizures a day, paralyzing headaches, and aching body pain. I lived under a waterfall of pharmaceutical drunkenness. It was a full-time job for Mike and full-time hell for me. Doctors had prescribed me every antiepileptic drug in the pharmacopoeia. These were really dangerous and addictive drugs—drugs that made me feel like I was crawling underwater, disconnected from this world and beaten down. They offered me more and more drugs, and none of them worked. I just kept having seizures. I couldn't read, thoughts just tumbled around in my head. My illness was devouring me. It was cavernous and I was falling deeper. I wanted a way out.

I was often hospitalized, and it was on one of my weekly or monthly visits to the emergency room in 1974 or 1975 that Mike read in a medical journal about a study with laboratory-induced seizures in rats that had been successfully treated with marijuana. You can imagine our skepticism. Neither of us could quite believe that marijuana would be the answer, especially since the expensive neurosurgeons I saw so often couldn't find one.

But, of course, we decided to try it, and it wasn't long before we began to see the difference. I began to see the "epileptic" part of myself differently. We carefully monitored my marijuana intake and tried to apply the use of it in a very regulated manner. I would try a certain number of joints or puffs and record the results. I always carried a rolled joint in my pocket, and I used it to ward off seizures when I felt an aura. I took it a number of times each day and carefully tracked that information. Soon we found that I could keep the seizures at a distance by maintaining a certain amount of marijuana in my body. This was the mid-'70s, and besides this one study, there was no other research available. But what happened was amazing, and I became convinced by the miracle of my own experience.

DAVID: How did WAMM begin, and what makes WAMM different than other medical marijuana organizations?

VALERIE: WAMM grew from being arrested. That jacked us right out of the closet. We had already worked with eighteen friends and family members who had died by the time of that first arrest in 1992—one of which was my Dad. After having successfully challenged the law (based on the "necessity" doctrine common law dating back to the Magna Carta), we were inundated with calls. There was a move to open a buyer's club like Dennis Peron's in San Francisco on Church Street in Santa Cruz. We were part of the original team of Santa Cruzans—a lot of remarkable activists and movers—but we never had the taste for the "club" idea, and our vision didn't really appeal to the local activists.

By mid-1993 we were veterans of two arrests and had to face a lack of available medicine. Having to buy it made it painfully clear that we weren't the only ones who couldn't afford to pay black market prices. We wanted to create an organization where there was access to marijuana that didn't cost very much money. That was really the impetus—that it shouldn't cost a lot of money. Illness is sobering. People read of our victory and began to contact us. It was a very organic beginning. The more people called to ask about it, the larger it became, until I was driving around town with a trunk full of medicine that we grew, giving it away. It is important to know that Mike and I have been growing and breeding marijuana for nearly thirty years, and Mike is a genius in the garden. I began spending the afternoons with the most extraordinary people, most of whom happened to be dying. It was a humble beginning. Those folks in our original group have long ago jumped out of this life into whatever lay beyond, but not without leaving behind precious jewels of teaching. WAMM is made up of the most courageous people, my mentors.

WAMM became an alternative service in our community. So we needed to find a larger place where we could conduct our weekly Support and Supply meetings. At one time the Santa Cruz City Council allowed us to conduct them at the Community Center. We grew to total 250 before the September 5, 2002, raid. Intimacy is a very important part of the success of our organization. Smaller cares better. In this way we notice each other, we see that, while we may come initially for the medicine, it is not long before we recognize ourselves in each other. There is so much that we share because we are both so diverse and yet we share similarities.

But there's a balance, as we also felt that there were more possibilities in a bigger group. There's more camaraderie. There's more protection. There's more juice, more of the sounds working together to make something better, something stronger and more rich. A lot of people that contacted us were dying, so there wasn't this idea that there was going to be a big long future of interaction. Although we've grown many crops, that really wasn't necessarily it. It was just people coming together who happened to be sick. Some happened to be dying. Some happened to be more able to do physical labor. Others were able to donate money, goods, tools, paper plates, toilet paper—whatever it was that they could bring. Their time. Their energy. This was not so much about the procurement of medicine as it was about the interaction of people working together to make it happen.

We are many things, but WAMM members are courageous. Illness can be a formidable demon. Its pain can be exhausting and grueling. And being sick can be very isolating. Not that your friends don't love you. They do. It just all changes when you're ill. You can't do the same things. But in working together, we relieve some of the burden from each other. Some of the loneliness. It's a perfect way to move from our own "suffering," to getting rid of it—or at least have a great chance to do so. And that is the subtle work of the collective—to mix it up. It changes what we are used to. Like my friend Robert Anton Wilson says, what you do everyday becomes your habit.

Around 140 of our friends have died, and in the nineteen months since the raid 23 have danced right on out of here. And we have to find a place for our grief, so that we make room for dying to be okay. Ram Dass constantly reminds us take another perspective, without the expectation of how death should look. It's a challenge and it's an honor. And while I have had the opportunity to sit with many of my friends, I honestly know nothing about death—though I sure am getting good at wiping butts and just hanging out. It's good practice. I can't say for certain, but it appears to me that the way we live is the way we die. Having observed this offers me some strange sense of comfort when I think of George Bush and John Ashcroft. Ah, that would be the evil Val saying that.

. . .

DAVID: Could you talk a little about how you've seen marijuana help people with serious illnesses?

VALERIE: In all the ways you can imagine and know to be true already. The nausea and vomiting from cancer or AIDS chemotherapies, convulsions related to epilepsy, the quivering of a paraplegic or quadriplegic, to induce hunger and stave off wasting, pain—intractable, phantom, ocular, extremity, internal, and emotional pain. But above all of this valuable and important aid, I've made the most extraordinary observation. Many people have reported to me that marijuana has affected the way they look at their death. They tell me it has opened a door for them, or even a peephole, to allow them to accept death more willingly. There is nothing more important in this life than to be able to court death as a lover, to change our view and dance with her. This is our most profound opportunity.

DAVID: What role you think the shift in consciousness that comes from using marijuana plays in its medicinal or healing value?

VALERIE: I believe that of all the things that marijuana does, the most important is that it shifts your consciousness. It might relieve some pain, or awaken your appetite. It may slow down your neuropathy tingling sensations and let you walk more normally, instead of with drunken legs that won't behave. But the way that it works the most remarkably is that it allows people to think differently about their illnesses and their symptoms. It really opens a possibility of looking at the illness in a different way. And, personally, I think that that's one of the most profound and important effects that it has. It's really the gold as a tool.

Marijuana is not only a great tool for relieving many symptoms and inducing hunger; it also offers an opportunity to shift the way we perceive what's happening around us. I think that of all the things that marijuana does, I feel that this is the most important to speak about—because this is where we find opposition around us. Marijuana alters our consciousness. People might react when they hear that it gets you high, or that you just want to feel better. What are people to think? What are young people to think if they see you trying to change the way you feel for only recreational reasons? Well, it's hard to separate those things when you're ill. It's hard to separate feeling better from feeling good. And isn't that really the intention of all of us in our lives—to have a better life, to do better, to feel better?

I think it's a practice. It is a tool, and this tool can be even more profoundly effective by using it to open or awaken your consciousness. I think that that is probably its most profound ability. It offers the most profound opportunity. When you don't feel well—when you're vomiting, or when you're in pain—and you take something to alleviate that pain, and then it starts leaving . . . leaving . . . leaving. The difference between not feeling good and feeling good is in and of itself a high. It's more than a gift. It is a wonderful feeling. It is elating, and it can produce great joy in somebody—to not feel good, and to feel good. To take that step into feeling better—wow, isn't that great? Isn't that amazing? Isn't that a high?

I don't see that as being any different from what I might seek in any practice, like if I'm practicing to speak in front of people, to play music, to write, to cook, to dance, or to be in church and feel the fullness. I don't know what all of us are doing, but I think people want to feel good. People want to feel better. And that's really an important part of creating a kinder collective, a kinder neighborhood, a kinder society, a kinder world—more allowance and more tolerance. And do I think marijuana is the answer to that? No, of course not. I don't say that. But I see that it offers people a remarkable capacity for opening their consciousness—if we want to do that, if we're not too afraid.

It doesn't even have to be what somebody wants to do with it. I know many people who use marijuana and absolutely do not get altered. They use it for a specific reason, for a specific purpose, for the moment where they relieve the pain, and that's it. They don't go beyond that place, because to do that is not effective for them. So I'm really talking about something else. I'm talking about the importance of consciousness. The reason that I talk about this is because I look at this moment in a big picture. This is a moment to laugh, but it's also a moment to practice for the moment of death—because the little death in this moment allows us to let go. It's not like death is somewhere else, but that in this moment I can be okay and I can accept it.

DAVID: Why do you think there is so much resistance from the U.S. government regarding the use of marijuana as a medicine?

VALERIE: It's really not a question of a democratic process. If this government and this administration were interested in the republic, and if they were interested in supporting a democracy, they would respect the will of the people, and they would allow for an avenue of law that reflects that will. They would not presume, nor would they have the courage even to say to us, that we do not know—that we, as people, do not know our life experience, and cannot trust that experience. And if we have that encounter, then we should not be trusted. The reason for that, from my little worldview, is because of power. It is not about the acceptance of a democratic state, and state's rights, or about people in small groups, where their voices are heard, being able govern themselves. This is not about a reflection of a true democracy, nor the support of a republic. It's about acquiring power and acquiescing nothing—only threats and fear.

So this marijuana struggle is so much about the way that we struggle as human beings. As we struggle against illness, we struggle to find a path in this life that leads us through it in a way that tastes of its harmony—not in the life I live alone, but in everywhere I walk. So I don't live with that government. I live in a land that gives me all, and that provides an opportunity for me to share that, and give witness to that, and observe it in other people. So the more freedom that we have, the more freedom we must protect. We must observe the importance of protecting it. What we're really talking about is obviously more than about marijuana. What does it free us up to do? It frees up our muscles and it frees up our pain. It frees up the epilepsy and the glaucoma. It could reduce the nausea. And ultimately it will free our minds and our hearts. But I think this government is terrified of any other power, and that's why we needn't let it rest with them, or in their hands.

. . .

DAVID: How has working with dying people affected your view of life?

VALERIE: It's helped me to uncover some things about the dance of life and about approaching the unknown. It's taught me that the unknown isn't stalking me because it's unknown, and that I'm only an observer. I hang around a lot of people who know a lot about dying, so it's been helpful.

DAVID: What do you think happens to consciousness after death?

VALERIE: Can you define consciousness?

DAVID: Simply awareness of one's self. The internal experience of existence.

VALERIE: This an interesting question, because for maybe about five years in WAMM we tried to define those words and make a distinction between awareness and consciousness. We never could do that. Some people would talk about awareness as being an awareness of something that hurt, or their suffering. Some people would talk about awareness as in the self, the place where we observe from.

DAVID: In the realm of consciousness, I understand that there are many subtle (and many not-so-subtle) distinctions that one can make when defining levels of awareness, but I just mean it in its simplest sense—your basic sense of "I." What do you think happens to that after death?

VALERIE: Certainly not one thing. I don't think that one thing happens. I really feel like my experience of dissolving that I described earlier felt like the most natural thing. I would say that my observations lead me to think that it's kind of a dissolution, but I don't think there's a distinction between who I am and what I dissolve into. Will I still know that I'm dissolved after it happens? Will I know that I'm part of something greater? Will I feel that? I have. So that's what I think.

DAVID: What is your perspective on the concept of God?

VALERIE: I don't really speak about God. When we talk about God, I think that we talk in riddles. I don't have a relationship with God as though God is something separate from myself. And yet, on this day—the eve of the resurrection [Easter Sunday]—I feel like there's a possibility for anything. It's a resurrection of my own ability to be able to observe what can be done. It's not even my ability—it's beyond it. Anything seems possible. I don't really see "the God," and I don't relate to "the God." I think of it in terms of metaphor. I don't have an Almighty. I think maybe God is who you always give it away to, and as long as you can give it away, you don't need to have it be a particular god. It's an allowance maybe.

DAVID: How has your experience with psychedelics influenced your perspective on life?

VALERIE: It's been a profound tool for me, and generally people can say that—or not. (*laughter*) I owe a lot to psychedelics. I think it opened my life, and changed the possibilities for me. Although I had that altered experience that I described earlier, I might have gotten caught thinking that that was the only way—that there was a certain path—and then gotten caught in the path. Psychedelics helped me to see the vastness, the nondimensional, the altered dimensional, and that it wasn't one way. It wasn't any single way that I could see. For me, it has been a tumbling of awareness, a tumbling out and through it. And again, probably the greatest and most significant possibility was really through allowance. It takes us out of the realm of being in control—so it's fabulous for all of us control freaks.

DAVID: Do you think that the human species will survive the next hundred years, or do you think we're in danger of extinction?

VALERIE: That's such a funny question, because everyday somebody dies. Every moment somebody dies. There's always some sense of extinction. So it could happen, and I don't know if it matters that much. I don't mean it to be callous, but I think that it could happen. And if we're concerned about saving people, we have a really good opportunity right now to do that. We have a really great opportunity.

DAVID: What do you think is the biggest threat to the human species?

VALERIE: Fear. Being self-serving.

DAVID: Assuming that we do survive, how do you envision the future evolution of the human race?

VALERIE: Oh, I don't mind how it comes out. You know, three breasts (*laughter*), one blue eye, one green eye. I don't mind. I'm just hopeful that we won't hurt each other, and that what we create we create out of love and kindness. Certainly being able to dissolve whatever ideas I come up with are pretty important in the realization of that. I think it's important that we all dissolve our notions of what we think we know is best or right, or how it should be. I think it's a pretty perfect world. But in all of its madness and suffering, what's so perfect about it? This moment—that we can be in that vastness. There's possibilities all around us at anytime. I don't think I'd either congratulate or blame humanity for what comes next. But I think that in our longing, and through the faith and belief that we can achieve a sense of goodness now, we find the possibility to do it. I think it's really important that we see it around us, and that we see it in others. It's not something anybody can do for the rest of the world, or lead the rest of the world into. We are infinitely fortunate beings to have these possibilities in front of us right now.

. . .

DAVID: What gives you hope?

VALERIE: Oh, you know there's really only hope. I live in this perfect world. I live in this amazing world. What reason would there be to not be full of hope? Because I see it everywhere around me. I see people facing death, and I see them hoping. I see them knowing that there's something greater. I see them witnessing greatness in their own lives. And, in my own life, I can see great fortune everywhere I look around me. It's just beautiful. We are alive in an extraordinary time, where everything is possible with no reason to think anything less. But it is essential that we understand the impact of our actions on our world, our world mind, our world culture, our world nation, our worldview, our world, if we take only what we need and we give all what we can, everything will be taken care of and there will be enough for everyone.

Magic, Magick, and
Shamanism

An Interview with Jeff McBride

Jeff McBride is recognized as one of the most talented and respected stage magicians in the world as well as a foremost innovator in contemporary magic. He was awarded the title "Magician of the Year" by Hollywood's famed Magic Castle for his remarkable sleight-of-hand abilities, and he performs regularly to standing ovations at some of the world's most spectacular theaters—including Caesar's Palace in Las Vegas, Radio City Music Hall in New York, and Her Majesty's Theater in London. In addition to his conventional magic shows, McBride also regularly leads ceremonial rituals at large outdoor gatherings, where he blends performance magic with alchemical "magick" and traditional shamanic rituals, sometimes for several consecutive days and nights. McBride has appeared in numerous television specials, and the Fox television network even devoted a Star Trek Deep Space 9 *episode to McBride's mind-bending illusions. McBride also founded the Mystery School, an organization of magicians who are interested*

in exploring "the deeper sides of the art of magic," and he coauthored the book Mystery School: An Adventure into the Deeper Meaning of Magic.

*   *   *

DAVID: What do you enjoy most about performing as a magician?

JEFF: It's different in different contexts. As Timothy Leary would say, it's the "set, setting, and dosage" that determine the experience. At different settings it's a different experience. When I perform at a festival or at a fire ritual, it's a very different type of magic than I perform at Caesar's Palace in Las Vegas.

In Las Vegas there's a certain kind of contract with the audience that this needs to be an entertainment spectacle that doesn't pull the audience member too deeply into uncomfortable territory. So, in a more conventional theater setting, my show is orchestrated so that it doesn't push people too far into the Mystery—although a lot of the symbolism and language that I use is hermetically-encrypted.

When I'm at a festival or a ritual, the intention is to go deep, deep, deep into the Mystery. So my rituals, what I call "trance-formances," have a very different flavor to them and a different intention than my stage performances. A lot of times I utilize my magical training in ritual space to create an illusion that hypes the dynamic of the ritual. The goal is to create a liminial space, a space between the worlds, where anything can happen. So, my shows on stage are very different from my ritual working in their intention. My public shows are very different from my private shows.

DAVID: How has your understanding of psychology and your interest in philosophy affected your performance?

JEFF: Everything that I learn and find valuable, I try to incorporate into my magical work. The more that I explore, especially in the realms of ritual magic and alchemy, the more I realize what I'm doing is creating a container of sorts, an alchemical vessel. At the fire rituals we're creating this container, which is very similar to an alchemical flask. The people come in, either through the front door or at the ritual smudge gate, bringing their life experiences with them. And through their creative process and the fire of the performance, a vessel is created that has the potential to affect people's lives, to transform their personal lead into gold.

Now, when I'm performing on stage, all of the different philosophies are not stated. They're encrypted through the symbolism that I use in the show. When I'm performing in ritual space, the language and the symbols are much more overt, because the people are initiates. They're much more ready for the type of experience at hand. So, to use a Hollywood show-biz term, sometimes I have to "dial down" my magic for the public and "dial it up" in ritual space.

If you start using words like "intention," "transformation," and "alchemical change" in a show in Vegas, people are not going to hear those words. There's that mind-set, and the physical setting that doesn't allow for the depth. That's why my shows in Vegas are an hour long, while these magical ritual workings are three, four days, sometimes a week long.

At the same time, all of the lessons that I learn in ritual space, I bring to my public performances through informed magical intent. In the early days, when I didn't have the guidance that I have now from my teachers, I guess I would be a little bit preachy to the nightclub audience, trying to encourage them, or cheerlead them, to go out to these fire festivals. Now I've really stopped that.

. . .

DAVID: Can you tell me more about the Mystery School, and how it came about?

JEFF: The Mystery School was an experiential magical retreat that was held for ten years, all over different parts of the country, that brought magicians together to explore magic's roots, the history of magic, and ritual theater. I had been going to pagan, shamanic, Druidic, and Native American gatherings, and participating in a lot of events where there were elders with profound wisdom teachings, and I didn't see any of that existing in the society of magicians that was around at the time. So it was my vision to create some sort of elders' wisdom council and to gather together the wisdom keepers in the world of magic. It was a gathering of progressive magical thinkers, historians, philosophers, and performers that were trying to make sense of all this, and who came together in a retreat setting where we could create a container for the exploration of magical consciousness. That's how the Mystery School came to be, and the work that we did there is still rippling out into the world.

DAVID: What inspired you to put the book *Mystery School* together, and what you think people can learn by reading it?

JEFF: I think they get a sense of possibility with magic. That magic is more than just tricks, gags, or illusion. That there's this incredible history of magic, that if you follow goes all the way back to the roots of the shaman, tribal culture, and the position of the magician/healer/wonder-worker/storyteller/bard. Their position in society was a crucial part of keeping the culture together, and now, in the last few thousand years, that's been radically changed. The wise man of yesterday has become the wise guy of today, and a lot of the depth of magic was lost. So by reading the *Mystery School* book, they get a sense of the history of magic, the mystery of magic, its lineage in society and its position in our culture today, and relevance to our culture today. We worked on the book for ten years, and it was created by many of the students and teachers at the Mystery School.

DAVID: Have you been influenced by occult philosophers like Aleister Crowley or Robert Anton Wilson?

JEFF: I've read Crowley's works. I've read *The Equinox, The Book of the Law, Magick in Theory and Practice*. I own an extensive collection of Thelemic literature that has informed my ritual work. I've also read a great number of Robert Anton Wilson's works—some of my favorites being the *Cosmic Trigger* series, *The New Inquisition*, and some of his plays. Robert Anton Wilson is a real trickster guru. You're never quite sure you know what's real. He's been an influence on my work as well.

DAVID: British biologist Rupert Sheldrake told me that he thought it was possible that psychic phenomena might be more likely during a stage magic performance because the audience enters into a state of "suspended belief." However, because stage magicians see how easily people can be fooled by sleight of hand, many—like the outspoken debunker James Randi—see all claims of psychic phenomena as a sham. I'm wondering if you've ever noticed any unusual events when you were performing that you couldn't easily explain.

JEFF: I would say this is more likely to happen in ritual space when performance magicians are creating magical illusion than in "conventional theater venues." The reason for this is setting and mind-set. You go to the theater, or the casino, and there's all of these conventional procedures that kind of lock in to the participants for a audience. There's a big difference between audience and ritual participants. There's a different contract. When you walk into a conventional theater, there's all of these like—you know, getting your tickets, going to your seat, getting your program. That kind of distances the audience. That puts them in an objective state of mind. For me, personally, it's much harder to create the sense of real magic in a theater than it is in a ritual circle.

DAVID: When you say "real magic," what have you noticed? Is there anything you can describe that you've noticed among participants, like some type of telepathic or psychic experience?

JEFF: The major thing that happens in ritual space is synchronicity. You notice the synchronicity. For me, yes, I could name instances for you that, in recounting, might seem minor but that had thunderous impact internally. You know, you can never really measure interior depth by recounting the surfaces.

I'll give a specific instance. Recently, at a five-day Fire Dance gathering, I did a piece of magic toward the end of the gathering. I do a piece where I throw a paper streamer, a huge spider-web streamer, out over the ritual fire, and sometimes this spider-web paper is carried hundreds and hundreds of feet up into the sky. It changes into a big paper dragon as it floats around, and people will see various things in that.

It's a piece of magic that I could never do inside of a theater, because you have this raging fire, and the heat and the convection pull this fifty-foot piece of streamer paper up into the air. It circles around and makes patterns, and looks like an enormous fifty-foot dragon in the sky. Often what happens is, it'll float and waft around for maybe five minutes. Then the wind currents will carry it off into the distance.

Well, this is something that happened. We're doing Fire Dance—it's a five-day drumming event. Midnight fire lightings until about ten in the morning, nonstop drumming, dancing, chanting, prayers, people from all different traditions. I throw the paper out in the morning toward the climax of the event. The paper takes off, and now I'm outside the circle, tracking the paper, because the paper will eventually come down, and I like to catch it.

So the paper flies out of the circle, well behind everyone's line of sight. No one can see this paper except myself and one other person. And I track it out into the field, and this one little piece of paper comes floating down. I catch it on my fan, and at that moment all of the drumming and dancing from the entire weekend stopped.

Again, from recounting it externally, it seems like a very minor incident. But for me, it was just an affirmation of the magic we'd been weaving all weekend. Everybody was on the same page at the same moment, responding to the same energy field—the paper, myself, the drummers, the dancers. It was as if Spirit said, This is the closing moment, the paper hit the fan, and the music just went out. There was only one other person witnessing this experience that totally got it, the synchronicity. All of the drummers, all of the dancers, were well up at the circle. No one could see what was happening to this paper or me.

DAVID: This was completely unplanned for everyone to time it this way?

JEFF: Absolutely. This is five days of drumming, stopped on this moment. Again, this is just one instance that something extraordinary happens like this. But these sort of synchronicities happen because of the Group Mind that's formed in a ritual space. People will begin chants at the same moment from across the fire circle. Is that thought transference? Is it mind reading? No. There's this field set up of the Group Mind that has tapped into Spirit.

There's occurrences happening continually throughout the evening—people entering trance states through dance and drumming and rhythm. People being able to all of a sudden have these incredibly cathartic breakthroughs during the evening. Or drum or dance in ways they've never thought possible before, taking risks with their physical body, their void, or their musical instruments that they would never even consider during the day.

Yet during the evening, the field of empowerment and possibility is so high that people can do these extraordinary things, that may be perceived from an outsider to be minor, but are of tremendous impact in the internal world of who's ever in the magic of the moment. So, for me, performance magic on stage is, at best, a shadow and retelling of what happens at these fires.

DAVID: What type of relationship do you see between stage magic and "real magic" (magick), shamanism, or this type of ritual magic that you're describing?

JEFF: A lot of this piece is drawn from my research in the history of magic and shamanism. One of the most influential books on my personal philosophy on magic is a book called *The Death and Resurrection Show* by Rogan Taylor. Rogan and I collaborated on the *Mystery School* book that we talked about earlier, which is an anthology of magic and illusion from the Mystery School magicians, that explores this area between performance magic and ritual.

Rogan Taylor's thesis is that all show business has its roots in shamanism. When the first Paleolithic fires were lit, people would dance and sing and gather in the night to do these healing seances, to do these healings on each other, for rhythm, dance, and movement. This is where the shamans would gather, and this is where the tribe would gather. This was the hearth, and this was the first nightclub. But there was no differentiation between the ritual. There was no theater yet, because theater needs an audience. In ritual everyone's participating.

So Rogan goes on to say that these bands of musicians, shamans, people that could do extraordinary things by handling hot coals, or juggling, or acrobatics, would band together to celebrate together. They enjoyed doing this so much that, after they got tired doing it for themselves, they would take it to neighboring villages and do this. They would sing the songs, and do the chants and healings on neighboring villages.

This became the origin of the traveling medicine show, developing over the years into the circus and other forms of theater, although they were originally ritual devotional work. But the important thing here that I've learned is that the birth of the audience is the death of ritual. That is, if you have people sitting in an objective space, they cannot be subjected to the magic. And that's where you get theater. People are objectively witnessing events instead of subjectively participating and entering into the mythos. That's why I have such a fascination with ritual theater, and that's where I spend most of my free time. Most of the time that I'm not performing in theatrical venues, I'm working on these four or five days of experiences.

Personally, I have seen great theater. I spent twenty years in New York City. But nothing has affected me the way that ritual theater has, where I'm participating in the event. Now, this isn't for everyone; if everybody was out at shamanic events in the woods there would be no one left at home to bottle Coca-Cola for the rest of the world. So, this isn't for everyone, but it is for some folks, and it is for me.

The rest of the year I travel around in nightclubs and theaters doing my magic show. And after the show, a couple of interested people will come and talk to me, and I'll tell them where I feel that I experience magic. On stage, doing "stand-and-deliver shows" in Las Vegas, where I have to get up there and be the star. But night after night after night is a really different experience. I honor that experience, and there's a great beauty to doing a wonderful magic show.

And for me, in my Hermetic way, I encrypt as many of the symbols, and even words, into the script. And images in my show that will hint at these experiences, because that's the way it's always been done in the Hermetic traditions. I consider myself a Hermeticist.

DAVID: Do you try to blend shamanism in your stage magic performances?

JEFF: Yeah, and to the Hermeticist, or the people that are slightly switching on to a magical current, or expanding their horizons on what they perceive magic to be, they'll light up, and they'll get it. When I do my piece with the grail, or when I do my shamanic initiation with a young man from the audience, or when I do my kind of shamanic journey of death and resurrection with the mask, people can see this. Or if they're on the verge of getting it, it will stir a chord inside of them, and there will be maybe a little e-mail, maybe a little conversation after the show, and that's where I can tell them about these other events.

So, for me, the big stage, the television work, the Las Vegas work, the touring work, becomes outer court. And at the same time, some of the best performers, and the best musicians that I meet at these fires, I take and tour with. I tour with them in my show. So if I meet some great drummers, dancers, or acrobats out at the fire, I'll plug them into my show for a while, and we become the traveling medicine show in the truest sense. I've met drummers at a Rainbow Gathering that I've taken around the world, on cruise ships, first-class hotels, and theater tours. So there's a crossover there.

DAVID: Speaking of medicine shows, I've heard that in South America, the Ayahauscaros—the traditional shamans who use the ceremonial hallucinogenic jungle juice ayahuasca—in healing sessions, will often mix some sort of sleight-of-hand-type magic with the real healing work that they're really doing, because it helps to create a state of suspended belief. Do you have any thoughts on that, on the healing potential of suspended belief and how it relates to what is known as the placebo effect in modern medicine?

JEFF: These shamanic healers are sometime called sucking doctors. One of the old shamanic techniques was that the shaman would put his mouth on the affected area and suck. Then he would spit out all kinds of weird bits of bones, bugs, twisted tumor, and things like that, to, I guess, create a placebo effect. Now, in the magical belief system, or ritual contract of these healing seances, that's fair game. And that has changed into what's called psychic surgery. South America and the Philippines are famous for their psychic surgeons. Sleight-of-hand magicians have a different take on this. People like James Randi and the other debunkers and skeptics see these shamans as con artists.

I see it a bit differently. I think that, yes, I would say that 80 to 90 percent of them are using sleight-of-hand technique. But given the culture, and the surrounding mind-set, and group belief system that these "healings" are taking place in, they can possibly result in a placebo effect which leads to a genuine cure.

That's very different from what I do at ritual theater. When I pull a beam of light from my heart and I place it on your heart, I do not expect you to believe that I have tapped into the cosmic force of nature and am able to pull a light beam from my heart and place it in your heart. It's a way of connecting with you through a magical illusion.

What this does is it creates a symbol, and a metaphor, for us sharing light from our heart with each other. Now, I can do that very same thing at a magic show in Las Vegas, and people will go, How did you do that? At a ritual, when I offer this light from my heart to a person that I may have had conflict with, and I take it out and I place it in their heart, then they'll say, I'm so glad you did that, and not even think of the how. There are ways of using magic in symbol and metaphor that can create an altered state of consciousness. And in that moment of altered consciousness, a profound psychic experience can occur that influences how we frame the way we live and work in the world.

DAVID: Do you view your magic performances as consciousness expanding?

JEFF: Yes, I absolutely do. Again, I'm very much a believer . . . Believer is a strange word. I'm very much a follower of the set, setting, and dosage school of thought of Timothy Leary.

DAVID: Have you ever had a psychedelic experience, and if so, how has it affected your perspective on magic?

JEFF: The answer to that is yes. It has changed the way I do, where I choose to do it, and how much I do. Set and setting and dosage. In Las Vegas the setting is a casino. The mind-set is, let's see how good this guy is. Or let's go kill an hour before we lose our wallets at the gaming tables, right? And the dosage is, you have to hit these people over the head. They're pretty jaded, because in Las Vegas they have to walk down the street, past exploding volcanos and giant water fountains. So to even reach their aesthetic awareness, you have to kind of bombard them with images and visuals.

DAVID: Because they're so numb from all the sensory overload.

JEFF: Exactly. The way I do this is by meeting that demand at the top of my show. Then I put on the brakes and go into complete stillness and silence, challenging that in a conventional theater setting. I do things in my Las Vegas show that no magician has ever attempted.

DAVID: Like what?

JEFF: Total silence. No music. No movement. No action on stage for four minutes, and see if I can totally entrance the audience. And I have stunning results with it—because they are expecting one thing, and as soon as I deliver the expectation, I can take them into new territory, which is stillness.

DAVID: When you say "stunning results," what are you referring to?

JEFF: Standing ovations. And the type of magic that I do isn't the big-box, lion-and-tiger, explosion magic. All of what I do is sleight-of-hand and skill magic.

And all of this, all of my repertoire, speaks to deeper metaphors and symbols of magic. I don't do any fluff in my show. And that's the thing. When I show up at some of these rituals, they say, What, are you from Vegas? You do a magic show? And they automatically pigeonhole me as some second-class, box-pushing lion tamer. Not knowing my history, and not knowing my experience.

And that's the same thing that happens with the audience in Las Vegas. Oh, this guy's going to be some razzmatazz sort of guy. So I come out, and I razzmatazz them into a total trance. Then I get them out of their social trance and deeper into my magical shamanic trance, using all of the tools of the shamans. Using the rhythmic music. Using masks. Using repetitive motion. Using call and response with the audience. I get my audience clapping in rhythm and doing call and response with me. Every tool that I've learned over the years that works, I've tried to apply to my theatrical performances. And all of the magic that I've learned for theatrical entertainment, I try to utilize at the fire circles and sacred art circles that we do.

DAVID: What do you think happens to consciousness after death?

JEFF: I can't explain it, but I've seen it. It's a painting by Alex Grey in his first book *Sacred Mirrors*.

DAVID: Which painting was it?

JEFF: It's "Death," and the man laying there in bed, with his spirit ascending, twisting and turning into the Net of Indra.

DAVID: You see a background composed of eyes?

JEFF: Yes. And again, it can't be put into language. But visionary artists like Alex Grey can paint it, and it is there for us to see.

DAVID: So, you think that after the death of the body there's an aspect of your consciousness that survives?

JEFF: Yes. However, whether the ego remains, I would say no. Consciousness in its unexplainable form, yes. I had an interesting conversation with my friend Joshua Levin last night. I forget the exact numbers that he used, but he says, you know all this reincarnation stuff? I can't figure it out, because if you go back a thousand years, what was the population of the planet then versus now? Where are all these people coming from?

DAVID: Well, the Hindus would say they're coming up from the animal realm. They evolved up through the lower animal realms into the human realm.

JEFF: Rumi has a wonderful take on that too. I'm paraphrasing it. He goes, Once I was a rock, and I died. Then I was an insect, and I died. Then I came back as an animal, and then I died. Then I came back as a human, and I died. What have I ever really lost from dying?

DAVID: That reminds me of an old Sufi saying that goes "God sleeps in the rock, dreams in the plant, stirs in the animal, and awakens in man." Jeff, what is your perspective on God?

JEFF: Spirit. You know, the word "God" is so loaded, and archetypically it just—bang—puts this big guy in a chair for me, having been raised a Roman Catholic. I've been examining my personal lexicon and I prefer the word "Spirit," because it embraces all gods. I love gods. There's tons of gods that I really identify with, that are really wonderful. Hermes and Mercury, and Thoth—these are gods that really capture my imagination and my heart. I study as much as I can about the Hermetic tradition, as far as the teachings of the gods go. To use a Ken Wilber phrase, "Spirit transcends yet includes God." So I prefer to use the word "Spirit."

DAVID: Just because it's so culturally charged and emotionally loaded.

JEFF: Yeah, it's a really loaded word, with a capital G. I think as consciousness evolves, the language evolves. I think language is one of things that helps consciousness evolve. And right now, the people that I spend most of my time with use the word "Spirit" in place of "God."

DAVID: Yeah, that was one of the things that Terence McKenna used to stress—how our language shapes reality.

JEFF: Right, and I think Ken Wilber explores this as deep as any writer that I've encountered does.

DAVID: Do you think the human species will survive the next hundred years, or do you think that we're in danger of extinction?

JEFF: (*laughter*) I think we'll survive. I think we're just a bit smarter than cockroaches, and look how long they've lasted. (*laughter*)

DAVID: What do you think is the biggest threat to the human species?

JEFF: I think it's humans themselves, quite simply put. I think there's a kind of increasing paranoia toward global nuclear holocaust. But my hope is that, through people exploring magic and alchemy, they'll find some way to turn even nuclear waste into some sort of wonderful energy source.

DAVID: Assuming that we do survive, how do you envision the future evolution of the human race?

JEFF: Daniel Quinn, in his book *Beyond Civilization*, sketches a map that intrigued me. It was a reexamination of tribal culture—not in the sense of that we all throw the keys of our BMW into a ditch and walk away barefoot into the Paleolithic—or Paleo—terrific—past ideals, I should say. (*laughter*) But that by exploring what works about tribal culture, we'll develop a new way to interact in community. So I see that as a viable option, and something that we explore in our festivals and our retreats.

. . .

DAVID: So, part of what you're saying is that you see your stage magic as an important aspect of your own spiritual path.

JEFF: Yeah, of course. You know, the Hindus say it best—all is maya. All is illusion. And I remind people of that continually through my work—that what we think is real is just our perceptions. And it's challenging people's perceptions—in a friendly magical way—and opening them up to the greater possibilities that exist within them and around them.

Sacred Reflections and Transfigurations

An Interview with Alex Grey

Alex Grey is a visionary artist recognized the world over for his unique paintings. His work has been exhibited at many museums and galleries, including the New Museum and Stux Gallery in New York City and the Grand Palais in Paris. His paintings have been featured on many posters, greeting cards, and book and magazine covers, and as album art for such bands as Tool, the Beastie Boys, and Nirvana. Grey attended the Columbus College of Art and Design and the Boston Museum School, and he spent five years at Harvard Medical School working in the anatomy department studying the body and preparing cadavers for dissection. Grey was an instructor in artistic anatomy and figure sculpture at New York University. He teaches courses in visionary art at the Open Center in New York City and the Naropa Institute in Boulder, Colorado. Many of Grey's paintings have been collected in his books Sacred Mirrors *and* Transfigurations. *He is also the author of* The Mission of Art, *which traces the*

evolution of human consciousness through art history and reflects on the creative process as a spiritual path.

* * *

DAVID: Is there a connection between your early childhood interest in monsters and death and your later interest in altered states of consciousness and mystical visions?

ALEX: I had a particular interest in whatever was strange. Monstrosities, fetal abnormalities, genetic malformations became strong interests. They were like real monsters. The caprice of God, as a designer in these various genetic strains, was quite an amazing and fascinating thing—that we could have two heads, or flippers instead of feet. And it's really miraculous that we don't. We live our lives within normal routines. Altered states of consciousness are condensed experiences that provide crystallized insights. Like dream experiences, they run counter to normal experience and let us see our life in another context, from the vantage point of the altered state. The monster recontextualizes reality and shows you that life could be another way. A monster is an alternative being, rather than an alternative state of consciousness.

DAVID: What was your religious upbringing like?

ALEX: Every week, when I was young, my family went to Methodist church, and I always respected the teachings of Jesus. But I never got hooked into a sincere spiritual search until my parents left the church. My parents left the church in a huff of disillusionment and became agnostic atheists. That's when God and spirituality started to interest me.

. . .

DAVID: What was it like working as an embalmer in a morgue?

ALEX: I worked in a morgue and a museum of anatomy. I created displays on the history of medicine and disease . . . Then there was the funeral home morgue work. I would accept bodies when the funeral home brought them in. It was a medical school morgue, so we prepared the bodies for dissection. When a new body came in, if no one else was there, I would do a simplified *Tibetan Book of the Dead* ritual, calling their name, and encouraging them to go toward the light.

DAVID: Was this on your own that you did this?

ALEX: It was not with the permission (*laughter*) of the medical school. "Oh, he's over there reading the *Tibetan Book of the Dead* to the dead guy." No, it wasn't standard operating procedure there at the morgue, but I couldn't with full consciousness accept these bodies as pieces of meat. Their spirit might still be hovering around the physical body.

DAVID: You felt presences around you?

ALEX: Oh, I definitely felt it. Maybe it's a projection of my fear of death. I might die today or maybe tomorrow. It's going to happen, but I don't know when. There's also a simultaneous repugnance and fear—terror in a way—of awesome energy, the Mysterium Tremendum of one's life. Life's limitations are confronting. Basic questions of selfhood arise. Who am I? What am I? If life and mind goes on after death, where does it go? All those questions come, like a freight train, through your mind whenever you're with dead people.

There was the work-a-day stuff that I did. I had to pump the bodies full of phenol and formalin, a kind of embalming fluid. I didn't drain the blood before putting in the embalming fluid, like in a commercial morgue. Gallons and gallons of embalming fluid would saturate the body, and it would puff up. All kinds of nauseating substances would ooze from every orifice during that process. Then it would drain off a little bit, and you'd wrap it up. Put a little lanolin on the hands and face, wrap them like a mummy, and stick them in the freezer. Occasionally there would be a request from a professor for only particular organs, or particular appendages, like hands were needed once to train hand surgeons. I had to hacksaw off dozens of pairs of hands. If there was a convention of hand surgeons doing a workshop, they needed a lot of hands to study and dissect.

DAVID: These people had donated their bodies?

ALEX: Right. But the hand surgeons, for instance, didn't need the whole body, so somebody had to go and hacksaw off the hands, or the head. Now, the head—that was a more intense thing. They had a kind of chainsawlike device and you could create kind of a sculpture bust—down the shoulders and then across the middle. You'd have a head, which you'd stick on a tray, and take to the place. That was wild. That was too much.

. . .

DAVID: How did this affect you emotionally?

ALEX: It was an unforgettable experience. I felt like I probably could have declined, but then I would never have had that experience in this lifetime. It's doubtful, except in the case of a psychotic murderer, that anyone would have that experience outside of a medical school where dismemberment is part and parcel of the daily activities. Maybe if you were a Tibetan funeral preparator doing sky burials, you chop up the bodies.

. . .

DAVID: In Carlo McCormick's essay in your book, he compares you to a shaman, and says that it was a necessary part of your journey to go through the darkness.

ALEX: Metaphorically, the path of the wounded healer or the journey of the shaman has very important implications for the future of spirituality. No other metaphor sufficiently deals with the journey of humanity. We are wounded, and whether we're going to be the wounded victim or the wounded healer is our choice. We have wounded the planet. We have wounded our genes. We've wounded the coming generations. Whether we make some remediation to the environment, and to our psyches, is something that only time will tell.

We need transcendent vision to guide us, and the vision of a common good to motivate and drive our creative efforts. That's critical. Another role that is critical at this time is the role of the Bodhisattva, because this is an archetype of ethical idealism. In Buddhism, the Bodhisattva, one whose being is enlightenment, expresses his or her compassion by working for the benefit of all sentient beings. Bodhichitta is altruistic positive motivation in all ones' actions. These Mahayana Buddhist teachings emphasize a universal compassion and responsibility, and are the logical consequence of realizing that we are all connected and that we can't turn our backs on a suffering world.

I love the yogic and shamanic path as a metaphor. A lot of my work is related to those paths. My early performance work started with an animal, the dead dog pieces, Secret Dog and Rendered Dog. That was my power animal that opened me up to the world of mortality and decay and led me to the underworld of death.

After the morgue pieces and a positive reorientation, my performances dealt with the possibilities of global death from nuclear war and ecotastrophy. I think that everyone with a conscious sense of responsibility carries around a heavy sadness, fear, or guilt about these possibilities. My daughter at age five made a little book about the Earth. It started with the a happy Earth from the earliest times when Adam and Eve were around. The globe had a happy face. Then the Earth was being trashed and the trees and people were dying. The Earth was dying. It frightens everyone. Even young children know the fear.

. . .

DAVID: What do you think happens to consciousness after death?

ALEX: I accept the near-death research and Tibetan bardo explanations. Soon after physical death, when the senses shut down, you enter into the realms of light and archetypal beings. You have the potential to realize the clear light, our deepest and truest identity, if you recognize it as the true nature of your mind and are not freaked out. If you don't, you may contact other less appealing dimensions. No one can know, of course, until they get there. Some people have had experiences which give them certainty, but consciousness is the ultimate mystery. I'd like to surrender to the process on its deepest level when death occurs, but I will probably fail and be back to interview you in the next lifetime. (*laughter*)

DAVID: What's your concept of God?

ALEX: My daughter said the other day, "God must think it smells down in the sewer." I thought that was an interesting statement. She said that because God is everywhere, and God is everything, God would be in the stinky places too. God is the infinite oneness. Oneness, but also infinite. That is the meaning of nondual. God is love. While we were tripping we thought, Love is the part of the all that's all of the all. Divine love is infinite and omnipresent, but our experience of it is partial and incomplete from day to day. If you have a loved one, you have access to the infinitude of divine love.

Even though Buddhists would not use the word "God," the nondual nature of mind, voidness, clarity, and infinite compassion, as described in the Buddhist teachings, is not different than the experience that I call God. Ken Wilber uses the ladder metaphor. There are different rungs, the material realm, the emotional, the mental, then the psychical, and progressively more spiritual hierarchies of states of consciousness and awareness. The highest rungs of the ladder give one the highest context, wherein the entire ladder is seen. The experience of God is the highest rung, and also the entire ladder. That's the transcendent and the immanent aspects of God. God is the beyond and also the manifest world—"the entire field of events and meanings," as Manjushrimitra [Dzogchen master] puts it. One without the other is not the full picture.

DAVID: You're describing God as a state of consciousness. Do you see there being any type of intelligent design in the universe?

ALEX: Absolutely. Wilber says that the materialists can't offer more than a "whoops!" theory for the universe manifesting. Whoops, it occurred by some chance. That's an infantile orientation to the complexity and beauty of the evolutionary design of the Earth and cosmos. I think we can come up with something deeper. Spirit, God, Primordial Nature of the Mind, whatever you call it, is the source and goal of it all.

DAVID: How have your experiences with psychedelics influenced your work and your perspective on life?

ALEX: When I came back from the north magnetic pole, I knew I was looking for something. I was twenty-one, and I was searching for God. I didn't know what that was. I was an existentialist. Within twenty-four hours of returning from the pole, I was invited to a party by an acquaintance who would become my wife. She invited me along with our professor, so the professor took me there. On the way, he offered me a bottle of Kahlúa laced with a high dose of LSD. It was the end of school, and I decided to celebrate. I drank a good deal of it. Allyson, my future wife, drank the rest. That was my first LSD experience.

Tripping that night, I experienced going through a spiritual rebirth canal inside of my head. I was in the dark, going toward the light, spinning in this tunnel, a kind of an opalescent living mother-of-pearl tube. All paradoxes were resolved in this tunnel—dark and light, male and female, life and death. It was a very strong archetypal experience. The next day, because it had been my first trip, I called Allyson up, to talk to her about it. I asked her out that night, and we never left each other. It's been over twenty years.

Within twenty-four hours of announcing that I'm looking for God, an LSD experience opened me up on a spiritual, evolutionary path, and I had met my wife. It was miraculous. My prayers were answered. Allyson and I have maintained an ongoing psychedelic sacramental relationship. We have often tripped laying in bed, blindfolded, or in a beautiful environment. Then, coming out of blindfolds, we write and draw.

DAVID: Have you ever actually tried to do any work while you were tripping?

ALEX: A little—the results are interesting and remind me of the trip, but it's not my most successful work. My work takes a steady mind, eye, and hand to accomplish. The psychedelic helps me to access the infinitude of the imagination, allowing me to see countless interpenetrating dimensions. William James says that no model of reality can be complete without taking these alternative dimensions of consciousness into account. Since I want to make art dealing with the nature of consciousness and spirit, I have to experience higher dimensions of consciousness.

During a trip I will have visions that are crystallizations of my life experience, or something completely surprising. You may enter a dimension that you've never known before, and it seems very real, more real than this phenomenal world. That "other" reality seems to be tinkering with this one, or acting like a puppet master to this one. I want to reveal the interrelationships between the different dimensions in my work.

DAVID: To act as a bridge between dimensions?

ALEX: Consciousness is that bridge. Making interdimensionality visible validates it for people who have had that experience. They can see a picture outside of their own heads and say, It was something like this. I'm not crazy. There's plenty of people who've had those experiences. Perhaps the work can be useful in that way. I've talked to people who use my paintings as a tool to access the dimensions that are represented. Some people trip and look at the book, or look at the art, and key into the states that are symbolized there. That is a psychedelic or entheogenic full circle. I glimpsed the visions while tripping, came back and made the work. Then people trip and access the higher state that produced the vision. The painting acts a portal to the mystical dimension. That is the real usefulness of the work, and it is the great thing about any sacred art.

. . .

DAVID: Have your dreams inspired you?

ALEX: Sure. I had a dream that I was painting the *Transfiguration* painting before I actually did it. I did DMT a few weeks later, and I was immediately thrust into the space of that painting I had dreamed of. I was experiencing what it would be like inside of the painting and what state of being I would try to project. Having seen it in a dream, I could clarify certain elements. It became clearer, although not all questions were solved. Shaving half of my hair off was an image that came in a dream as well. In the dream, I opened up a garbage can and saw myself with this haircut.

DAVID: Are there any other avenues that you use to access the unconscious, and what else has inspired you?

ALEX: Oh, sure. Creative visualization is surprisingly effective. Also shamanic drumming can be a pathway to expanded, imaginative territories. Sometimes doing nothing at all you can receive powerful visions. Once I was waiting for the subway, tired after a day of teaching, and I saw the *World Soul* piece which I then worked on for two years. I was in no altered state and was not anticipating anything in particular. I like to keep the "door open" and be permeable to these transdimensional blow-darts of vision. I believe that I am being used by the Logos. The images are sent to me.

DAVID: Do you feel like sometimes you're not really doing it, like it's just happening though you?

ALEX: No, I know that I'm physically creating the work. But the vision is being given as a gift. Other creative and receptive people are receiving other visions, but these are my gifts, and I'm supposed to manifest them.

· · ·

DAVID: What are your views on the evolution of consciousness?

ALEX: It seems to me the universe is like a self-awareness machine. I think the world was created for each individual to manifest the boundless experiences of identity with the entire universe and with the pregnant void that gives birth to the phenomenal universe. That's the Logos. That's the point of a universe—to increase complexity and self-awareness. The evolution of consciousness is the counterforce to the entropic laws of thermodynamics that end in stasis, heat death, and the loss of order. The evolution of consciousness appears to gain complexity, mastery, and wisdom.

Lessons are learned over a lifetime—maybe many lifetimes. And the soul grows and hopefully attains a state of spiritual awakenedness. Buddha was the "Awakened One." To be able to access all the simultaneous parallel dimensions, and come from a ground of love and infinite compassion like the awakenedness of the Buddha, is a good goal for the evolution of consciousness. The spiritual "fruit" in many spiritual paths is compassion and wisdom.

DAVID: So then, are you optimistic about the future evolution of humanity?

ALEX: That's a big leap. (*laughter*) I have some optimism about the potential for human beings to manifest Buddhic qualities of compassion, spiritual heroism, and reverence for all life. There's always problems in this phenomenal world, but if we maintain ideal ethical views, we can cause less harm. There's hope for a future to hand our children, and their children. There is also despair over the deludedness and the catastrophic disasters that human beings have created.

I don't like vacillating between fear and hope. The Buddhist teachings caution against entrapment in those emotions. But we're in samsara, and subject to emotions. Ultimately, I'm optimistic because the primordial nature of mind will never change no matter what happens. Our consciousness may appear in another universe, or in another dimension, but in some form the energy will be around. Consciousness just recycles.

. . .

DAVID: Do you think that the human species will survive the next hundred years, or do you think we're in danger of extinction?

ALEX: Yes, I think we are in danger of bringing down much of the web of life with us. We are a drunken suicidal adolescent species. Nevertheless, what better time to wake up, get over ourselves, forgive and love each other, and fix the mess we've created?

DAVID: Assuming that we do survive, how do you envision the future evolution of the human race?

ALEX: Self-illuminating nondual mystics, dedicated to the repair of the water, air, and soil, and nurturing the species that still remain.

Glossary

anandamide: A naturally occurring brain chemical that binds to the same receptors in the brain as THC (tetrahydrocannibinal), the primary psychoactive component in marijuana. From the Sanskrit ananda, which means "inner bliss."

Artificial intelligence (AI): The field of research that attempts to emulate human intelligence in a computer.

ayahuasca: A hallucinogenic plant brew used by South American shamans that contains the powerful psychedelic substance DMT. (See *DMT*)

Ayurvedic medicine: The traditional medicine of India. The word "Ayurveda" is based on two Sanskrit terms: *ayu* meaning "life," and *veda* meaning "knowledge" or "science." The practice is said to be around five thousand years old.

axon: A thin neuronal branch that transmits electrical impulses away from the body of a brain cell (neuron) to other neurons (or to muscles or glands).

bardos: According to the *Tibetan Book of the Dead*, the bardos are the intermediate states of consciousness, or realms of existence, that lie between death and rebirth.

Bell's Theorem: A mathematical proof derived from physics demonstrating that whenever two particles interact, they are thereafter connected in a mysterious faster-than-light way that doesn't diminish with time or distance and can't be shielded. Also known as the mechanism of nonlocality.

bifurcation: The splitting or branching of possible states that a system can assume due to changing parameters.

blog: Shorthand for Web log.

cephalomancy: A form of divination that involves interpreting the skull or head of a donkey or goat.

CFC: Chlorofluorocarbon. A compound consisting of chlorine, fluorine, and carbon that is responsible for depleting the ozone layer. The ozone layer protects land-based life on Earth from the deadly effects of ultraviolet rays from the sun. CFCs are commonly used as refrigerants, solvents, and foam-blowing agents.

chemokine: A type of peptide that acts as a chemical signal and attracts specific immune cells, such as white blood cells, to infected parts of the body.

darshan: A Sanskrit term that means direct visual contact with a deity.

dendrites: Tiny treelike branchings at the electrical impulse-receiving end of a neuron (brain cell).

directed panspermia: Francis Crick's theory to explain the origin of life on Earth. He hypothesizes that spores traveling through space on meteorites seed planets throughout the galaxy.

DNA: Deoxyribonucleic acid—the long complex macromolecule, consisting of two interconnected helical strands, that resides in the nucleus of every living cell and encodes the genetic instructions for building each organism.

DMT (N,N-dimetyltryptamine): An extremely powerful, short-acting hallucinogenic molecule found in the South American shamanic brew Ayahuasca. DMT is also found naturally in the human brain.

endogenous: Found naturally within the body or produced within an organism. The opposite of *exogenous*.

endorphin: Meaning "endogenous morphine"; the brain's naturally produced neuro-transmitter, which binds to the same brain receptors as opiate drugs.

EPR: In 1935 Albert Einstein and two colleagues, Boris Podolsky and Nathan Rosen developed a thought experiment to demonstrate what they felt was a lack of complete-ness in quantum mechanics. This so-called EPR paradox (named from the first letters of their last names) has led to much subsequent, and still-ongoing, research.

exogenous: Derived or developed outside of the body or organism. The opposite of *endogenous*.

excitatory: Excites, speeds up. Used to describe a type of neurotransmitter.

field: A region of physical influence that interrelates and interconnects matter and energy. Fields are not a form of matter; rather, matter is energy bound within fields.

fractal: Computer-generated images corresponding to mathematical equations that repeat self-similar patterns at infinitely receding levels of organization.

Gaia hypothesis: A model for interpreting the dynamics that occur in Earth's biosphere as being part of a single, self-regulating organism.

Ganzfeld Experiment: A telepathy experiment that uses a sensory deprivation technique, or an unchanging sensory environment, so that the nervous system of the subject becomes more sensitive to faint information.

genome: The complete set of genetic material or genes for a single organism.

haruspicy: A form of divination that involves interpreting animal entrails.

Hermetic: Related to the Gnostic writings or occult teachings of Hermes Trismegistus, a philosopher, mystic, astrologer, and alchemist who lived around two thousand years ago in ancient Egypt.

information: Nonpredictable patterns that carry a message.

infophobia: A term coined by Robert Anton Wilson, meaning "the fear of information."

infophilia: A term coined by Robert Anton Wilson, meaning "the love of information."

left brain: The left hemisphere of the human brain, which is associated with language and symbolic thinking.

lucid dreaming: The phenomenon of being conscious and aware that one is dreaming, while one is in the process of dreaming.

magick: Spelled with a "k" to distinguish it from stage magic, this is Aliester Crowley's term for "real" magic. Crowley defined magick as "the art and science of bringing about change in accordance with one's will."

MDMA (methylenedioxymethamphetamine): A psychoactive drug, commonly referred to as "ecstasy," that is chemically related to both amphetamines and mescaline, although its pharmacologic action is unlike either. Users of this controversial drug report feelings of empathy, sensory enhancement, and enhanced communication.

media virus: A term coined by Douglas Rushkoff, meaning "a media story that carries a cultural message beyond the actual story." An example of a media virus would be the Rodney King videotape, which was first and foremost a media story not about Rodney King, but about the tape itself, that is, about media being used in a new way.

meme: A term coined by Richard Dawkins, who defines it as "a unit of cultural inheritance, hypothesized as analogous to the particulate gene and as naturally selected by virtue of its 'phenotypic' consequences on its own survival and replication in the cultural environment." Memes can be political ideas, religious philosophies, catchphrases from songs, cultural fads, or any unit of cultural information that spreads from person to person.

morphic field: According to Rupert Sheldrake, this is a region of material influence—similar to a magnetic field or an electric field—that organizes the way that forms occur in nature. These hypothetical fields organize the characteristic structure and pattern of activity of natural forms—ranging from crystals and organisms to herds and societies. The fields are influenced by the form and behaviors of past morphic units of the same kind, as the fields contain a kind of memory and tend to become increasingly habitual over time. This term includes fields at all levels of complexity—biological, behavioral, social, cultural, and mental.

morphic resonance: The influence of previous structures of activity on subsequent similar structures of activity organized by morphic fields.

morphogenesis: The coming into being of form.

morphogenetic field: A nonmaterial region of influence that guides the structural development of organic forms.

nanotechnology: Atomic engineering—the ability to devise self-replicating machines, robots, and computers that are the size of molecules.

natural selection: Charles Darwin's theory of biological evolution, based on the survival and replication of the fittest and most adaptable genes, through competition over limited natural resources.

neurogenesis: The birth of new brain cells.

neuropeptide: Peptides are natural or synthetic compounds consisting of two or more amino acids linked end to end—or, in more technical terms, linked with the carboxyl group of one amino acid and the amino group of another. The body uses peptides as ligands, or chemical messengers that communicate information between systems in the body. Neuropepides are those peptides that were found initially in the brain and nervous system, but are now known to exist elsewhere in the body.

neurotransmitter: Chemicals that transmit impulses between nerve cells or between nerve cells and effector cells.

ornithopter: A machine that flies by flapping its wings, in the same way a bird or insect flies.

paradigm: A model for explaining a set of data; a belief system.

paradigm shift: A change in the way one perceives information.

paranormal: Phenomena that cannot be explained through conventional science.

peptides: A compound consisting of two or several amino acids.

polymerase chain reaction (PCR): A technique developed by Dr. Kary Mullis that allows chemists to replicate as much precise DNA as they need. PCR revolutionized the study of genetics and won Dr. Mullis the 1993 Nobel Prize in Chemistry.

Psi research: Scientific investigation into the effects of psychic phenomena, such as telepathy, precognition, and telekinesis.

psychical research: The older, more traditional term for research into psychic phenomena.

quantum physics: The scientific study of subatomic reality.

robotics: The science and technology of designing and manufacturing robots that combines mechanical engineering with artificial intelligence.

right brain: The right hemisphere of the human brain, which is associated with pattern recognition and nonlinear holistic thinking.

samadhi: A nondualistic state of consciousness described in Buddhism and Hinduism that occurs when all other mental functions pause except for consciousness. There are various stages of samadhi, the highest of which is *nirvikalpa-samadhi*, union with one's own consciousness.

samsara: The cycle of birth, suffering, death, and rebirth (or reincarnation) that Buddhists and Hindus seek liberation from.

Second Law of Thermodynamics: The law which states that the entropy (chaos, randomness) of particles in the universe may increase but never decreases and that disorder is perpetually increasing in the universe.

sidhis: A Sanskrit word from the Yoga Sutras that means psychic or occult powers. According to the Yoga Sutras there are eight sidhis that develop as a result of yogic practice—such as the power to become invisible to the external eye, and the power to make the body heavy as one wishes.

SMIILE (or SMI²LE): Timothy Leary's acronym for Space Migration plus Intelligence Increase (or intelligence squared) plus Life Extension, which Leary saw as the primary goals of the evolutionary process.

synchronicity: Carl Jung's term for a "meaningful coincidence."

teleology: The study of evidence for intelligence or design in nature, and a doctrine that ends or final causes are immanent in nature. An explanation of phenomena by reference to intelligently designed goals or purposes.

Thelemic: Relating to Thelema, a Greek word meaning "will" or "intention," that also refers to a spiritual philosophy largely developed by Aliester Crowley.

theory of Formative Causation: The hypothesis that organisms or morphic units at all levels of complexity are organized by morphic fields, which are themselves influenced and stabilized by morphic resonance from all previous similar morphic units.

Ubi-Comp: Refers to a state where almost all physical objects are embedded with computer chips that measure their surroundings in some way and wirelessly communicate with each other.

Internet Resources

To find out more about the people in this book, please visit the following Web sites.

David Jay Brown
www.mavericksofthemind.com
www.sexanddrugs.info
www.animalsandearthquakes.com

George Carlin
www.georgecarlin.com

Noam Chomsky
www.chomsky.info

Deepak Chopra
www.chopra.com

Deepak Chopra Photo by Jeremiah Sullivan
www.jeremiahsullivan.com

Valerie Corral
www.wamm.org

Alex Grey
www.alexgrey.com

Paul Krassner
www.paulkrassner.com

Ray Kurzweil
www.KurzweilTech.com
www.KurzweilAI.net

John E. Mack
www.passporttothecosmos.com
www.centerchange.org

Jeff McBride
www.mcbridemagic.com
www.firedance.org

Edgar D. Mitchell
www.edmitchellapollo14.com
www.noetic.org

Hans Moravec
www.frc.ri.cmu.edu/~hpm/

Kary Mullis
www.karymullis.com

Candace B. Pert
www.candacepert.com

Clifford Pickover
www.pickover.com
(where you can find his Reality Carnival web log: RealityCarnival.Com)

Dean Radin
www.psiresearch.org

Ram Dass
www.ramdasstapes.org

Ram Dass Photo by Jean Hanamoto
www.garlic.com/~artworks/marijuana_art/

Douglas Rushkoff
www.rushkoff.com

Peter Russel
www.peterussell.com

Rupert Sheldrake
www.sheldrake.org

Bruce Sterling
http://blog.wired.com/sterling/

Robert Anton Wilson
www.rawilson.com
www.gunsanddope.com

About the Author

David Jay Brown is the coauthor of two previous volumes of interviews with leading-edge thinkers, *Mavericks of the Mind* and *Voices from the Edge*. He is also the author of two science-fiction novels, *Brainchild* and *Virus*. David holds a master's degree in psychobiology from New York University and was responsible for the California-based research in two of British biologist Rupert Sheldrake's books on unexplained phenomena in science: *Dogs That Know When Their Owners Are Coming Home* and *The Sense of Being Stared At*. To find out more about David's work, visit his award-winning Web site: www.mavericksofthemind.com.

Photo Credits